SHOWDOWN

SHOWDOWN

SHOWDOWN

THE INSIDE STORY OF THE
GLENEAGLES
RYDER CUP

IAIN CARTER

First published 2014 by
Elliott and Thompson Limited
27 John Street
London WC1N 2BX
www.eandtbooks.com

ISBN: 978-1-78396-064-4

Plate section picture credits:
Page 1: John Raoux/PA Images; Page 2: John Angelillo/PA Images (top);
PA images (bottom); Page 3: Peter Byrne/PA Images; Page 4: Peter
Morrison/PA Images (top); Hugo Philpott/PA images (bottom); Page 5:
Alastair Grant/PA Images; Page 6: Matt Dunham/PA Images; Page 7:
Matt Dunham/PA Images (top); Alastair Grant/PA Images (bottom);
Page 8: Scott Heppell/PA Images

9 8 7 6 5 4 3 2 1

A catalogue record for this book is available from the British Library.

Typesetting: Marie Doherty
Printed in the UK by TJ International Ltd

For Sarah and Ollie

Contents

Foreword

By Graeme McDowell

There is nothing quite like the Ryder Cup. For us players, it provides an adventure unlike anything else we experience on the golf course. In a game that is steeped in individuality, the feeling of being part of a team is something magical. Competing in front of vast, partisan crowds pumps your adrenaline from start to finish. It is such a rarefied atmosphere, it's almost impossible to describe what it does to you. You see displays of emotion from players which are so out of character that you realise that they are playing the game with a totally different mindset. It is inevitable that once you get a taste of playing for Europe your number-one objective is to retain your place for future Ryder Cups.

The 2014 match at Gleneagles was my fourth appearance in continental colours. Once again, it was amazing to be part of such a huge event. We were lucky enough to have, in Paul McGinley, the standout captain of recent times. I don't want to take anything away from Sir Nick Faldo, Colin Montgomerie or José María Olazábal, under whom I played in my first three matches, but Paul was a natural born leader. His attention to detail was second to none and he instilled a subliminal message in the heads of all the players, focusing them intently on the job at hand. I had been one of those who advocated his appointment as skipper and he thrived in the role of trying to beat his boyhood hero, Tom Watson, who led the American team.

This Ryder Cup victory was the culmination of so much hard work from Paul and his team of backroom helpers. We players were motivated and inspired to play at our very best, despite it being the end of an exhausting summer of golf.

It was a year full of intrigue as both teams took shape and new personalities like Victor Dubuisson came on board. It became clear early in the year that the captain intended me to partner Victor and prepare him for the stage that is the Ryder Cup. It seemed merely a coincidence that Victor and I were paired together for the first two rounds of the French Open, where I successfully defended my title. But unbeknown to either of us, it was down to Paul. Even though this was only June and the Ryder Cup wasn't until September, the captain had already set the wheels in motion for me and the young Frenchman to form a powerful bond.

We won both of our foursomes matches together at Gleneagles, contributing to record-breaking session scores on both afternoons, and then I had the honour of leading out Europe on the final day. It was an awesome responsibility, if not a little intimidating. The scenes on the first tee were unbelievable but, having gone three down to Jordan Spieth early on, I had to dig very deep to turn the match around. Thanks to a raucous crowd, some great golf and a couple of mistakes from Jordan, I managed to secure a point, of which I may be most proud. It was one of many highlights from a Ryder Cup I will never forget.

It capped a year in which we saw Tiger Woods struggle in vain to overcome injury and take his place in the US team. On our side of the pond, my old partner Rory McIlroy stepped into Woods' shoes, with two major wins. My relationship with Rory was put under some strain too, but our friendship emerged stronger than ever. We also reinforced that unique bond that goes with being Ryder Cup teammates.

I was an outsider looking in when I first encountered one

of these biennial transatlantic tussles. In 2006 I was an up-and-coming European Tour pro and I joined Iain Carter in the BBC Radio commentary team at the K Club, where Europe thrashed the Americans to retain the trophy. By the end I didn't want to be holding a microphone again. I had been inspired to push for a playing role and I made my debut two years later at Valhalla.

It's a source of great pride that I have played in every match since. I'm happy to leave the commentary to Iain and his 5Live colleagues and already my aim is to push on for the next Ryder Cup at Hazeltine in 2016. Who knows what stories that one will produce? All I know is that there were plenty generated by the build-up to Gleneagles and during the contest itself.

I hope you enjoy reading them in this book.

Prologue

29 September 2014,
Gleneagles Hotel, Perthshire

'Aha! The morning after the night before.'

The Irish brogue was familiar, but a touch more hoarse than usual. This was the victorious captain, at 7.30 a.m. the day after his job was completed. Just five hours of sleep passed before he walked purposefully into the room that had been his team's base for the previous week. It was situated in one of the wings of the magnificent Gleneagles Hotel.

The area was bedecked in blue and gold. The colours of Europe. The walls were blue and gold, the carpet was blue and gold. He wondered what would become of the carpet. Hundreds of tropical fish swam in their tank. They, too, were either blue or gold. Photographs hung on the walls, depicting great scenes from previous Ryder Cups. Others, carrying messages of inspiration, had already been taken down and packed off to be exhibited in the captain's native Dublin at a later date.

A handful of media and marketing officials milled around. There was a bar. It had been busy earlier that morning.

There was a tight-knit eating area. Just like the team; tight knit. There were sofas and a coffee table. Upon it were neatly arranged newspapers. They all bore similar images of the champagne-drenched victors in their moment of triumph.

On top of the papers sat a trophy. The Ryder Cup. That was pure gold.

A caddie came into the room. Bleary-eyed, he stretched and let out an expletive. His head hurt, but his heart was full of pride. The caddie's mate arrived. He wanted a beer. 'No, sorry,' came the polite reply from the waitress. 'Why not?' the man asked. The caddie intervened. He said it wasn't possible because it was now 7.30 a.m. in the morning. 'But I haven't been to bed, it's still party time for me,' came the plaintive reply.

The waitress left, the caddie's mate wandered over to the bar and helped himself to a beer.

The captain shook the hand of the caddie. Whispered words of gratitude. Tight knit. They smiled and the caddie sipped his coffee. Then his boss arrived, a player of great distinction. More smiles, more handshakes, emphatic gestures reflecting a job well done. The player departed, off to pursue his solo career, but forever a part of a winning team. Another golfer and his girlfriend popped in. The same routine. Smiles, handshakes and knowing nods. They had got it right.

The phone sitting on a table next to the door that said 'Team Europe' sprang to life. A BBC Radio producer answered and then handed it to the captain. He sat on the chair next to the phone and sighed before that hoarse voice was pressed back into action.

It was time to tell the stories of the night, and of the days before, to the audience watching breakfast television. The answers were sharp, concise and eloquent. Millions of viewers entranced by the events of the previous day hung on his every word.

There was no hangover for the captain. These precious memories were not to be lost in a fog of alcohol. It had been just the same when he had holed the putt to win the trophy 12 years earlier, when he heeded his wife's advice not to drink too much. He drank it all in, but in a sober fashion.

Over the next hour he talked to various BBC Radio stations, telling them all the same triumphant story. He dealt with the questions regarding the way the Americans had disintegrated on and off the golf course. There were stories to be told about all of that, but it wasn't for him to say. Other eyewitnesses could recount those tales. It had been clear the opposition were anything but tight knit by the end. And this despite a radical idea to involve a legend of the game – the triumphant captain's hero, no less – to try to halt their run of defeats.

For the victorious skipper, though, there was just a feeling of immense satisfaction. When it came to the showdown, the biggest event in his sport, the masterplan had come to fruition.

It had been a long road. Gaining the opportunity to do the job had not been straightforward; indeed, it had been contentious and controversial. The victory had been nearly 24 months in the making.

In that time, the golfing world had not just evolved, it had turned on its head. There was a new order. The old guard were fading; injured, out of form and unable to maintain their winning habits. The younger generation had taken over and this process contributed massively to the story of how that gold trophy came to sit on that coffee table, among those newspapers, in that room, on that morning.

The captain had been wrong. This wasn't the morning after the night before, this was the morning after the two years before – the period since the 'miracle' that occurred the last time these two great golfing entities had locked horns.

On this occasion it was not miraculous, it was meticulous. This was the product of a plan, an extraordinarily detailed plan, that rode the dramatic swings of fortune of the golfing calendar.

And this is how it happened.

CHAPTER 1

Watson's story

*'He thinks that in 2014 not only do we have to win,
we need to go over there and hammer these guys.'*
Ted Bishop, President of the PGA of
America, on Tom Watson

For America, losing their biennial clash with Europe's top golfers was nothing new. Their defeat in 2012 meant they had lost seven of the last nine Ryder Cups. But this one was the hardest to stomach because they had squandered a seemingly unbeatable position.

Golfers are among the most resilient of athletes. One of the mantras on tour is 'there's always next week' and an immediate chance to atone for each and every disappointment. This loss, however, was different.

Keegan Bradley made a sensational Ryder Cup debut at the Medinah Country Club. He revelled in the atmosphere and won three out of a possible four points. Yet in the wake of the match he could not bring himself to switch on the Golf Channel, the network that provided his usual viewing. 'It was too difficult,' Bradley said. He didn't even unpack the bags that had carried the clothing he wore throughout his Ryder Cup debut. They lay at home, the zips firmly locked.

Jim Furyk, who had played in every American team since 1997, called it 'the lowest point', while the even more experienced Phil Mickelson said: 'We thought we were going to win; we were playing well. It was one of the biggest disappointments I've had to deal with in my career.'

Late into the Saturday afternoon fourballs, the US team led by 10 points to 4 and were ahead in one of the two remaining matches. The vast Chicago crowds swarming over the Medinah course were in celebratory mood. They had only 24 hours to wait until the famous trophy would be back in American hands.

They had won it only once this century – in 2008, at Valhalla – and only twice since 1993, the other triumph for this golfing superpower occurring at Brookline in 1999. The thirst for victory was insatiable.

Throughout this barren period for the US, the Ryder Cup had sustained its position as the highest-profile event in golf. Europe celebrated their successes with gusto while American despair grew ever more apparent. Medinah was the most painful defeat by far.

There is no hiding from the Ryder Cup. It defines the professional schedules in Europe and America. Much of the modern game is centred around its qualifying processes. Every two years it is contested over three autumn days, when golf is showcased in its most exciting and dramatic form.

One of the key benchmarks for any American or European player is where they stand in those qualifying tables. A big win in one of the majors – the Masters, the Open, US Open or PGA – is hugely significant in its own right. More often than not, however, it is also seen in the light of what it does for a player's Ryder Cup chances. Within minutes of winning his second Augusta green jacket in 2014, Bubba Watson was asked for his thoughts on all but sealing his Gleneagles place. The same happened a couple of months later when Germany's Martin Kaymer ran away with the US Open at Pinehurst.

In short, the Ryder Cup galvanises golf. It draws in the casual sports fan where most other tournaments are restricted to die-hard enthusiasts. It attracts huge crowds, prepared to pay top dollar for the experience. The revenues generated through ticket sales, sponsorship and, most significantly, television rights effectively underwrite the European Tour, while in the US they go a long way to funding the PGA of America.

The reason the event generates such vast sums is because the Ryder Cup can always deliver sport of the highest calibre. Two 12-man teams go head-to-head with cut-throat intensity. On the Friday and Saturday they compete as pairs in alternate-shot foursomes and fourball contests. Here, each player plays his own ball and the one who makes the best score wins the hole. The respective captains decide who plays with whom and in what order. This provides a heady cocktail of tactics, hunches and second-guessing, and adds a compelling sense of intrigue to the spectacle.

On the final day it's every man for himself, over 12 singles matches. Again, the skippers try to read each other's thoughts as they finalise their playing orders. In total, there are 28 points to play for, with 14½ points enough to win outright a cup that has been the precious prize of these transatlantic jousts since 1927.

The format captures the magic of inserting an individual performer into a team environment. Some prosper, others perish. The process of determining which side of that fence a player will fall invariably involves huge sporting drama.

It also plays to the tribal instincts that help give team sports their captivating edge. That is why so much excitement was being generated on Saturday, 29 September 2012. For those American supporters, there was a genuine expectation that something monumental was in the making. And they would be proved correct – but not, as it turned out, in the way they either expected or wanted.

At one stage at Medinah, Davis Love III's team led by six points during the Saturday afternoon and needed just four-and-a-half more for the skipper to lay his hands on the trophy. There were two more fourballs to complete, then 12 Sunday singles; a total of 14 points still up for grabs. Europe, led by José

María Olazábal, needed to win 10 of those to retain the trophy. That meant winning 71 per cent of the remaining action – precisely matching America's winning percentage up to that stage of the contest. Put another way, a total reversal was required.

Europe seemed to be out for the count. Walking the course while commentating for BBC 5Live, I could feel the mood. The only remaining question was by how many points America would win. Could they emulate the record-equalling thrashings handed out by Europe to claim the 2004 and 2006 matches, by 18½–9½? It looked a distinct possibility.

Except that Europe had in their ranks a man called Ian Poulter.

No one quite connects with the Ryder Cup like the English golfer from the unpretentious town of Hitchin, just north of London. He had made his debut in 2004 at Oakland Hills and returned to the team as a controversial wildcard pick four years later. He would confound his critics by emerging as the top scorer in Sir Nick Faldo's losing line-up at Valhalla, taking four points out of a possible five. Two years later, he claimed three out of four in Colin Montgomerie's victorious team at Celtic Manor.

On Saturday evening at Medinah, Europe were barely breathing. America had won all but one of the six matches completed that day. The one they lost had been down to Poulter's morning partnership with Justin Rose, the Englishmen beating Watson and Webb Simpson on the final green. It had been one-way traffic ever since. Mickelson and Bradley had set the template by crushing renowned Ryder Cup stalwarts Lee Westwood and Luke Donald with six holes to spare. Watson and Simpson bounced back from their pre-lunch defeat to thrash Rose and Francesco Molinari. By the end, they were five holes ahead with four to play.

It was the kind of hammering that only seems to be handed out when a team is being swept along on a tide of optimism and confidence. Graeme McDowell, the man who claimed the winning point for Europe in 2010, commented: 'It was hard, very hard to ignore the red on the board. There's blood in the water. They're up for it.'

And so it took a truly astounding spell of play to put any kind of brake on the runaway success of the home team. Poulter was in the last match, partnering world number one Rory McIlroy. They were up against the in-form duo of Jason Dufner and Zach Johnson and the Americans were two up with six to play. McIlroy birdied the 13th to halve the arrears and then his inspired English partner took over.

An astonishing run of five straight birdies ended when Poulter holed the winning putt from 12 feet on the final green. Associated Press columnist Tim Dahlberg called it 'a fist-pumping, gut-roaring, bug-eyed display'. It rescued a precious point and silenced the home support to such an extent that it inspired Donald and Sergio García, the only other Europeans left out on the course. They also won on the final hole, beating Tiger Woods and Steve Stricker.

The catalyst for this late fightback was Poulter – the man they call 'The Postman' because he always delivers. 'He just gets that look in his eye, especially when he makes one of those big putts . . . he's fist-pumping and he will just look right through you,' said McIlroy.

Afterwards, Poulter marched into the team room and told his colleagues: 'Now we have a pulse.' That pulse was still weak, but it was regular and beating more reliably than it had for most of the first two days.

It also spelt trouble for America. Now they led 10–6, with the singles to go. It remained a commanding position, their biggest Saturday evening lead for 31 years and one that still promised victory. 'Being up four is nice,' Woods said. 'We are in a great spot right now to win the Cup.' The home team, indeed, had not lost a session.

But their momentum had stalled. Chants of 'U-S-A, U-S-A!' had gradually given way to optimistic strains of 'Olé Olé!' from the travelling European fans. Unquestionably, there was still a battle to be won.

The final day is remembered as one of the most dramatic ever seen at a Ryder Cup. Europe fed off Poulter's heroics from the previous morning. They were quickly ahead in the first five matches. They needed to be. Eight out of the dozen points on offer would retain the trophy. As the holders, a 14–14 tie was enough.

Scoreboard pressure is everything in the Ryder Cup. Players are told to ignore the standings and concentrate on their own ball and their own match. But that is impossible. Crowds are either energised or silenced by circumstance. The mood is tangible, dictated by whichever way fortune is flowing. And it was now taking a decidedly European course.

One by one, the points were being delivered by Olazábal's team. In the top match, Donald beat Watson. Behind, Poulter saw off Simpson, McIlroy accounted for Bradley (even though McIlroy had arrived late at the course, travelling in a State Trooper's patrol car after misinterpreting his tee time) and Rose sensationally beat Mickelson. Scotland's Paul Lawrie had already delivered his point with an emphatic 5 and 3 win over Brandt Snedeker. For the United States, the two Johnsons — Zach and Dustin — provided welcome victories, as did Jason Dufner. But García somehow got the better of Furyk on the final green and Westwood beat Matt Kuchar 3 and 2.

All of this meant that if the previously out-of-form Kaymer could beat Stricker, Europe would reach the magic 14-point mark. The German duly obliged, despite charging his initial putt across the home green and six feet past the hole. Kaymer held his nerve coming back and, as the American crowds headed for the exits, he leaped into the arms of his disbelieving yet ecstatic teammates.

Woods then conceded a half to Molinari. Europe had not only retained the trophy but won the match 14½–13½ to repeat their victory of two years earlier by the same margin. They had come back in astonishing style to inflict the most painful American defeat in Ryder Cup history.

Europe called it the 'Miracle at Medinah'. For the US, it was a 'Medinah Meltdown'.

So when the 2014 match at Gleneagles came around, the United States' desire for victory had never been greater. 'Are we in a desperate situation? Yes, that's a fair statement,' admitted Ted Bishop, the President of the PGA of America. 'I mean, we are real tired of losing. All due respect to the Europeans, they've deserved to win these Ryder Cups, but those guys would feel the same way as we do if they'd lost as many times as we have. We are sick and tired of it.'

Even before the US capitulation at Medinah, Bishop had been addressing the issue of his country's inability to win the event in the modern era. It seems ironic now that it was a suggestion made by America's greatest golfer, Jack Nicklaus, that had helped make the trophy so hard to regain. The 18-times major champion felt the Ryder Cup would become an irrelevance if it remained a match between the United States and Great Britain and Ireland. These contests held no jeopardy; America won them with ease. Nicklaus recognised that interest in golf was spreading beyond the shores of the British isles. Why, therefore, should America not face the whole of Europe instead? At least the matches would be closer.

The golfing continent of Europe came together for the first time in 1979 and was captained by the hugely respected former player and teacher John Jacobs at The Greenbrier in West Virginia. It remained a predominantly British team but was supplemented by a young Spaniard called Severiano Ballesteros and his compatriot Antonio Garrido.

The outcome did not change, though. America won easily,

just as they did at Walton Heath two years later. On that occasion, Dave Marr's team swept to a record 18½–9½ triumph. It was probably the greatest American team ever assembled, containing the likes of Nicklaus, Tom Watson, Johnny Miller and Lee Trevino. Only Bruce Lietzke, no slouch with 13 wins on the PGA Tour, did not have a major title to his name. Europe had no answer to such strong opposition. But two years later, in 1983, it was a different story.

At the PGA National Golf Club in Palm Beach Gardens, Florida, Europe's true potential was revealed for the first time. Inspired by Ballesteros, and supplemented by fellow Spaniard José María Cañizares and Germany's Bernhard Langer, Tony Jacklin's team came within a point of inflicting America's first home defeat.

Ballesteros told his disconsolate teammates this was just the beginning and he was correct. Two years later at the Belfry in the English Midlands, Europe marched to a five-point triumph. It was the first time America had been beaten in 28 years. Between then and Gleneagles there had been 12 Ryder Cups. Only four were won by the United States. Furthermore, they had not won an away match since 1993.

This was the statistic that most concerned the incoming President of the PGA of America. He had every reason to make a plan to redress the balance. Ted Bishop is the General Partner and Director of Golf at the Legends Club, a facility he founded in Franklin, south east of Indianapolis. Golf has been his life since graduating from Purdue with a degree in Agronomy and Turf Management in 1976.

For 17 years he was the superintendent at a municipal course in the coal-mining town of Linton, Indiana. He was innovative and enterprising and not afraid of approaching big names to help further the interests of the game in the area. Bishop ran the Phil Harris Celebrity Tournament and attracted the likes of Vice President Dan Quayle and astronaut Neil

Armstrong to the field. Celebrated pros came along, too, Dave Marr, Toney Penna and Doug Sanders among them.

These successes helped Bishop make a name for himself. He is charismatic and smart, and has the reputation of being an 'ideas man'. When, aged 58, he became PGA President he was fearless in challenging rule-makers like the R&A and USGA over their plans to outlaw anchored putting techniques. He blogs regularly and maintained a high profile throughout his tenure.

Bishop left Linton in the early 1990s when he bought farmland and transformed it into the Legends Club. People liked the fact that he could think 'out of the box' when seeking new ways to grow the game. It was clear that he was destined for high office at the PGA of America, which administers the club game in the US. A member since 1985, he had served as President of the Indiana section. Bishop was elected to the PGA Board of Directors in 2006 and served as Secretary for the two years prior to becoming Vice President in 2010.

As well as looking after club professionals, the organisation is also responsible for the Ryder Cup in the United States. Bishop was slated to become its 38th President, which meant taking over in the wake of Medinah and overseeing America's challenge at Gleneagles – as well as naming the next captain.

For whatever reason, the PGA of America had previously followed an unofficial doctrine which stated that Ryder Cup captains had to be major champions, had to have played on multiple Ryder Cup teams and needed to be in their mid- to late-forties.

'So there was this unofficial list of guys that met this criteria that would almost be handed down on the back of a napkin from president to president. You just picked the next guy and went on,' said Bishop.

Davis Love and his immediate predecessors Corey Pavin, Paul Azinger, Tom Lehman and Hal Sutton had all ticked those boxes but, of those, only Azinger in 2008 had emerged a winner.

Bishop assumed he would go down the familiar process of picking the next skipper. 'I started doing a lot of research and I went back through the past 15 years and I created this matrix of major champions. I looked at all the Americans who had won majors.

'You had a group that had won and never played on a Ryder Cup team (John Daly, Todd Hamilton, Lucas Glover, Shaun Micheel and Mark Brooks). So they're not potential captains. Then you had someone like Payne Stewart, who would have been an ideal choice but is sadly no longer with us [Stewart was killed in a plane accident months after winning the 1999 US Open. He had also played in the Brookline victory that year]. All of a sudden, when you started looking at this list of possibles, there were only maybe six or seven guys.

'This was because of the number of Europeans and other foreign players who were now winning majors, plus the number Woods and Mickelson had won in this era. So our list was pretty short and I thought if ever there was an opportunity to do something different, 2014 offered the chance.'

Bishop had an alternative plan, one that had been in the making since 2009, the year of his first visit to an Open Championship. He went to Turnberry, on Scotland's Ayrshire coast, and witnessed the most improbable challenge for a major that golf had ever seen. At the age of 59, Tom Watson came within an eight-foot putt of winning his sixth Open, what would have been his ninth major in total. The story of a man of such senior years claiming one of sport's elite titles would have been remembered for evermore.

'What a first one to go to!' Bishop recalled. 'I'll never forget this. I was on the course on the Sunday with my wife and I said to her towards the end of the front nine: "You know what? Let's go back." We were staying in Ayr and I wanted to watch the

BBC call the last nine holes. I wanted to hear what Peter Alliss would say because I really thought Tom was going to win.'

As it turned out, Watson missed that eight-footer, failed to par the last hole and the great Alliss never had the chance to marry his magical words to a moment that would have transcended the game. Instead, Watson had to settle for a four-hole play-off with Stewart Cink which was convincingly won by his younger compatriot.

Nevertheless, the story of Watson's odyssey was brilliantly captured by the late American broadcaster and writer Jim Huber in his book *Four Days in July*, published in 2011. At that year's PGA Grand Slam event in Bermuda, Huber handed a copy to Bishop.

'I read it on the flight back to Indianapolis,' Bishop said. 'I really have to credit Jim Huber for tripping the switch in my mind. As I was reading the book, I thought: "Hey, this is Scotland, why not Tom Watson for captain in 2014?"'

Watson had been the last man to captain America to Ryder Cup victory on European soil back in 1993. He had won four of his five Opens in Scotland and, as was shown at Turnberry in 2009, he still commanded immense popularity in the country that would stage Europe's next home Ryder Cup.

His caddie since 2003 has been his great friend Neil Oxman, a full-time political strategist and regular lecturer at the University of Pennsylvania and at Oxford in the UK. Oxman is also a fine golfer and occasionally plays friendly matches with Watson. 'We talk a lot about the Ryder Cup because I caddied for Tommy Horton in the 1975 match when it was just GB and Ireland versus the US. When I play against Tom, I always make myself Sir Henry Cotton. We actually always play Ryder Cup matches,' he revealed.

Oxman was at Watson's side at Turnberry and could feel the crowds' adulation for his boss. He says the reaction is magnified in Scotland, but that the response he generates throughout the

United Kingdom is sometimes hard to handle. 'Thousands of people would just stand and applaud, for no reason. You would literally get tears in your eyes. Even as a caddie you feel the emotion. Tom had to say: "Boy it's hard for me to play, I've got to concentrate and it's hard."

'All the crowds in the UK are like that with him – especially now that Arnie doesn't play and Jack doesn't play and Gary doesn't play and Trevino's stopped coming. He's kind of the last guy, the last living legend who still plays. But he's not playing ceremonial golf. He's playing real golf. He keeps playing well.'

At Turnberry, the standard of his play was so high that it prompted Huber to write the book that had such an effect on Bishop, on his way home to Indianapolis. 'I got back to the house and straightaway sent Jim an email and asked him if I could call him at the weekend,' Bishop said.

'We spoke on the Saturday and I said to him I had an off-the-wall question. What would he think of Tom Watson for Ryder Cup captain at Gleneagles in 2014? Other than my wife, Jim was the first person I threw the idea past. I was aware Jim knew Tom better than I did. He probably had a good idea what was inside Tom's head, as to whether he would be interested. When I posed that question there was a pause. Then he gave me a one-word answer. He just said: "Brilliant."

'Then he gave me Tom's cell phone number. Jim was funny. He said: "When you call Watson don't tell him where you got this number."'

Bishop spent the next fortnight mulling over the idea. Watson's number was now safely stored in his cell phone. It was on the 180-mile journey from Chicago back to Indianapolis when the PGA Vice President decided it was time to make his approach.

'I was nervous about it,' Bishop admitted. 'You know, Tom Watson is Tom Watson. He's one of the sport's icons and I didn't really have a lot of history with him. None, at that point in time. I also knew we had staged a Ryder Cup captains' dinner in Savannah the previous May and Tom was one of the few who didn't go.'

The call didn't begin particularly well. 'I told him who I was and I could tell he was outside. You could hear wind blowing through the telephone. He said: "I'm pheasant hunting in South Dakota, could you call me back tonight?" When I called back later that evening, the conversation started with him saying: "Tell me your name again?"'

Bishop explained that, having missed him at Savannah, he would like to pick his brains on America's lack of recent successes in the Ryder Cup away from home. 'Ironically, you were the last winning captain,' he told Watson. 'Why have we not won over there since?'

Watson was typically blunt. 'Well, for one thing the Europeans have played better than we have,' he said. 'Maybe they have better players during the week of the Ryder Cup.'

It was clear that Watson was energised by the conversation. Bishop revealed: 'He got into the fundamentals of the players' swings and he said: 'You know, I've watched our guys and their guys and I'm not so sure their swings aren't better, which helps them hold up in bad weather.' He went on to talk about the familiarity the Europeans have with the golf courses, because they usually play Tour events on them.'

Watson also reasoned that the American players were often exhausted because they came to the Ryder Cup a week after the season-ending Tour Championship in Atlanta. 'That's kind of the way the conversation went,' Bishop said. The chat lasted around three-quarters of an hour. 'At the end I said: "Well, here's the million-dollar question. Would you ever have any desire to be Ryder Cup captain again?"'

'He said: "You know Ted, this is the phone call that I've been waiting on for years. I might be very interested."'

Their discussion took place in November 2011. The

Medinah Ryder Cup was still more than 10 months away and Gleneagles nearly three years off. Watson had not attended the event since leading his country to victory almost 20 years before.

Back then, he had been the one to initiate captaincy talk. 'It was different,' Watson recalled. 'Chuck Rubin was my manager in those days. I asked Chuck: "I would like to be a Ryder Cup captain. Can you make contact with them? And if you do, please request that I am a captain overseas, because of the record that I've had over there." '

Rubin carried out the request. This was 1992 and, a few months later, Watson received a call from the PGA of America and was summoned for an interview. Within 15 minutes Watson was offered the job. It was a no-brainer. He had a legendary status in the game, having won five Open Championships in 1975, 1977, 1980, 1982 and 1983 to go with Masters victories in 1977 and 1981 and his US Open triumph at Pebble Beach in 1982. He played in four Ryder Cups, recording 10 wins, four defeats and one half. The tied 1989 contest at the Belfry was the only Ryder Cup he had been involved in that America had not won.

Furthermore, he was a consummate ambassador for the game. Watson was regarded as someone who would always do or say the right thing. He had learned his golf at the Kansas City Country Club but resigned in 1990 when he discovered that a businessman called Henry Bloch had been denied membership because he was Jewish. 'I felt it was a religious issue and I cannot live with that,' Watson told the local newspaper. 'I feel more than uncomfortable. I think it's wrong. It's more than my conscience could bear.'

As Oxman observed: 'He's a gentleman. He was raised a certain way. There are guys you see on a golf course who are "hot dogs", and Tom's not like that. I think he saw how gracious Jack Nicklaus always was in defeat. One of the great golf writers wrote that Jack was even greater in defeat than he was in victory, in terms of his graciousness. With the exception of Augusta, he turns up at every tournament thinking he can win. But he doesn't do it in an obnoxious way. There's no swagger about it, there's no chip on the shoulder.'

Back in 1993, he was a natural choice. For the 2014 match, it was much more a decision from left field.

Bishop and Watson finished their conversation with an exchange of email addresses. The next morning Bishop was up early, heading to his office at Legends. On his arrival the first thing he saw in his inbox was a message from the man with whom he had been conversing the night before. 'I'm thinking: "Uh-oh, maybe he doesn't want to do it."' Bishop admitted.

But Watson had emailed to say he would like to speak again that morning. The call lasted two hours. 'Tom was asking me questions about the 2010 Ryder Cup in Wales,' Bishop said. 'He was trying to determine the similarities and the differences between today's Ryder Cup and the one in 1993. It was fun. He was asking all the questions and I was giving all the answers.'

The two men stayed in touch over the coming months but Bishop's next big move wasn't until 10 days after Medinah. American golf was hurting like never before. The feeling that a radically different approach was needed had been reinforced.

Bishop flew to Watson's ranch in Kansas City and briefed his prospective skipper on all that had happened during those dramatic days in the Chicago suburbs. 'We met for probably six hours that day,' Bishop said. 'We did that and it was basically a handshake and I said: "Okay, we will see you in a month or so."'

Bishop, meanwhile, had drawn up an 85-page document to support his notion that someone who would be in his mid-60s when the next Ryder Cup came around was the man to lead America's quest for the trophy. The dossier was effectively a campaign manifesto to woo votes for this unorthodox course of action from his senior colleagues.

The only potential blight on Watson's reputation was that

he had had a problem with alcohol, but even that became an indicator of his inner strength. In the 1990s he became increasingly dependent on drinking and his marriage to childhood sweetheart Linda was unravelling. They divorced after 25 years, having wed in the wake of his graduation from Stanford University.

In 1998 Watson tackled the problem head-on and brought an end to his reliance on the bottle. 'I stopped all by myself,' he later revealed. 'Drinking is a choice. It's a social issue, a peer-pressure issue. If I'd had trouble giving it up, I would have gotten some help. But I managed.'

The alcohol issue featured in Bishop's document. So did the fact that Watson was now happily married to his second wife Hilary, who had been a pillar of support in the wake of the 2009 Turnberry loss. The incoming PGA President was determined to see this through and break from the norm. Yes, it was a move outside the box, but he was convinced he had the right man for the job.

'The thing I love about Watson is that winning is number one on his priority list,' Bishop said. 'It's just all about bringing the Cup back here. He would tell you that he thinks in 2014 not only do we need to win, we need to go over there and hammer these guys. We need to send a message loud and clear that we are going to bring back the Ryder Cup in style. And I think that what really drives these comments is that we had a sizeable lead going into Sunday at Medinah and we didn't put them away.'

A month later Bishop, Vice President Derek Sprague, Secretary Paul Levy and brand new PGA Chief Executive Peter Bevacqua flew to Kansas City for the formal interview process. Watson was going to be the next Ryder Cup captain, the first to do the job for a second time since Nicklaus in 1987. The fervent hope was that Watson would be more successful than his great friend and rival had been on his return. Nicklaus was the first skipper to lose a home match, a result that went a long way to inspiring Europe's current domination.

Still, the move was top secret. Few outside the PGA's inner circle were aware of the radical plan. Watson carried on playing a mixture of seniors and main tour golf around the world. He played in the 2012 Australian Open and shot the lowest round of the final day, a week before the announcement of America's new skipper on 13 December.

Oxman was one of those who knew what was about to happen. 'Tom and his wife went on safari in South Africa. Then he played Sun City and the Australian Open. So we literally went round the world in one trip. We left on separate planes – I went back to Pennsylvania and he went to New York, where it was announced that he was going to be Ryder Cup captain. He was really excited about it, it was a big deal.'

Most observers were expecting David Toms – a major-winning, multiple Ryder Cup player in his mid-40s – to succeed Davis Love. If it was to be someone from the older guard, then maybe the nod would go to Larry Nelson, a three-times major winner who had won five out of five Cup matches in 1979.

The fact that both men categorically denied they had been approached offered the only clue that something different might be afoot. In Sydney, Watson was asked if he was interested in the job: 'It would be a great honour if I was tapped on the shoulder,' he replied.

This alerted the American media and while Watson was in the air on Tuesday, before the scheduled Thursday announcement, *Golf Digest* broke the news. The best-kept secret in the game was out of the bag.

Watson was unveiled alongside Bishop on NBC's *Today* show before a set-piece news conference on the 80th floor of the Empire State Building. Bishop told reporters: 'We feel he's certainly the perfect person to do this, based on his playing record in Scotland.

'The other key thing is how this gentleman is revered there. He's got a tremendous understanding of the culture, the country and its people. We also know about the unique weather challenges that Scotland will probably present and I think he is recognised as one of the top players under challenging conditions. We certainly hope that will translate to our team.'

'The way I look at being a captain, it's like being a stage manager,' Watson said. 'That person has to prepare the stage for the actors and that's what I do as captain. My job is simply to co-ordinate and maybe inspire a little bit.'

Watson fronted up to the accusation that he would be too old. 'I can deflect that very simply,' he said. 'We play the same game. I play against these kids at the Masters. I play against them at the British Open, the Greenbrier Classic. We play the same game and they understand that. I understand that.'

It was a forceful and impressive display from the veteran, who showed no signs of fatigue despite having flown from Kansas to Cape Town, then to Sydney and back to New York in the preceding week. As Oxman says: 'The guy is pretty young – you wouldn't know what his age is.'

Watson's message to Europe was emphatic: 'We are going to pull out all the stops to beat you guys. I will do it in the style and grace in which we play the game. We're tired of losing. I learned to win by hating to lose. It's about time to start winning again.'

The one area of concern was Watson's relationship with America's best player. He had been outspoken in his criticism of Tiger Woods when the 14-times major champion became embroiled in scandal after his multiple affairs went public in 2009. Watson had said: 'I think he needs to clean up his act and show the respect for the game that other people before him have shown.'

But Watson gave a very different message to the world's media assembled at the Empire State Building. 'You can bet that he's going to be number one on my pick list. My relationship with Tiger is fine. Whatever has been said before is water under the bridge, no issues. He dominates this game unlike anybody in the history of the sport. So I want him on my team.'

Woods reacted swiftly with his own statement: 'I think he's a really good choice. Tom knows what it takes to win and that's our ultimate goal. I hope I have the privilege of joining him on the 2014 United States team.'

Little did Woods know how what was to become a vain hope would form a substantial part of the narrative in the build-up to Gleneagles.

America, though, had made a bold statement. They were daring to be different or, as Roger Warren, one of Bishop's predecessors, suggested, they had no choice. 'It's like the definition of insanity. You can't keep doing the same thing over and over again and expect a different result.'

Hence this radical route. It was a match the US had to win, like never before. They had turned to one of the game's legends to reverse their fortunes. The questions now were: would he be up to the job, considering his age, and how would Europe respond?

CHAPTER 2

Watson as captain

'I want players with heart. I want people who can
make that five-footer. That's what I'll be looking for –
those are the types of players that win Ryder Cups.'
Tom Watson

Tom Watson came into the room full of apologies. He was
late, but with good reason. Everyone, it seemed, wanted
to talk to him as he prepared to compete in the British
Senior's Open at Royal Porthcawl in July 2014.

'I'm sorry to delay you so much, I feel like Jack Nicklaus,'
he joked as he took his seat. Nicklaus, with a record 18 major
championships to his name, is regularly held up by well-wishers
and admirers whenever he is anywhere near a golf course. It
was the same for Watson, particularly in the build-up to the
Gleneagles showdown. Not only was he a legendary golfing
figure in his own right, but now the 65-year-old was leading
the US in its quest to wrestle back the precious Ryder Cup.

We had scheduled our conversation in the company of
Bernard Gallacher, who had been Europe's captain the last time
Watson had led America, back in 1993. That had also been the
last occasion that the US had won an away match. From the
outset, it was evident that this little gold trophy, at the heart of
the September contest in Scotland, has always mattered hugely
to Watson.

'My main goal was to be the best player I could be,' he said.
'But it was also to make the Ryder Cup team. It really was a
goal of mine – I wanted to play for my country. One of the best

experiences I can remember was making the team for the first time in 1977 and watching the American flag go up, with the 'Star Spangled Banner' being played at the opening ceremony on that grey afternoon at Lytham and St Annes.

'Having that feeling that I'm part of a team for America. That was a very, very special time for me. It really sent chills, I mean, I was teary, the emotions were really, really hot,' he added in the interview for BBC Radio.

The idea of the meeting was to provide the opportunity for Watson and Gallacher to reminisce. They had played each other in the 1983 singles, when Europe came so close to victory on American soil for the first time. Watson won 2 and 1 to deliver a crucial point in a Ryder Cup effectively settled by Lanny Wadkins' brilliant approach to the last which forced a half against José María Cañizares. Nicklaus was the US captain on that occasion and Watson recalled: 'That was the most animated I ever saw Jack on the golf course, the way he hugged Lanny after that shot.' Gallacher nodded in rueful agreement.

But Watson did not want to dwell on old times. Unprompted, he brought the conversation up to date in a way that indicated how the mission to win back the trophy was at the forefront of his mind. 'The American team has to get back on track,' he said. 'The loss at Medinah should stick in their craw. All those playing in the Ryder Cup team this year, it should stick in their craw and they have to take care of business, to basically get even.'

Watson wasn't at Medinah but still felt the pain of American defeat acutely. 'One of the things I recall is having an empty feeling for three or four days after that Ryder Cup defeat. I really did. I've never had that empty feeling, ever, playing for myself. My gut was hollow and it was just so disappointing that we lost.

'It basically came down to one hole with [Phil] Mickelson and [Justin] Rose ... Rose did great things.' Rose had closed out an epic match on the 18th green after holing a huge putt to win the 17th with a birdie.

'The beautiful thing about the Ryder Cup is I see more holed shots and more great shots than in any other event,' added Watson. 'You just don't see it in individual tournaments. When they're playing for their team it's like they are holing from everywhere. The shots they are making are spectacular, the players rise to the occasion.'

Watson's appointment as captain for 2014 received popular acclaim. Few people felt he was too old. Nevertheless, it was a subject that he was touchy about. Watching him in press conferences throughout the year of the match, it was evident he was keen to shut down any talk of him being aged or out of touch. This was especially the case after he appointed Andy North, who was 64, and Raymond Floyd, 72, as vice captains.

'Are you too old to be a Ryder Cup captain? The way I answer that, and I believe this with all my heart, is that these players know Raymond, Andy and myself,' Watson said. 'We've been there. We know what Ryder Cup pressure is all about. Raymond and I have been captains. We know what's going on. And to have that trust and respect from the players that we know what's going on, that can help them. So the age difference, actually, it's kind of like a professor. You go to learn from a professor. He's been there, he knows, he has the experience, he has the knowledge; and that's what we bring as captains and vice captains to the Ryder Cup.

'When these players look at Raymond, they know he's been there and they know he's been successful. They know he wants to win. I don't really need anything else. We need those players to understand that we are there to support them. We have their back. Whatever they need, we'll bring it to them,' Watson added.

Gallacher, meanwhile, feared the impact that Watson's appointment might have on the American team. He also believed such a revered figure would be able to breathe new life into the match. 'I just thought it was a masterstroke from the American PGA,' the Scot said. 'We won at Celtic Manor and Medinah. If anybody can keep the interest going on the American side, it is Tom. It's not just about the players; you're really thinking about the American public, keeping them interested. If it's important for Tom to be captain, trying to get back the trophy, then it should be important to the American golfing public.

'Of course, it's in Scotland as well,' Gallacher added. 'Tom is better known in Scotland than anybody else in the world! He's so respected and well liked . . . If anybody can turn around the American side, you would probably think of somebody like Tom Watson to do it.'

When Gallacher and Watson locked horns as captains in 1993 it was in a match that followed the infamous 'War on the Shore' at Kiawah Island. That had been a thrilling contest that wasn't settled until Bernhard Langer missed from around six feet on the final green against Hale Irwin. It had been marked, though, by ill-feeling between the teams. Some US players, including future captain Corey Pavin, wore military-style caps because the first Gulf War was underway. It was a crass gesture that took no account of the fact that troops from European nations were involved as well. The atmosphere from the crowd was hostile and a local radio station made prank early-morning phone calls to disturb the sleep of European players. All this meant that the two captains in 1993 had to make sure the contest at the Belfry was played in the right spirit. Gallacher and Watson proved the perfect ambassadorial figures for such a task.

Ryder Cups, though, are always a partisan business. Players and fans become more demonstrative than in any other form of the game. Watson remembered being shocked by this dimension when he first took part.

'I was playing with Hubert Green on the first day,' he said, recalling the Lytham match of 1977. 'We had Tommy Horton and Brian Barnes six down after 10 holes. I knocked it on to the par-5 11th in two and they were scrambling. Tommy hit it to 15 feet and although I was on in two I didn't make a good putt. It came up four or five feet short. Tommy made his putt and I missed and a cheer went up from the crowd. I didn't like that. I did not like that at all.

'But I looked at it logically and actually it motivated me, and the other hand is, you know, if I'm pulling for that other team, it's actually okay to cheer for a missed putt. I don't mind that. You don't do that at an Open Championship when somebody misses a putt, but in the Ryder Cup it's okay. But the thing is, you don't want people yelling at them on their back swing.'

Watson wasn't lying when he told PGA of America President Ted Bishop that he had waited 20 years for the call to re-assume the captaincy. Ever since his appointment, this seemingly most youthful 60-something relished the prospect of returning to the US team room. He couldn't wait to impose his Ryder Cup philosophies on a side that, once assembled, would boast an excellent mix of youth and experience.

'Golf is an individual sport, Ryder Cup is a team sport, although you are playing individually,' Watson explained. 'Bottom line, you are still playing individually. You are playing the golf course the best you can as a player, but the team rooms are wonderful places to be. The camaraderie is great because we share a level of pressure together. I've talked to past captains – Davis Love, Tom Lehman and Corey Pavin – about the team rooms and they just say how spot on it is. It's just the nature of everybody, so gung-ho to play in the Ryder Cup. Being in the team room is different than playing for yourself and it is a joy.'

Giving an insight into the way he intended to manage his golfers, Watson stressed the importance of lightening the mood and empowering them to perform an invaluable role. 'In 1993, Payne Stewart was carrying that ball for the team,' Watson revealed. 'He was the gung-ho guy, he got in people's minds. And then there are the quiet people, who every now and then put a line out and make everybody laugh. Under all that pressure, laughter is the greatest way of reducing it to a degree which is tolerable. You have to release the players, and humour is just great for that.'

As Watson found out when he grilled Bishop about what a modern-day Ryder Cup entails, the event has grown massively. But the returning skipper saw no reason to change the methods that resulted in his team coming from behind to beat Gallacher's side 15–13. 'I haven't changed my way of thinking about the Ryder Cup. As a captain, what I can bring to the table, very specifically, is putting the teams together, the right players together. You assess how they are playing and how to change the teams if necessary. Prior to that, you pick the three players who are going to complete and help your team. The bottom line is that I'm not there to motivate. If they're not motivated to play, they're in the wrong business and I know 100 per cent that everybody will be motivated. I may be able to inspire them a little bit . . . there's a lot of pressure going on and to try and create a place of respite for the players with humour and ease, that's my job. Clear the obstacles and make it easy for them to go out and perform.

'The pressure won't be any different,' Watson continued. 'You are playing on the Ryder Cup team and the players who've been there before recognise what pressure is all about. The players who haven't played before, well, the players who've played before will tell them – that's the way it works. They won't ask me so much, but if they do I'll talk to them about it.

'You hope all your players are playing to the best of their capabilities – which is never the case,' he added with his trademark gap-toothed grin.

Controlling the controllable was the Watson mantra throughout his captaincy. Repeatedly, he returned to the message that he was a stage manager, enabling his actors to go out and perform. Equally, he also seemed detailed and meticulous in his preparation, as his wife testified.

'Hilary Watson was saying at dinner the other night how fussy Tom is being about the rainsuits,' Ted Bishop told the *Global Golf Post* e-magazine. 'He has sent them back three or four times for modifications to the zippers, the logos and the waterproof ability. She said he puts one on and goes and stands in the shower for up to an hour at a time. She would say to him: "Tom, what are you doing?" and he'd say: "I'm giving this thing the ultimate test." That speaks to his preparations.'

By continuing to play a handful of PGA Tour events and the majors for which he remained eligible – the Masters, Open and, as Ryder Cup captain, the PGA Championship – Watson was able to keep close tabs on the leading Americans as his team took shape. He also took the opportunity to play practice rounds with the younger, less familiar golfers who forced themselves into contention. He was looking for those with the temperament to deal with the unique pressures that come with the Ryder Cup. 'The way I'm looking at it, we have an away game,' Watson said at the Gleneagles news conference marking a year to go before the match. 'The home team has an advantage from a crowd standpoint and familiarity standpoint. I think we are going to go in as underdogs, because of the past records of the Ryder Cup. But don't tell that to my players!

'I said in 1993 I hope the players are all playing well going into the matches. If you are lucky enough to be a captain on a team like that, then you have no worries at all. Where you have worries is when some of your players aren't playing well. You know, the Ryder Cup pressure does a lot of things to players and their ability sometimes. That's where picking the right players for the team comes into play for me. I want players with heart. I want people who can make that five-footer. That's what I'll be looking for – those are the types of players that win Ryder Cups.'

The dynamics of the biennial jousts had changed greatly from the days when Watson first came into an American side that routinely beat Great Britain and Ireland. He acknowledged that now that the continent of Europe provides the opposition, it is a different proposition for the US team. 'It really opened the eyes of the American public, because, hey, we're supposed to win this thing,' he said.

'It's great theatre and because people have seen this theatre several times, where it comes down to one of the last two or three matches, it just holds their attention and people love to watch that and they expect that now from the Ryder Cup. Before, it was a yawner and now it's something that people really look forward to.'

Watson is a patient, gentlemanly figure with a fierce competitive steel running through him. It was ironic that he was now getting a second chance at captaincy courtesy of the most glorious loss of his career – the 2009 Open at Turnberry. It was his remarkable attempt to win a sixth Open at the age of 59 that generated Huber's book that, in turn, put Watson in Bishop's mind.

Neil Oxman was at Watson's side for that gallant bid for glory. What few people know is that it was someone with whom Watson would ultimately become inextricably linked at Gleneagles who helped ease the pain of Turnberry.

'How about this for a story?' Oxman said to me. 'When Tom loses the play-off to Stewart Cink on Sunday, the following day at noon we played a practice round at Sunningdale. Tom hadn't played there in a long time and that's where the Senior British Open was the next week. I drove through the night to be there and he flew down and we played with Bob Gilder. And who walked round with us for 18 holes? Paul McGinley.

'Paul lives there and just walked round with us. And it was

really, really nice. No one bothered us, there were no crowds. When I say there was not a single spectator on the course I am not exaggerating, but Paul McGinley came out, found Tom and spent four-and-a-half hours with us. Is there any better human being in the world than Paul McGinley?

'It was great, it was fun. Just a normal day of two players, two caddies and Paul McGinley walking inside the ropes.'

And, of course, McGinley was the man at the heart of Europe's response to Tom Watson's appointment as America's captain.

CHAPTER 3

McGinley's story

'Dad, you'll never guess who
I've just driven in the buggy...'
Paul McGinley, during his time at university

T
hey were a talented bunch of boys — one of those special school years where athletic genes had combined to
create a crop of youngsters capable of topping leagues
and challenging for representative honours. Golf was not their
obsession, though. No, their passion was reserved for Gaelic
football, one of two national sports in Ireland (the other is
hurling. The boys were good at that as well).

Among them was a small, bright and determined figure,
popular with his mates and known as a tenacious competitor.
He was good at school — not a genius but constantly making the
grade in his exams, no mean achievement for someone more
pre-occupied with his chances of playing at the mighty Croke
Park, Dublin's national stadium, than doing his homework.

He loved being in a team, sharing the craic and banter with
his mates in the dressing room. On the field, he would be the
one inspiring the others, getting them into a huddle and leading the team talks. He was the corner forward, the one who
scored the points, and he wanted the best from the guys who
would provide his scoring chances.

It didn't go unnoticed. The talent scouts knew all about
Paul McGinley. They could see he could make a name for
himself in sport. At that secondary school stage, though, there
was little notion that it would be in golf that he would prove

himself, both as a player and leader. Back then, in the 1970s, it was all about the football for this son of the Rathfarnham district of Dublin.

He had inherited strong sporting genes from his father Michael, who had played representative football for County Donegal. McGinley senior was also a keen golfer. From the age of eight, he had been a regular at the unprepossessing Dunfanaghy Golf Club where he would earn pocket money as a caddie. Michael then took up the game and by the time he reached adulthood he was down to a scratch handicap. He wasn't an elite player but good enough to compete in amateur tournaments of note. When his eldest son, Paul, came along he found he had a ready-made assistant. 'I was playing in the amateur championships in Ireland and we'd go out to Portugal and Spain maybe once or twice a year. I always brought him along to caddie for me because I couldn't afford a full caddie,' Michael recalled.

'In those days, golf wasn't like it is today. When you finished your game you generally didn't go out and practise that much unless you were doing horribly badly. Although I was never a drinker, you'd go in the bar and meet the guys and you'd have dinner and it was all fun.'

But for the young Paul there was more enjoyment to be found elsewhere. 'When I'd be doing that, he'd be out practising all the time. He'd go away and he'd practise on his own. That didn't go without notice by some of the very good players of the time,' Michael explained.

At this stage, though, Paul was no better than an 18-handicapper. His sporting eyes were still firmly trained on becoming the main man for the legendary 'Dubs' football team. Golf was merely an enjoyable pastime, though still an outlet to help satisfy what was to become a lifelong quest for self-improvement. Gradually his handicap would fall. He was in the high single figures in his teenage years but his play was largely limited to the school holidays – when there was no football or hurling.

'Paul showed his skills playing football and hurling in the primary school. He represented his school in both codes. In the Dublin area they regularly won their championship,' Michael said. 'He did a bit of soccer as well and he was captain of his team. That was his first captaincy. But he was primarily Gaelic football and hurling. He was obsessed with it. He played regularly in Croke Park as a youngster from around the age of 11 and 12. He was much better than his age at the time. He won tournaments at Croke Park, which is the biggest stadium we have here in Ireland.'

Paul's mother, Julia, added: 'He was lucky to be involved with a lot of good players ... There were a lot of them who went on to play senior football for Dublin. When they were training at Croke Park, he'd be the one in the middle getting them all going, getting them up for the challenge.

'It wasn't golf that he was interested in. He only really went with Michael when he was on school holidays in the summer time. When he was at school it was all about the football. He didn't play golf in the winter. But he was lucky to be around a lot of the good golfers of the time and he watched them.'

Paul attended secondary school at St Enda's and his arrival coincided with a prophetic coincidence. 'When he went to that school there was a teacher called Mr O'Donnell who was a golfer and, without knowing the ability of the youngsters, he got a team going,' said Michael. 'It turned out there were a lot of boys whose fathers played, just like Paul. And so they had a pretty successful team. It was anything from probably 10 or 12 handicap up to 24. That gave it a team ethos as well.'

Exams were passed and education continued. Paul was now studying for a diploma at the Dublin College of Marketing. There was still the passion for football and hurling but a growing enthusiasm for golf too, especially after he had tasted the team dynamic.

Then the fates took over.

It was the mid 1980s, Paul was 19 and, despite suffering from a worryingly sore knee, he was on the verge of being picked for Dublin's under-21 Gaelic football team. That August, there was a hurling game to be played as well. 'He went off to play in north Dublin. It wasn't a very good pitch,' his father remembered. 'He jumped up to hit the ball and he landed in a hole in the ground and twisted his knee. And then he got a crack of the hurley [stick] which broke the kneecap. That was effectively the end of football.

'We took him to the Blackrock clinic, one of the major hospitals in Dublin, and he had an operation. The surgeon put it back with four screws. He would have taken it out altogether but he knew about Paul's sporting career, so he put it back with the screws.'

This athletic, sports-obsessed teenager was suddenly stuck on crutches with his ambitions in ruins. Paul had a bike machine installed in the back room at home to speed up his rehabilitation. But it was still a long process. He joined the Grange Golf Club two minutes from the family house. Football was essentially gone from his life and, even though he was only an eight handicapper, golf suddenly took on much more importance. That desire for self-improvement, allied with a voracious appetite to practice and perfect, meant he was able to make rapid strides.

'It was sheer hard work,' Michael said. 'Getting back into the game again after being out for about 18 months. It was sheer grit as well and having the mental attitude to be successful at golf. At that stage he played the odd football game, but not very much.'

Members at the Grange recall how the youngster came close to wearing out their putting green. 'He'd leave these big footmarks on one corner,' his former teammate David Walker, now a club professional, told the *Irish Sun* newspaper. 'He could be there for hours, grooving the same putt over and over. A few of the members complained because they were afraid that he was going to wear a bare patch. He had a fantastic drive to succeed.'

Even at that age, Paul was separating himself from the rest. 'He hit shots we could never hit,' said his close friend Brian Shaw. He told Irish journalist Brian Keogh: 'He never wasted time. He loved the craic the same as anyone else and he has a great sense of fun, but he was always working on something.'

Paul attended a trial for the provincial Leinster under-21 team and played himself straight into the side. 'There was a tournament called the Leinster Youths Championship. The likes of Ryder Cup hero Philip Walton were former winners ... It was a high-quality field and, at that stage, there was a big difference between youth and senior golf. You'd be 30 before you could be that good to represent your country. He ended up winning by about 10 shots,' Michael added.

One day, the McGinleys heard their eldest son announce he was heading to Brussels to continue his education. He had been offered a posting to the European Union headquarters. A life in international business was beckoning. But the move didn't do his golf any harm either.

'The EU guys out there were saying: "This Irish fella's arrived and he's a very good golfer,"' said his father. 'There were some Irishmen in very senior positions. All of a sudden he was away golfing with them nearly every day. There was a guy called Eamon Gallagher who was a senior official and a golf fanatic, without being a very good player. He would send a black limousine to collect Paul and take him out to the Royal Waterloo golf course.' The young McGinley was seeking to learn French and the ways of continental business, but his game moved on rapidly too.

The next step saw him head to college in America with the twin aim of developing his education as well as the sport which had now become an almost all-consuming passion. One destination in particular caught his eye. San Diego, in Southern California, offered the perfect climate as well as good opportunities to continue his studies. All he needed was the money to make it possible. Once he was out there, Paul was confident his golfing prowess would earn him a scholarship. But, to start with, he would have to pay his way.

He needed to raise £6,000 (Irish Pounds) and his father's business contacts proved invaluable. 'At that stage I was head of Motorola in Ireland. It was a good bit of money to find then, in the early 80s. I knew a guy who suggested we should go and see the Bank of Ireland Private Banking. So I met Paul in the city and we went to see two gentlemen at the headquarters. They laid on a nice lunch for us in the private suite. We were there for about 10 minutes and in that room was a pitching wedge and a few golf balls. I said to Paul: "These guys must be golfers."

'So the introductions were made and then Tom Finnegan, who was the boss, called Paul and said: "Can you give me a pitching lesson? I'm having terrible trouble with my pitches. I'm stubbing the club in the ground." So Paul gave him a few lessons. A few minutes later he looked up, after three or four pitches, and he says to his colleague: "Give these guys whatever they want." And that set him on the way to America.'

McGinley's parents were heartbroken at the prospect of their son leaving but Paul was determined to make the most of his time at the United States International University. He certainly emerged with much more than a Masters degree in international business. From the women's golf team he met Alison Shapcott, who would later become his wife and the mother of their three children. He bought a small car to get around and readily made what have proved lifelong friends.

He also caught the eye of a golf coach who was obsessed with horse racing. Gordon Severson, a former club pro from Auburn, Washington, took the newly arrived prodigy under his wing.

'He was very fortunate to meet Gordon,' Michael McGinley said. 'He was a very good coach.' Severson would go on to help found the TaylorMade golf company, with which Paul has had a long-term deal to play their clubs. Severson later became a successful racehorse owner, before his death at the age of 63 in 2006.

As a university golf coach he was capable of identifying thoroughbred talent as well. He could see the young McGinley had something special about him and Paul would go on to lead the USIU Gulls team to four straight tournament titles in 1989.

All the while he was working on his technique and trying to learn from the best players he could find. His father recalled: 'Typical of Paul, he started to play with the professionals out there. As an amateur, there were only vouchers for him to play for in competitions, but he was playing for more than prizes. He was continually measuring himself. Was he good enough for the pro game? This was the real key. "Am I good enough to get on the tour and make my living on it?" He had to prove that for himself.'

Paul, then in his early 20s, was in San Diego for two-and-a-half years. On his return to Ireland he beat Portmarnock's Niall Goulding 3 and 2 to win the 1989 final of the Irish Amateur Close at Rosses Point in County Sligo, an event boasting such winners as Padraig Harrington, Rory McIlroy, Graeme McDowell, Darren Clarke and Ronan Rafferty.

The victory catapulted McGinley into the Irish amateur team. Despite having missed out on national duty at age group levels, he was now leading an Irish team that included future Open champions Harrington and Clarke. They won the home internationals against England, Scotland and Wales. It was the first time Ireland had won the title away from home soil.

This success added to Paul's belief that he could make it as a professional player. Further confirmation came when he was picked for Great Britain and Ireland against the US in the 1991 Walker Cup at Portmarnock. The match was won 14–10 by the Americans but the locals still remember McGinley's magical wedge to the last in the foursomes, a gloriously judged approach to a couple of feet which secured a one-hole victory with partner Liam White over a highly promising left-hander called Phil Mickelson and his teammate Bob May.

With his 25th birthday fast approaching, McGinley knew that he was ready. His performances had impressed an up-and-coming agent in the burly shape of Andrew 'Chubby' Chandler, who was already looking after Clarke's affairs. Chandler wanted to add McGinley to his International Sports Management stable as soon as he turned professional and so made sure the player was well-prepared for the transition. He recruited an experienced caddie for the player's one and only visit to the European Tour's Qualifying School. McGinley made the grade with ease and, at the end of 1991, could officially call himself a touring professional.

He didn't need to wait long for his first cheque and he knew what to do with it. He picked up £15,000 for winning the World Under-25 Championship. 'The Irish Sports Council had helped with financing San Diego and with that 15 grand he paid it back to the Irish Government,' his father said.

It was a gesture typical of the man. He is someone who always wants to do the right thing, and he recognised just how important his time in California had been. Paul had taken full advantage of the facilities and climate to ensure he would be capable of making his living playing sport. That was what he had always wanted, even if he had originally dreamed that it would be Gaelic football rather than golf.

Even so, his biggest sporting hero had always been a golfer – a man with a ready smile, a fierce competitive streak and a determination to do things the right way. Paul McGinley had plenty in common with Tom Watson.

America's 2014 Ryder Cup captain was still in his playing prime when Paul was based in San Diego. Naturally, the student Irishman was keen to be involved whenever the PGA Tour landed at the city's Torrey Pines course. He was recruited to drive buggies to ferry players from the practice ground to the first tee. Michael remembers well a breathless phone call home from his son.

'The tournament was there in February time. Paul had got his job down there, driving the buggy. He rang me, all excited: "Dad, you'll never guess what happened! I was driving Tom Watson down to the first tee in Torrey Pines!" Paul was so thrilled. Watson was his big, big hero and there he was, sat in his company for the first time. It's amazing how your path in life evolves.'

CHAPTER 4

McGinley's path to captaincy

'I knew how important it was.
I knew it was for the Ryder Cup.'
Paul McGinley, 2002, The Belfry

The most important round of Paul McGinley's professional career began in a rather eerie atmosphere. It felt as though it was being played in a parallel universe. Huge roars and cheering echoed over the course, but none were for him or his opponent. Only a handful of spectators, indeed, were watching the Irishman making his Ryder Cup singles debut against the doughty American Jim Furyk. The hoards were elsewhere.

Up ahead, they swarmed around Colin Montgomerie in the lead match against Scott Hoch, Sergio García versus David Toms or Darren Clarke's clash with David Duval. And if they weren't with those games, they were hanging back to watch Tiger Woods and Phil Mickelson finish on the range before playing the final two contests.

McGinley and Furyk were not the box-office ticket. They knew their match could be pivotal in an event where the scores were level going into the final day. Indeed, every one of the singles matches in 2002 was potentially vital, but when this one started it was still hard to imagine it would hold any great significance. Not that the two protagonists would have agreed, as reflected in the grim determination etched on their faces.

Furyk was playing his third Ryder Cup. He was firmly established as one of the leading players in the US and was months away from winning the US Open at Olympia Fields. McGinley had less idea of his standing in the game. He arrived at the Belfry, in the English Midlands, badly out of form.

Most players are at the top of their game for the biennial jousts, their good play having earned them their place in the team. This match, though, was different. It should have been played a year earlier but was postponed because of the September 11 attacks on the World Trade Center in New York. McGinley had his breakthrough season in 2001, cracking the top-10 in the European Tour's Order of Merit for the first time. He banked more than £1 million in prize money and, for the only time in his career, averaged under 70 strokes per round. He was well worth his place in the European team led by Sam Torrance.

A year on, it didn't feel that way. McGinley had managed only two top-10 finishes and barely scraped into the top-60 who contested the year-end Volvo Masters. Throughout that season he battled to rediscover his game in the knowledge that September was fast approaching. Regardless of how he was playing, he would be thrust onto golf's most public stage. It was stressful. Lee Westwood was in a similar, or even worse position. All semblance of form had deserted him.

Neither player was eligible for the big-money WGC American Express Championship being staged in Ireland in the lead-up to the Ryder Cup. Torrance arranged instead for them to accompany him on an early visit to the Belfry. The skipper was keen to inject some confidence and it proved a masterstroke in man management. It also provided the foundations for an enduring relationship between the Irishman and the Scot. But, heading into the 2002 contest, few would have anticipated quite how significant the Ryder Cup would prove to McGinley's career. At the time, he just wanted to fight off the demons that had infected his game and prove his worth to the team.

The Irishman rookie sat out the morning foursomes on the first day and then in the afternoon fourballs partnered his fellow Dubliner Padraig Harrington. This was no surprise – Torrance had told them well in advance that they would play together. McGinley's compatriot, however, was not at his best and they fell to a 2 and 1 defeat to Furyk and future Open champion Stewart Cink.

Afterwards, Harrington asked to be taken out of the firing line to work on his game, leaving McGinley without a partner and expecting to be benched for the second day. But captains need to be flexible in their thinking and Torrance ripped up Plan A. He paired McGinley with Clarke for the bottom match on Saturday afternoon. They were up against Furyk and Hoch. This was just the contest McGinley needed.

He was revelling in the team environment. It was like his schoolboy days at Croke Park. He fed off the camaraderie, and his boyhood dreams of playing in front of thousands of spectators were reawakened. Okay, it wasn't his beloved Gaelic football and it wasn't the Irish capital, but it was for the team, and thousands were imploring him to succeed. He wasn't nervous. He never suffered from nerves on Ryder Cup duty. The only emotion was excitement and the memories remain vivid. 'I was playing with Darren,' McGinley recalled. 'I had just hit my tee shot down 16. The crowd was 10-deep around the hole. And there was a guy leaning in on the left side. His eyes were bulging out of his head. He wasn't drunk but he was high on adrenaline and excitement. "Come on Paul, come on Paul!" he was screaming. He had a suit and tie on as well. I looked at him and thought: "Wow!". I loved that he was so into it.'

McGinley and Clarke battled out a tense half in the gathering gloom. Europe lost the session 2½ points to 1½ and America had the momentum heading into Sunday's singles. They had been behind throughout the first two days and now they were level. Statistically, the Americans were stronger in the singles and the common perception was that Europe needed to be leading at this stage to have any chance of regaining the trophy that had been lost at Brookline three years earlier.

Torrance has a gambler's instinct. He knew he had to pack the top order of his singles with his best players to try and swing the momentum his way. It meant, though, that he would have to rely on his less-vaunted men in the later matches – rookies like Niclas Fasth, Pierre Fulke, Phillip Price – and Paul McGinley.

At breakfast, this group of players met to discuss the day ahead. 'Myself and Pierre Fulke and Phillip Price talked about it,' McGinley said. 'One of us is going to finish it. It was unlikely that the first six matches would all be won. It was going to filter down to us, whether we were going to win the Cup or not.'

McGinley and Furyk faced each other in the ninth singles match and all the early running was made by the American. Before the match's sparse gallery, McGinley was only just clinging on during the early exchanges.

Up ahead Montgomerie, Bernhard Langer, Harrington and Thomas Bjørn were posting European wins. The outcome was still too close to call, though. Toms had beaten García and Westwood fell to Scott Verplank. As McGinley's match progressed, the crowds began to swell and the realisation grew that this might prove the defining contest. Price, sensationally, beat Mickelson on the 16th green and Europe moved 14–11 ahead. They needed just half a point to regain the trophy.

Michael and Julia McGinley had walked every step of the match but, by the 16th, the crowds were too great to afford a decent view. 'I left Julia out there and headed back to the clubhouse,' Michael said. 'When I got in there I found Sam's dad, Bob Torrance, and his wife June. They could hardly watch. It was only then that I realised just how big a deal this Ryder Cup thing is.'

McGinley and Furyk were all square coming up the final hole. Furyk was frustrated he hadn't finished off the contest earlier but admired his opponent's tenacity. 'I got up on him early. I played very well,' Furyk said. 'I slipped a little bit in the middle. I made some poor decisions on 8, 10 and 13. He won those three holes, although I was still leading at that time. And I played very solidly down the stretch, not making a bogey and making a couple of birdies. He made about a 10- to 12-footer on 17 for birdie. He came up with some big putts when he needed them.'

The home player had missed the final green to the left and pitched to around nine feet. Furyk then played a brilliant bunker shot to two feet. McGinley thought: 'Wow, he could miss that' but indicated to the American not to bother marking the ball. The putt was good. He conceded the par even though it was a potentially tricky downhill tap-in. 'I just wanted clarity,' McGinley said. 'I didn't want any doubt. I knew I had a putt to win the Ryder Cup and it made it simpler if there was no doubt surrounding it.'

The remaining matches on the course offered no guarantees so the putt had to drop. 'I just couldn't wait to hit it,' McGinley said. He is a man with a quick, busy manner. As he sized up the most important stroke of his life, this characteristic was exaggerated further. He just wanted to hit it. Get it done. Enjoy the moment. This was why he played sport. 'I knew I would hit a good putt,' he said. 'I didn't know whether it would go in, but I knew I would strike it well.'

Back in the clubhouse, his father turned to Bob Torrance – McGinley's coach as well as the European captain's dad – to find that the Torrances had turned away from the television. 'I told them Paul had this putt to win the Ryder Cup. Emotions were running so high, they wouldn't watch.'

McGinley settled over the ball. His teammates were watching by the green, willing him to make it. The Americans were rooting for a different outcome.

'I just remember thinking: "Of all the people to have that putt, why does it have to be Paul McGinley?"' remembered Harrington. 'If ever there has been an unlucky putter, it is Paul. Growing up together and playing with him for Ireland, I can remember so many putts that have looked brilliant and yet not dropped. They've found a way to lip out or inexplicably turn away from the hole.'

Not this time.

McGinley's ball made a positive, sure journey into the hole. 'The cheers went up, we could hear them in the clubhouse,' said Michael McGinley. His son's arms rocketed skywards in celebration; his barrel chest swelled with pride, his brilliant smile lit the green and his teammates swarmed on to the putting surface. He had been handed a four-leaf clover ball marker at the start of his round by former Ryder Cupper and now American TV commentator David Feherty. All that concerned the hero was keeping the marker safe, because he knew where he was headed.

In celebration, his teammates grabbed their man, the rookie who'd delivered the crucial half, and threw him into the lake beside the green.

'I knew how important it was, that it was for the Ryder Cup. I said I'd love to have the opportunity, and fortunately I did,' an elated McGinley said. 'I knew the line and it was a matter of having the nerve to hit it on the line, and fortunately I did.'

Furyk was magnanimous. 'I actually played against Paul in three matches. He's a wonderful gentleman. I never met him before. I told him afterwards that I felt like I'd made a new friend. He's a wonderful man.'

More significantly, McGinley's place in Ryder Cup history had been assured. From bit-part player to centre stage in one extraordinary afternoon of golf. Until he got to Gleneagles in 2014, this was to prove the defining moment of his career. His heroics at the Belfry added star quality to an otherwise steady and well-remunerated European Tour career. He had won the Wales Open in 2001 and would go on to claim a huge victory at the Volvo Masters at Valderrama in Spain four years later.

Throughout this period, though, his biggest motivation was retaining his Ryder Cup place. The lure of the team environment was immense and continued to grow in the wake of the Belfry triumph.

For the next match at Oakland Hills, McGinley had to dig deep to remain in the European team. He played 10 weeks in a row from the French Open in June to secure his spot in Langer's side. He was fifth at the Irish Open, runner-up in Holland the following week and recorded his best major finish when he tied for sixth at the PGA Championship a week later. McGinley ended the qualifying period with a share of sixth at the BMW International Open in Munich and it was enough to retain his Ryder Cup status.

No longer a rookie, McGinley was able to relish another crack at the Americans and this time it was in their own backyard, in Detroit. Europe surged to a record win by 18½ points to 9½ as US skipper Hal Sutton's plan to pair his biggest two names, Woods and Mickelson, totally backfired. Europe, by contrast, were marshalled with astute intelligence by the unflappable Langer. The German's meticulous and intelligent approach left a lasting impression on McGinley.

He partnered Luke Donald in the opening sequence of fourballs and they battled out a tense half against Chris Riley and Cink. He then had to wait until the Saturday afternoon foursomes when he teamed up with Harrington.

Sutton abandoned the Woods/Mickelson experiment after it failed to yield a point in two matches on the opening day. Woods, then at the height of his powers, had won in the morning alongside Riley and had been put alongside Davis Love III in the afternoon. They would form the opposition for the ebullient Irishmen.

It is a popular misconception that McGinley and Harrington share a great golfing chemistry. Yes, they are good friends and yes, their careers have intertwined. They won the World Cup together in 1997 at Kiawah Island, a career highlight for both men, and McGinley strode the fairways a decade later to support his compatriot as he won a play-off against García for the Open at Carnoustie. But they have contrasting characters.

'We are totally different,' McGinley said. 'He's all about preparation and wants to get to the course hours before he tees off. I just want to get there, have a quick stretch, put on my spikes and hit a few balls.'

Put them together, though, and they make a potent partnership. Langer knew this. They also attracted huge support from Detroit's Irish community.

All the momentum was with Europe. Langer had completely out-thought his opposite number and Sutton – who had forgotten how many children he has during his speech at the opening ceremony – was being made to look ever more hapless. That Saturday afternoon, Europe were going for the jugular and McGinley and Harrington were at the forefront.

Closing in on victory, they arrived at the short par-three 13th. It was Harrington's honour and he wanted to hit a nine iron to reach the pin cut on the upper tier at the back. Langer arrived on the tee and quietly instructed his man to hit wedge. Harrington was reluctant. He knew he couldn't reach the flag, but the skipper was insistent. He duly hit wedge and looked nonplussed as he found the front portion of the green, nowhere near the flag.

Woods then stepped up and launched his tee shot, which flew all the way to the hole. It took a hard bounce and careered into the back bunker.

Langer had known how the balls were landing and that it was impossible to hold the upper portion of the green. Love had no chance of getting the bunker shot anywhere near the flag and a bogey became an inevitability. The European pair, meanwhile, had a routine two-putt par to win the hole.

Langer's intervention was inspired captaincy that stayed with McGinley. He would be reluctant to interfere as a skipper but this incident informed him of the scope that existed to make a telling contribution. On this occasion, it meant there was no way back for the American pair and they ultimately fell to a 4 and 3 defeat.

It capped a magnificent couple of days for Europe. They led 11–3 going into the singles and Langer's side only needed 3½ points to secure back-to-back victories.

Sutton responded by sending out his team in the order they had qualified, with Woods at the top. Langer was more subtle, and used McGinley as an insurance policy. He knew the Irishman had come through for Europe at the Belfry and, if necessary, he would be well-qualified to do the same if the US mounted a fightback.

Given the raucous Irish support they had received on Saturday, Harrington and McGinley suggested they should be kept close to each other in the order. That way, the Irish crowds would stick together and ensure both players received maximum backing. Langer was happy to go along with the idea. Harrington was sent out 11th and McGinley just behind him in the anchor match.

Langer told McGinley to arrive at the course late because playing last against Cink would involve a lot of hanging around. The captain wanted him to conserve his nervous energy. McGinley was also instructed not to look at leaderboards, and to prepare just as he would for any important round.

He followed his captain's orders to the letter. In the locker room and on the range he steadfastly avoided any news of what was happening on the course. He did the same on the putting green, and it was only when he arrived on the tee that the spell was broken. As the handshakes were being made, one of the officials attached to Europe commented: 'Looks like we might need your point here.' McGinley glanced up at the leaderboard and found Europe were struggling.

'There was no blue at all. The Americans were fighting back,' McGinley said. Then he felt an emotion that he had never experienced before or since. He looked at Cink, his tall American opponent and the diminutive Irishman knew he would beat him. Whatever it took, McGinley would find a way to secure a point. 'I just knew I would win,' he said.

McGinley played brilliantly. Ultimately, the Cup was settled early as Europe collectively rallied and Montgomerie sank the winning putt with six matches still out on the course. McGinley was in no mood to let up, though, and, as they shook hands after his 3 and 2 victory, Cink told him he would have beaten anyone that day. The Irishman's point completed a record rout and he'd now played on two winning teams.

His victory at the Volvo Masters, just over a year later, was perfectly timed. Qualifying for the Ryder Cup was still McGinley's top priority, especially as the 2006 match was the first to be played in Ireland, at the K Club in County Kildare. Europe were led by Ian Woosnam, the US by Tom Lehman.

Understandably McGinley was desperately keen to retain his place in the continent's team and experience his favourite form of golf on home soil. His victory at Valderrama came early in the qualifying period. It was the most important win of his career, coming in a season-ending tournament restricted to the elite top-60 money-winners on the Order of Merit. It also capped a fine end to the season in which he had been runner-up to US Open Champion Michael Campbell in the HSBC World Matchplay at Wentworth.

'In a funny way I think he under-achieved as a player,' said his former manager Chubby Chandler. 'But in another way Paul over-achieved. He should have won a lot more. I'm not sure he ever had enough belief in his game. He was actually a better player than he thought he was. He was never quite as good a putter as he should have been for a little bloke, though. You know, little blokes have to be good putters. But he's tenacious.'

The following year McGinley's form was patchy. It took a fourth place at the K Club in the European Open to ensure his place on the team. 'It was a relief to be able to hold on to my spot,' he admitted. 'It was the complete opposite of what I did two years earlier, when I stormed through the final stages of the qualifying process.'

In the previous Ryder Cup, Langer had been a cool, calm and analytical leader, in keeping with his character. Woosnam also stayed true to his personal traits. He, though, was fuelled by emotion and intuition. It started with his wildcard picks, who were not only fine golfers but, as importantly, two good lads for the team room. Westwood was always a popular figure but the real gamble was Clarke, who had lost his wife Heather to breast cancer six weeks earlier.

Woosnam felt Clarke was capable of riding what would be an incredibly emotional wave of goodwill generated by the Irish crowds. He believed this would help unite the European team. They would be doing it for Darren. And he was proved emphatically right.

The American team was not the strongest ever assembled. The inclusion of Brett Wetterich and Vaughan Taylor reflected the comparative lack of strength in depth in US golf at the time. Between them, they contributed a mere half point to the cause, when Taylor partnered Chad Campbell against Westwood and Montgomerie in the Saturday afternoon foursomes.

Lehman's side also had to contend with miserable weather and the raucous home crowds, who bubbled with enthusiasm. This was never more evident than when they roared their welcome for the grieving Clarke as he arrived on the first tee for the Friday morning fourballs. It was a noise the like of which had surely never been heard on a golf course before. Full throated and brimful of adulation, respect and compassion, it could only inspire the entire European team.

Clarke's partner and great friend Westwood struggled to keep tears from streaming down his face. The Ulsterman fought off watering eyes as well, finding a way to hit the most magnificent tee shot down the first fairway. It set the European pair on their way to a one-hole victory over Mickelson and Chris DiMarco that tipped the session Europe's way by 2½ points to 1½.

McGinley had been short of form and had shut himself away for concentrated practice the week before. He had headed to the range at Sunningdale, switched off his mobile phone and worked to find a cure for a swing fault that had crept into his game. 'Technically, I've got really out of position. I've been swinging too flat and laying off too much, from the ball coming up too much on the inside,' he explained.

'I'm raring to go. I'm sure the adrenaline and the excitement of playing in front of my home crowd, playing in the Ryder Cup and playing as part of the team will bring it to a new level.

'If Woosie says to me my role will be to play the singles on Sunday and that's all, I'm quite happy to do that. There will be no complaints from me whatsoever,' McGinley added. 'If you ask me to play five games, it will be the same. I'll do my best. I feel that I'm a cog in the wheel, one of 12 and very much a team player ... The most important thing for me is that we win this Ryder Cup in my home country.'

On the first day McGinley was saved for the afternoon foursomes. Harrington was his partner again and the two Irishmen battled out a tense half with Zach Johnson, who putted brilliantly, and Chad Campbell. The first three matches that afternoon were halved and Donald and García swung the session Europe's way by beating Woods and Furyk on the final green. At close of play the home side led 5–3.

Europe increased their lead in the following morning fourballs and afternoon foursomes. McGinley sat out the better-ball format and after lunch found himself again paired with Harrington. They fell to Europe's only foursomes defeat, losing 3 and 2 to Woods and Furyk. 'Obviously disappointed to lose,' McGinley said. 'Bottom line is we played numbers one and two in the world, both of them on their game, and when you do that you're going to have a tough day, and we did. We battled well. We fought hard. We both played what I thought was good golf.'

Nevertheless, Woosnam's side took a commanding 10–6 lead into the final day, where McGinley was sent out for the sixth singles match against J. J. Henry.

And Europe were ruthless. Montgomerie, Paul Casey and Clarke swept to victories. There was blue on the board everywhere and the overall result was never in doubt. It was just a matter of the margin.

Henrik Stenson sank the winning putt with his 4 and 3 win over Taylor, who was sadly out of his depth in such a rarefied golfing atmosphere. David Howell had won 5 and 4 against Wetterich and Donald took down Campbell at the 17th. Harrington was losing heavily to Verplank in the anchor match, but it didn't matter because José María Olazábal and Westwood were winning theirs.

Europe had every chance of beating the record they had set two years earlier at Oakland Hills. An unprecedented 19 points was within their grasp and it largely came down to McGinley's tense clash with J. J. Henry. When they arrived on the final green McGinley was on the verge of victory. A streaker, however, suddenly appeared and began running around the green. McGinley implored him not to run on the line of his opponent's 25-foot putt, which Henry needed to force a half.

Knowing the Ryder Cup was already won, McGinley pondered whether to concede the putt. The naked intervention had ruined his opponent's concentration. He asked assistant captain Des Smyth. 'He wouldn't help,' McGinley later said. So he took the initiative himself. As the streaker headed off to dive into the lake bordering the green, McGinley turned to his opponent and offered his hand. The match went down as a half, instead of the likely European win.

'I think it shows really what the spirit of this competition is all about,' Henry said. 'What a gentleman.'

McGinley said: 'It was a gesture done in the right spirit.'

As for Woosnam, he knew that the moment of generosity had cost him a record-breaking win. He still mutters about it to this day, though deep down he recognises that McGinley had done the right thing.

For the player though, the overall result was all that mattered. He said: 'I'm so, so proud. I'm very emotional. It's just wonderful. I'm proud not just for me and the team, but for the Irish people and the way they behaved this week . . . bar that clown on the last green.'

And why had it been possible to win three Ryder Cups in a row in such grand style? 'There's one reason and one reason only; it's talent. Nobody understands how good this team is and how good our Tour is,' McGinley replied.

With his golf and his eloquence, the Irishman was appearing ever more authoritative. He had played important roles in an unprecedented hat-trick of European successes, and more and more people were looking to him for intelligent, insightful analysis. He was, first and foremost, a golfer, but Paul McGinley was confirming himself as a fine ambassador for his Tour and the game in general. Indeed, he was starting to look like captaincy material.

CHAPTER 5

McGinley's appointment

'Congrats to Tom Watson, 2014 US Ryder Cup
captain. I would love to see Paul McGinley go up
against him as European Captain at Gleneagles!'
Rory McIlroy tweet

In the decade that followed Sam Torrance's 2002 captaincy at the Belfry, Europe chose its most successful golfers to lead the Ryder Cup effort. The skipper in 2004, Bernhard Langer, could boast two Masters victories among the 80 wins he had enjoyed worldwide. Two years later it was another prolific winner and former Masters champion, Ian Woosnam. The Welshman had been part of a double appointment that made Britain's most decorated player, Sir Nick Faldo, his successor for the match at Valhalla in 2008. Colin Montgomerie hadn't won a major, but had topped the Tour's Order of Merit eight times. He also was unbeaten in eight singles matches at Ryder Cups. The Scot was in charge in 2010 and was followed by a double Masters champion, José María Olazábal, for the Medinah match two years later.

Their achievements demanded that they be appointed as European captains. They represented a golden generation for the continent. Of those who dominated an era when European golfers came to the fore on the world stage, only Sandy Lyle missed out. The former Open and Masters champion was an assistant to Woosnam at the K Club but never won the vote to lead the side.

Captains were chosen by the European Tour's Tournament

Committee, made up of senior players and, since 2007, chaired by the Dane Thomas Bjørn. The committee would discuss all manner of policy issues but their most important decision came every couple of years – who should lead Europe in the Ryder Cup.

When Langer, Woosnam and Faldo were appointed, there was little debate. They were obvious choices. The decision to go with Montgomerie in 2010 required more discussion, because Olazábal had seemed the obvious choice. The Spaniard was worried about his health, though, and opted out of the running. Lyle fancied the job and, ironically, had Monty's backing, but the committee was less keen. Henrik Stenson was at the table for the decisive meeting at Abu Dhabi's Emirates Palace Hotel and he put forward Montgomerie's name. A couple of weeks later in Dubai it was no surprise when the Scot was officially appointed. Then Olazábal's arthritic condition improved sufficiently for him to become the obvious choice to succeed Montgomerie at Medinah in 2012.

It was all pretty straightforward. Appointing European Ryder Cup captains generated little controversy or intrigue. The choices were as obvious as they were sensible. There was no need for campaigning or electioneering. Indeed, such behaviour would have been regarded as being in bad taste and not befitting the position.

That said, it was well known that the role, although officially unpaid, was very lucrative. There are innumerable spin-offs for any skipper prepared to make himself available for corporate appearances on both sides of the Atlantic. It was a job well worth having, and one that stretched well beyond marshalling a dozen golfers for three autumnal days.

When it came to identifying who should lead the team in 2014, however, the picture, for once, was unclear. Historically this match had seemed earmarked for Montgomerie again. He would be 51 and at the end of a glorious career. He happens to live in Dunning, just down the road from the Auchterarder course in Perthshire. It seemed Gleneagles was made for him.

But the job was now regarded as a one-off assignment. Long gone were the days of Tony Jacklin leading the continent for four matches, before being succeeded by Bernard Gallacher for the next three. Monty had had his chance and took it with victory at Celtic Manor in 2010.

With Lyle now seen as out of touch with the modern game, this time the field for the Gleneagles captaincy didn't include any of the greats of the European game. Darren Clarke, having won the Open in 2011 and with a couple of World Golf Championships tournaments to his name, was the most decorated candidate. It was too soon for three-times major winner Padraig Harrington, 1999 Open champion Paul Lawrie had played at Medinah and would surely want to try to retain his place in the team and Bjørn also still harboured hopes of playing.

If Europe had struggled with a captaincy dilemma in the past, it was over whether someone should be appointed for their past excellence as a player or because they were the best man for the job. Langer, Woosnam, Montgomerie and Olazábal had been great players but it was felt they possessed the sort of acumen that would make them strong leaders as well. The same went for Faldo, although the six-times major champion proved a poor captain. Never did the committee feel that Lyle had the necessary leadership qualities to sit alongside his outstanding playing record.

Paul McGinley doesn't come close to his predecessors in terms of playing success. He never won a major title but he has been more than a mere journeyman, banking over £10 million in prize money. And who knows what he might have achieved if he had not been dogged by persistent knee problems, the legacy of the injury that dashed his dreams of competing at Gaelic football? He was good enough to force himself into three winning Ryder Cup teams and was a prominent and intelligent member of the Tournament Committee.

McGinley, though, also came into the reckoning for the captaincy for another reason – his leadership qualities. The bonding skills that he had learned on Dublin's football and hurling fields were those that made him stand out as a prospective Ryder Cup captain. Yes, he had decent playing credentials, but so did plenty of players. What separated McGinley was a desire to inspire and influence others.

Ironically, these qualities were initially noticed by Faldo. His first act of substance during his spell as captain was to appoint McGinley and Olazábal as vice captains in May 2007. Both men spoke of the honour of being asked to assist in Europe's defence of the trophy, but McGinley still harboured hopes of playing again.

Four months later, Faldo led the Great Britain and Ireland team to take on Continental Europe in the Seve Trophy. He had two wildcard picks and overlooked McGinley, selecting instead England's Simon Dyson and the Scot Mark Warren. The match was played at the Heritage course near Dublin. The event could have done with some Irish influence to help boost disappointing ticket sales but Faldo spurned the opportunity by ignoring the claims of a player he had chosen to help his Ryder Cup effort. Many observers felt this caused a rift between the two men that ultimately led to McGinley pulling out of his Valhalla duties.

McGinley, however, claimed Faldo's decision to omit him from the Seve Trophy team had nothing to do with his decision. He had been struggling and was only 70th in the Order of Merit. The then 40-year-old announced: 'On reflection, and after careful consideration, I feel it's in my best interests to concentrate on trying to play myself into the team. Now I want to play for Nick and bring the Cup back to Europe again.'

McGinley had spent the previous fortnight weighing up

his options after being asked to accompany Faldo on a scouting mission to the Valhalla course in Kentucky, which would host the 2008 match. Having resigned as vice captain, however, he still couldn't find the form to play in a fourth successive Ryder Cup.

Even so, the episode had put him on the captaincy map. When McGinley failed to qualify, Langer urged Faldo to reinstate him. The German former skipper felt Faldo needed more assistants than just Olazábal and he was right. But Faldo didn't share this view and his strategy was fatally flawed. Players were left exposed, with no support on the course. McGinley watched at home while figures like DJ Spoony – brought along to offer entertainment for the players – occupied the buggies that should have been used by properly qualified assistants.

When Montgomerie was appointed to succeed the beaten Faldo, one of his first jobs was to oversee the Seve Trophy match that would be played in the autumn of 2009. He installed Thomas Bjørn to lead a strong Continental Europe side and McGinley to take charge of the GB&I line-up.

For the match, played among the fallen apples from the trees that lined the fairways at Saint-Nom-la-Bretèche, the continental side boasted considerably greater experience. Stenson, Robert Karlsson, Søren Hansen and Miguel Ángel Jiménez had all played in Ryder Cups. Anders Hansen was a two-times PGA Champion at Wentworth and Gonzalo Fernández-Castaño was well-established on the Tour.

By contrast, McGinley's side had only Graeme McDowell and Oliver Wilson with Ryder Cup experience. The rest of the team included the likes of Anthony Wall, Dyson, Steve Webster and Nick Dougherty. There was another youngster as well – a lad from Northern Ireland called Rory McIlroy.

McGinley invested heavily in the 20-year-old sensation from Ulster, pairing him with compatriot McDowell and sending them out first in three of the four sessions. They won all three of those matches. They were then put out in the first two singles. McIlroy, in the top match, beat Stenson on the final green and McDowell took out Karlsson 3 and 2.

Every step of the way McGinley had the better of his opposite number Bjørn, in terms of tactics, motivation and public relations. The inexperienced Great Britain & Ireland team won by a resounding and prophetic 16½ points to 11½.

'Paul McGinley did an unbelievable job motivating the guys, keeping everybody in the loop, asking the guys where they want to play, who they want to play with,' said McDowell. 'He was a really, really good motivator. You know, they have the best team on paper, no doubt about it, but we were up for it.'

McGinley had proved himself to be a natural captain. He had come up with a system that got the best out of players who might not have otherwise been motivated. Compared to the Ryder Cup, after all, the Seve Trophy can be seen as an eminently forgettable beer match.

On this occasion, though, there was a captain who recognised its potential to unlock greater ambitions, for there was little doubt that McGinley would one day want to lead Europe into a Ryder Cup. He invited his players to his room every evening for team meetings to outline strategy and to keep them focused. He kept notes in his Filofax of what he'd said to players and how they reacted. Those scribblings remained with him and helped form the template for his future leadership style.

The GB&I captain revealed: 'I'm not a methodical kind of person, but I have had a notebook and of course I wrote down thoughts and other things, and a lot of the stuff I wrote down during the day was said at the team meetings at night. It's a small room, but it was a very energetic room. We had great meetings in there for half an hour every night at 7.30 before we went to dinner.

'I've always been a team player. My background, as everybody knows, up to the age of 19, really wasn't as a golfer. I was a footballer. I have always thrived on being part of a team. As I said to the guys at the start of the week, the most fun I've ever had playing golf has been as part of a team. If I can impart some of that fun onto them, and impart some of that experience that I've learned, I'd be delighted.'

It was always going to be a special week for McGinley. The match was the brainchild of the great Severiano Ballesteros with whom he had struck a firm friendship. The Spaniard couldn't be in Paris for the match that bore his name because he was battling brain cancer, from which he died in May 2011. 'He has always singled me out for special attention,' McGinley recalled after taking a congratulatory phone call from Ballesteros as the winning captain.

The victory generated hugely supportive headlines. 'Paul was always a very good player, always a deep thinker,' his former manager Chubby Chandler recalled. 'Always a bit of a team man, quietly. As soon as you saw him captain the Seve Trophy team, you thought: "Crickey, he's going to be a great Ryder Cup captain." Because not everybody gets it. Not everybody gets putting together the right team, the right partnerships, and imparting enough of their experience on them without suffocating the players, and I think that's what Paul does.'

And so, suddenly, McGinley was being seen as a prospective Ryder Cup leader. He was selected as a vice captain by Montgomerie for the Celtic Manor match in 2010 and a year later he again led GB&I to victory in the Seve Trophy. This time he beat a side skippered by Jean Van de Velde by 15½ points to 12½. One of his players was Darren Clarke, who was hugely impressed. He wrote to McGinley to say he wouldn't challenge him for a future Ryder Cup captaincy.

Olazábal had no hesitation in naming McGinley in his management team for Medinah. Indeed, he was chosen alongside Clarke and Thomas Bjørn. They were the three most likely figures to take over from the Spaniard for 2014. Bjørn could feel his form returning and still held genuine hopes of playing but Clarke, despite that letter, was a different case.

The veteran of five Ryder Cups since his 1997 debut under the leadership of Ballesteros at Valderrama, Clarke had by far the best playing record of the likely candidates. Although he had lost consistency, he remained capable of magical golf. This he proved with his Open victory at Royal St George's in 2011, after which he openly speculated that his success might prove to be the springboard for a return to the European team. He had not played for Europe since the K Club match in 2006. Lifting the Claret Jug proved a momentary bounce back to top form, but Clarke quickly returned to the status of an 'also-ran' at most tournaments. His most likely return to prominence appeared to be through becoming Europe's next skipper.

After the Medinah victory, it seemed clear that the race for the job would be between Clarke and McGinley. Clarke's post-Seve Trophy letter had long been forgotten, although McGinley was somewhat taken aback to find its author as his main rival. It would be between two Irishmen, one from north of the border, the other from the south.

They had grown up together under the umbrella of the Golfing Union of Ireland and had been firm friends. McGinley's wife Alison was very close to Heather Clarke and both men would often travel and practise together. They shared the same manager in the flamboyant Chandler. It was not an enduring friendship, though, and as the years passed in the wake of Heather's death, McGinley and Clarke spent less time in each other's company.

They were different in so many ways. Clarke was an exceptionally talented golfer, while McGinley's skills were hard-earned rather than God-given. Clarke is a big personality, happy to show off the trappings of his wealth. McGinley is more reserved, and more approachable. Both are fiercely ambitious. Both wanted to be Ryder Cup captain.

Clarke's great friend Lee Westwood played an exhibition event in Turkey a couple of weeks after Medinah. Chandler promoted the event, which attracted Tiger Woods, Justin Rose and a decent-sized media party. At the end of one of his rounds, Westwood was asked who he thought should be the next captain. It was clear he welcomed the question. 'There are a lot of good candidates but, if I was asked to pick, I would pick Darren,' Westwood said.

'He's been a Ryder Cup stalwart for many years. The one at the K Club will be remembered for him and his great performance under the stress of what he was going through at the time. He's a major champion, he's a very good public speaker, which I think has to be taken into account, tactically very astute. I think Darren has a lot of good things going for him.'

This signalled the start of the public phase of Clarke's campaign for the captaincy. 'I still dearly want to make the team, and even more so after being present in Medinah as part of Ollie's support staff,' he said. 'But unfortunately, the way things have been going with my game of late, that's not been happening. However, if it means going to Gleneagles as the captain of the team and not a [playing] member of the team, then I would accept that as a huge honour.'

During the autumn of 2012, McGinley was devouring every newspaper article on the subject that he could find. He was desperately keen to become captain and knew that his inferior playing record might be his undoing, despite superior captaincy experience. He was itching to have his say, but his wife urged him to maintain a diplomatic silence. Being seen to campaign for the job could be construed as disrespectful, such are the ways of golfing politics. He didn't want to do anything that might prove counter-productive.

The appointment of Tom Watson stunned Europe. Few anticipated such a radical move by the PGA of America. There could be no doubting the playing credentials of the man who would lead the US effort to regain the trophy. The decision upped the ante, with regard to what Europe might do in response. The holders were due to make their decision at the Tournament Committee meeting in Abu Dhabi in January 2013.

Three months earlier, on 9 October, the *Daily Mail* reported that 'Darren Clarke has won the race to be Europe's Ryder Cup skipper'. It was news to all concerned. The golfer denied the story on Twitter, adding: 'Would be a huge honour if asked.' Clarke then appeared on Irish television, on the *Late Late Show*. 'It's an awkward position because you've got my good friend Paul McGinley and myself both vying for the same position,' he said. 'One of us is going to be disappointed but, the way it's looking, Ireland is going to have its first Ryder Cup captain.'

As autumn turned into winter, European golf was split. There was a McGinley camp and one supporting Clarke. Most of the discussions occurred behind closed doors, with outside observers left to scan the make-up of the committee to try to judge which player would attract most votes. On 11 December, McGinley's fellow Dubliner Peter Lawrie was elected to the committee along with Italy's Francesco Molinari. Englishman Richard Finch, one of Clarke's International Sports Management stablemates, stepped down. Would this lead to a shift in opinion?

As it turned out, the most important figure was not even on the committee. It was a 23-year-old who was in the process of taking the game by storm. In August 2012, Rory McIlroy had romped to an eight-shot win in the US PGA Championship at Kiawah Island. He was now the world's number one golfer and that brought influence. He decided to exert it on 13 December, the day Watson was appointed.

McIlroy took to Twitter to make an intervention of huge significance: 'Congrats to Tom Watson, 2014 US Ryder Cup captain. I would love to see Paul McGinley go up against him as European Captain at Gleneagles!'

It was a bombshell tweet. Later he added: 'For the record, I think Darren Clarke would make a great captain in the US so would like to see him do it in 2016. Both guys deserve a go.'

That second tweet was of scant consolation to Clarke. Three days later he retweeted McIlroy's support for McGinley without comment.

Clarke knew that his campaign to land the Gleneagles job had been dealt a savage blow. He had always been happy to be seen as a mentor to his fellow Ulsterman, yet McIlroy had gone into bat for his main rival for the captaincy. Clarke was aware that the support of the world's best golfer would carry great weight. McGinley was now the favourite.

By this time Clarke's friendship with McGinley was at an end. All the indicators suggested that, if he was not going to be captain, then Clarke didn't want McGinley to have the job either. On 21 December the race took another dramatic turn. Clarke effectively took himself out of the running and threw his support behind Montgomerie.

'Whoever it is standing on that stage opposite Tom Watson needs a huge presence,' Clarke said. 'We do have an (unwritten) rule where we don't ask anybody to do it again, but we might have to look at that.'

Montgomerie spent Christmas and New Year wondering whether the captaincy was heading back to him. A Scot leading Europe in Scotland, a chance for a Ryder Cup colossus to add to his legend by beating one of the greats of the game. It was a heady prospect and of little surprise that, at the first opportunity in 2013, he said: 'If asked, of course I would accept.'

The Tour Committee meeting was scheduled for 15 January. The weekend before, Clarke formally ruled himself out. 'Now may not be my time,' he said. 'When I was initially mentioned as a potential captain in October, I wasn't playing very well.

I played much better at the end of the year and have been thinking long and hard about it over the Christmas break. I won one of the biggest prizes in golf by winning the Open and I am exempt for another three years on the PGA Tour. If I was given the opportunity to do the captaincy, I'd effectively be throwing two of those three years away. It's a tough one for me but, to be honest, I want to play golf.'

Clarke was speaking at the Volvo Champions tournament in Durban just before the Tour headed off to the crunch week in Abu Dhabi. Montgomerie was also at the South African event. 'I've always said that we need the best man for the job,' he commented. 'And if we're going for the best man for the job, that doesn't say you shouldn't do it again. I thought it was between Darren and Paul until Darren said something. Then my name was mentioned.

'I've never canvassed, as I didn't last time. I've not spoken to anyone about this but I've always felt that, if I was asked, I would do it. And that's still the case.'

The betting exchanges reacted quickly. The Scot was backed down to 6–4 and, in the hours leading up to the meeting, Sky Sports News quoted a source in the Montgomerie camp stating he was confident the job was his. Long-time manager Guy Kinnings, the most influential figure in 'Team Monty', shrugged his shoulders and gave a look of 'not me Guv' to play down the veracity of the Sky reports.

McIlroy had already dispatched another vital tweet. 'RC captaincy should be a 1-time thing. Everyone deserving gets their chance and then moves on. I would love to play under Paul McGinley in 2014.' He reiterated those sentiments at the launch of his multi-million-dollar Nike deal on the eve of the meeting. Playing under the Dubliner in the Seve Trophy had left a lasting impression.

Olazábal, the outgoing skipper, weighed in: 'The fear is that someone might miss out because there are just too many strong candidates who have yet to have their chance. I think it is only right to give those guys their chance.' The Spaniard added that McGinley had been a 'massive and vital help' at Medinah. Woosnam added his weight to the Irishman's cause, stating: 'In my opinion, it's a once-only deal.' Another former skipper, Bernard Gallacher, said appointing McGinley should be 'a no-brainer' given his record as a Seve Trophy captain.

It was a good half hour's drive from the Abu Dhabi Golf Club, which was staging that week's HSBC tournament, to the sumptuous St Regis Hotel on Saadiyat Island. First, there was a full meeting of the players in the early evening to discuss Tour policies. Most were staying at the hotel and, at the end, they trudged out to leave the committee with Tour executives to conduct their business. The key item on the agenda, of course, was the Ryder Cup captaincy.

The run-up to the meeting had been unusually contentious and, with Watson installed for the Americans, the committee knew there was no room for error. Of the 15-strong committee, 12 were present; Miguel Ángel Jiménez, Joakim Haeggman and Robert Karlsson were absent. That left chairman Bjørn, the Chilean Felipe Aguilar, Englishmen Paul Casey and David Howell, Clarke, McGinley, Montgomerie, Raphaël Jacquelin of France, Italy's Francesco Molinari, Spaniard Gonzalo Fernández-Castaño and the Swede Henrik Stenson to decide the outcome.

When it became time to discuss the captaincy, McGinley and Montgomerie were asked to leave the room. Both headed off to their respective bedrooms. McGinley sat with his brother Michael, nervously nibbling home-made biscuits and hoping his quiet campaign strategy had paid off. After a few minutes there was a knock on McGinley's door and he wondered how the committee could have made their decision so quickly. They hadn't. McIlroy and Shane Lowry had decided their preferred candidate could do with some company and they joined in on the consumption of biscuits in McGinley's room.

The committee discussed four candidates. Scots Paul Lawrie and Sandy Lyle were also given consideration, but it was essentially a choice between McGinley and Monty. There is no doubt that the support given to the Irishman by big names like McIlroy made a huge difference. Rose and Donald had also tweeted their backing.

After two hours of deliberation, waiting reporters became aware that the meeting had broken up. No one knew which way the vote had gone until the white-shirted Montgomerie was spotted leaving the building to return to the Westin Hotel next to the course. He had already offered a hand of congratulation to the new skipper. His departure was the biggest clue that the vote had gone McGinley's way. Moments later, he was coming down the escalator with media director Scott Crockett and, along with Bjørn and Tour boss George O'Grady, he was brought into the press conference room.

The quiet man had won. He'd seen off the brasher campaign of Clarke and the orchestration that had sought to return Montgomerie to the role. 'The best part for me was that all the lobbying that went on in the press and on Twitter was all down to them,' McGinley said of the players who had backed him. At the far end of the room stood McIlroy, Harrington and McDowell. Lowry was also there. Two months earlier, McGinley had visited him four times while he was suffering from shingles during the DP World Tour Championship in Dubai.

'None of it had anything to do with me. They did it off their own bats,' McGinley added.

His appointment was reported as a victory for 'player power' because of the support he had received from prospective team members. Clarke's only public support had come from his mate Westwood, and it had been the Ulsterman who had effectively brought Montgomerie into consideration.

'I had two goes at the Seve Trophy and both times came

through with teams that were underdogs on paper,' McGinley added. 'I have also been twice a vice captain in the Ryder Cup. They both went well. We won both times. So, from that point of view, I was the most qualified,' said McGinley.

'From a playing point of view I wasn't, though. But the point is there is no direct relationship between being a great player and being a great captain. It can and has happened, but there is no direct correlation.'

Harrington looked on as his old teammate held court as Europe's newest captain. 'Most of all, he possesses the same meticulous approach as his great hero in the job, Bernhard Langer,' the three-times major champion commented.

There was someone else to be factored in. Not only would McGinley lead Europe at Gleneagles, but he would do so against the golfer whom he had worshipped during his childhood. This was the same Tom Watson whom he had been thrilled to drive in a Torrey Pines buggy in his student days in San Diego. 'I'm a huge Tom Watson fan,' McGinley admitted. 'He was my boyhood hero. I have so much respect for him.'

Tellingly, though, McGinley made clear that there would be no more room for sentiment. He said: 'There has to be a hardness, too. That edge is vital to the Ryder Cup. It's what separates it from other team events. As much as I respect Tom, I know he is the ultimate competitor. So I'd like to beat him.'

For both captains, the quest for victory would start with the assembling of their teams.

CHAPTER 6

Woods and Walker

'I'd rather stay home. I think I could get a pretty
good job and make about the same amount of
money and enjoy watching my kids grow up.'
Jimmy Walker, 2014 Ryder Cup debutant

For the better part of two decades, no one has decorated the golfing skies more than Tiger Woods. At his best, he took the game to a new level, collecting more than 80 titles. From his first Masters win in 1997, he claimed 14 major titles in 11 years. The major victories only dried up after a dramatic fall from grace when, after his car crash on Thanksgiving in 2009, he was revealed to be a serial adulterer. Even so, Woods rebuilt his career and golfing reputation to the extent that he headed into the year of the Gleneagles Ryder Cup as the undisputed world number one.

In 2013 he won five times on the PGA Tour. They were big wins. He claimed a second Players' Championship on a revamped Sawgrass Stadium course that was thought to be too tight for his often errant long game. Before winning the tournament regarded as the game's 'fifth major', he had already come out on top at Torrey Pines, Doral and Bay Hill, all of which have been fertile venues throughout his glittering career.

Woods finished fourth at the Masters after controversially avoiding disqualification. He made an illegal drop on the 15th hole of the second round and should have signed for a score that reflected a two-stroke penalty. He escaped on a technicality – officials had failed to spot the error – but many observers felt the Augusta authorities had fashioned the rules to keep golf's biggest name in the tournament.

A couple of weeks later he won the Players, followed in August by the World Golf Championships Bridgestone Invitational at Firestone, which he won for an astonishing eighth time.

Throughout his career, Woods' name has rarely been out of the headlines and undoubtedly he remains the brightest star in the golfing galaxy. Even though his Ryder Cup record is modest compared with his successes in every other aspect of the game, he would always be the first name a captain would want on an American team.

Contrast Woods' role as a sporting icon with that of fellow professional Jimmy Walker. The Oklahoma City-born pro is three years younger than the man who has been the pre-eminent force of the modern era. Before making his way into Tom Watson's Gleneagles team, Walker had never been one of golf's stars. For 187 tournaments he failed to emerge from a black hole of anonymity. He was a largely unnoticed figure – he was better known for quietly seeking stardom of a more literal kind.

Walker's hobby is astro-photography and during his down time he is most likely to be found at a computer screen in his home in Boerne, Texas. That's where he processes images from space, captured by his telescopes hundreds of miles away. 'It's evolved to my gear being on top of a mountain at a place called New Mexico Skies, where I shoot every night, pretty much,' Walker revealed.

'I've got a computer sitting there that runs all the telescope components. I can set targets through a software programme and it can start running the telescope all night long.'

From layered images of outer space, Walker painstakingly creates spectacular pieces of photography. This artistic process provides the perfect antidote to the pressures of life on tour.

'He's created some really beautiful pieces of art,' said his wife Erin, a show-jumper whom Walker met when she was a volunteer at a Nationwide Tour event in 2004. 'It's amazing.'

Walker believes the instincts that drive his passion for capturing stars have also helped him reach for them in competition. 'You have this pretty picture we are trying to paint on the golf course and it's the same with astro-photography,' he said.

The key is attention to detail and a desire to unlock potential. While these qualities have created stunning images from outer space they have also helped turn him into a spectacular late bloomer in his chosen profession.

'I wasn't having much fun playing golf and I feel like I was out there killing myself and I didn't have a lot to show for it,' Walker said of his many years of struggle on the circuit. He graduated from the Nationwide Tour, where he won three times. In 2006 he started to play the PGA Tour full-time but made little impact. 'I wanted to win and it wasn't happening,' he admitted. 'I said: "I really have to figure out how to get better." And I remember also saying: "I'd rather stay home. I think I could get a pretty good job and make about the same amount of money and enjoy watching my kids grow up."'

But, deep down, Walker always had the feeling that he could make a success of his career. So instead of staying at home and taking a steady job, Jimmy and Erin fired up their motorhome and, along with their young sons Mclain and Beckett, they have been criss-crossing the US in pursuit of golfing glory ever since. In 2008 he broke into the top-200 earners, a year later he was in the top-150 and in 2010 he finished 72nd. Twelve months later Walker banked more than a $1 million for a season for the first time and, thereafter, he has earned seven-figure sums each year.

In 2012 he made another decision that took him to a new level. He enlisted the help of Woods' former coach Butch

Harmon. The son of 1948 Masters champion Claude Harmon Snr is one of the most respected teachers in the game. He was the man who fashioned Woods' swing when he held all four major titles at the same time in 2000–01, and he also turned Phil Mickelson into an Open champion at Muirfield in 2013. Harmon told Walker he was under-utilising his talents and set about finding a way to maximise his potential.

'Butch is great,' said Walker, whose initial payment to his coach was a $1,200 bottle of Château Margaux. 'He can watch two swings and see what is going on. He's very matter of fact and he's very confident in what he tells you and that's what I really enjoy about working with him. When he tells you something, he tells you with passion and purpose and makes you believe in what you are working on. I was playing well before I started working with Butch and I feel like I'm playing better after.'

The proof came in the very first event on the 2013–14 PGA Tour schedule. The new 'wrap around' season began in mid-October at the $5 million Frys.com Open at CordeValle Golf Club in San Martin, California.

Most of the big names skipped the event but, for Walker, it was the start of what proved to be the most successful season of his life. This was Walker's 188th event on the PGA Tour. Prior to it, he had taken three weeks off to attend a wedding in Canada and do some strengthening work in the gym. His golfing preparation consisted of little more than a couple of hastily arranged lessons with Harmon.

Sometimes that's all you need.

Walker liked the course and had finished fourth there 12 months earlier, having just recovered from knee surgery. He began steadily with rounds of 70 and 69 to move to three under par. Few were expecting a Saturday charge but it materialised with no fewer than 10 birdies in a spectacular 62 carded by the Baylor University graduate. Suddenly Walker knew he had a chance of claiming his first victory on the main tour.

But that looked an unlikely prospect after 11 holes of the final round. Walker was playing well, but not well enough. He went to the turn in a perfectly respectable 32, but trailed 23-year-old Brooks Koepka by four strokes. Walker was three months short of his 35th birthday and it appeared that his wait for that elusive first win would continue. It was Koepka, however, who lacked the winning knack. His putting stroke vanished and the young American's lead evaporated within four holes. Walker made birdies at the 13th and 15th before parring home for a two-stroke win over Hall of Fame member Vijay Singh.

Walker played the weekend with rounds of 62 and 66 to break his duck. It was a landmark moment, which also gained him entry to the Masters.

Walker had only been to the glorious Georgia venue once before, as a guest of a member called Paul Sarvadi. The businessman had invited Walker and his father, Jim, in the winter of 2009. They stayed in Arnold Palmer's cabin and the abiding memory was of his dad birdieing three of Augusta's four par 5s. Jimmy Walker inherited most of his golfing talent from Jim Snr, a scratch handicapper who once carded a round of 60 – something Jimmy had yet to manage. At least now he was a winner on tour.

Victory at CordeValle was also a vindication for Walker – he'd been right to stick at his chosen career, even though it had taken him until his mid-30s to finally start winning. 'I don't think my window is closing,' said the big-hitting Oklahoma native. 'I don't feel old. I don't think I'm old. I hit the ball further than these kids do, so I'm not worried about that.'

Walker was now into the world's leading 50 players and his win took him to the top of the early-season American Ryder Cup qualifying table. 'It is a goal,' he said of his prospects of making it to Gleneagles. 'I would definitely like to go and play Ryder Cup. It's something I've watched since I was a kid and it looks like the ultimate pressure and playing for your country, it's got a lot of history and I would love to be part of the team.'

If the 34-year-old was looking to the future with youthful verve and optimism, Woods, at 37, was feeling much older. Despite his five wins in the 2013 season, it ended painfully amid growing concern about his fitness to compete at the highest level.

Woods was the first golfer to pursue his sport with the mindset of an elite athlete. Yes, Gary Player, Greg Norman and Sir Nick Faldo accepted the need for disciplined diet as well as strength and fitness conditioning, but Woods totally embraced it.

It's clear he is obsessed with athleticism. He has often given off a sense of frustration that good golf can be played by people not in peak physical condition. Woods has always wanted to be like elite performers from more explosive sports – the likes of basketball superstar Michael Jordan and tennis's Roger Federer. He teased players like Darren Clarke (now, admittedly, a much slimmer figure) for being overweight and would undertake punishing fitness regimes. At his peak, Woods ran at least 30 miles most weeks, and he would constantly seek to maintain and build muscle mass by lifting weights.

As his former coach Hank Haney observed in his book *The Big Miss*: 'He liked the impression that his swing was so violently athletic that it put him on constant guard against injury.'

Haney also observed: 'I thought Tiger was more susceptible to the whole injury drama because of his self-image. It occurred to me that he never forgot being the skinny kid who was an outsider. Even though he was a golfing prodigy, he was never the popular jock or the big man on campus.' Haney went on to say: 'In that context, it's not surprising that Tiger overcompensated by putting big muscles on his narrow frame.'

When Woods underwent surgery to repair the anterior cruciate ligament in his left knee after winning the 2008

US Open, he was advised by the surgeon to reduce his weight to 165 pounds. According to Haney, the patient's response was: 'No way.'

Woods still wanted the lean muscle mass and figure of an explosive athlete, but such physiques can be prone to breaking down in their mid- to late-30s. Woods was an aged 37. His body had been swinging a golf club since he was two years old. He's been through four operations on his left knee, has had trouble with his Achilles tendon and his neck has been troublesome. And, by late summer in 2013, his back was starting to play up.

Arriving at the Barclays tournament in Jersey City on 21 August, he could manage only the most cursory of practice sessions. The long clubs were left in the bag and he chipped and putted his way round the Liberty National course. 'My neck and back are a little bit stiff,' he admitted. 'It was stiff this morning after a soft bed and just one of those things. Sleeping in hotels. I didn't want to push it, so just took it easy.' Woods played down worries of an underlying problem.

The next day was a long one. Woods had been up at 4 a.m., bad weather rumbled into New Jersey and there were three rain delays. Between the interruptions, he carded a fine 67 to lie three strokes off the lead. After a second-round 69, he admitted he was feeling increasing pain in his back. 'A little sore right now,' was his typically understated way of explaining how he was feeling at the halfway stage of the tournament.

He followed up with the same score on the Saturday and claimed his condition was 'all good'. But, to the spectators, it was clear he was struggling. Woods could only move gingerly as he bent to tee up the ball or retrieve it from the hole. 'It starts off great every day and then it progressively deteriorates,' he admitted.

Nevertheless, Woods remained in contention for a sixth title of 2013. He has always possessed an astonishing competitive instinct. Not only did he win the 2008 US Open with no anterior cruciate ligament in his left knee, he was also suffering from a stress fracture in the same leg. It is no exaggeration to say that he won that major, which included an 18-hole play-off and one hole of sudden death against Rocco Mediate (91 holes in total), on one leg.

So, despite being hampered by an ever more troublesome back, he harboured genuine hopes of kicking off the 2013 play-offs with victory. But on the 12th hole of the final round he felt a sharp, biting pain as he struck his tee shot. One hole later, there was no disguising his discomfort. Just a single stroke off the lead and beneath clear blue skies, he sized up his second shot on the par 5 from 258 yards out. It was a five wood that needed a controlled cut to find the putting surface. He shaped up to produce that left-to-right movement through the air, opening his stance and shoulders. It's a shot he has played hundreds of thousands of times. On this occasion, though, the ball flew straight left over a willow tree that appeared ready to weep in sympathy before careering into a waiting pond. Woods was on his knees, his face contorted in agony as his back cramped and seized up. 'Big time,' Woods stated when asked if it had gone into spasm. 'It actually started on the hole before, my little tee shot there started it and 13 just kind of accentuated it.'

Somehow he found a way to finish, and did so creditably with a gutsy 69 that gave him a share of second place. Ironically, his fellow runner-up was Graham DeLaet, who had recovered from his own bout of back trouble but only after undergoing surgery. The Canadian's protracted convalescence provided a benchmark for observers trying to chart Woods' chances of recovery in Ryder Cup year.

Woods managed to complete the rest of the 2013 season but rarely hit top form. A share of 11th place at the BMW Championship, where he opened with an excellent 66, was his best showing in the remaining play-off events. He claimed three out of a possible five points when the US took on the non-European International team for the Presidents Cup at Muirfield Village in Ohio at the start of October. He followed a light schedule, playing an exhibition match against Rory McIlroy in China before finishing third at the Turkish Airlines Open. His only genuine chance of a victory came at his own tournament, the Northwestern Mutual Challenge, a limited-field event in California at the end of the year. Woods enjoyed a second round 62 and led by four with eight to play but ended up losing a play-off to Zach Johnson.

Still number one in the world, he admitted that his fitness frailties were an ongoing concern. 'Any athlete who plays any sports is going to get injured and the longer you play it, the more likelihood you are going to get injured,' he said. 'I've certainly tried to curb my workout regime over the years. I don't run the mileage like I used to. I don't lift the way I used to. Things evolve. I'm not 22.'

Nevertheless, Woods, having just turned 38, was looking forward to 2014 more than any recent year. He felt the schedule offered him his best chance of ending a six-year drought in the majors. Always a threat at Augusta, where he had won four green jackets, he liked his chances there. Pinehurst would stage the US Open and he had been third and runner-up when the Championship had been played there in 1999 and 2005. Hoylake, the venue for the Open, was the scene of his last Claret Jug in 2006, and he also won the PGA at Valhalla in 2000. The major locations for 2014 were all happy hunting grounds and gave him great cause for optimism. 'Three I've won at and one I'm trending in the right way,' Woods said.

His clubs remained in the cupboard for the opening weeks of the year. The PGA Tour resumed in Hawaii with the Hyundai Tournament of Champions. For the first time, Jimmy Walker was eligible for the event, which is reserved for the previous year's winners on tour. He finished in an unremarkable tie for 21st before the circus moved to the Waialae Country Club in Honolulu for the Sony Open.

With wife Erin and their two boys in tow, Walker was at ease both with the surroundings and his newly elevated status in the game. He said: 'I want to keep the pedal down. I want to keep playing well. I was disappointed last week. I wish I would have played better, but I took some positives out of it and bring them into this week, and I want to keep playing well.'

He backed up rounds of 66 and 67 with a third-round 67 that put him firmly in the mix for what proved to be a tense final day during which he found his very best golf. With a couple of hours left to play, five players shared the lead.

It is not always birdie putts that spark a charge. Sometimes it is an unlikely par save that proves the catalyst. This was certainly the case when Walker sank a 12-footer to avoid bogeying the 14th. Now was the time to hit the accelerator. One behind leader Harris English, who was in the final group a hole behind, Walker birdied the 15th. Moments later, English failed to get up and down from a greenside bunker and dropped a stroke to provide a crucial two-shot swing. Pumped with adrenaline, Walker then lasered his approach to the 16th for a seven-foot birdie. At the next, his tee shot flew to six feet and he capitalised to move to 17 under par.

Walker completed the last in regulation figures, then had to wait to see whether third-round leader Chris Kirk could hole a 30-foot pitch for an eagle to tie the clubhouse lead. The American missed to the right and Walker had won for the second time in six starts.

'It took me a long time to do it,' he reflected on his 187-tournament wait before securing the first of those titles. Now, though, he knew what it took to become a champion and he'd become a repeat winner. 'I felt very calm and controlled. That's what you have to feel and do when it's time to win. It's easy to say and hard to do, but today was awesome.'

Woods' season, meanwhile, began at the scene of his most astonishing major victory. Even though he won the 1997 Masters by a record 12 strokes and romped to a 15-stroke victory at the 2000 US Open at Pebble Beach, his win in the 2008 running of America's national championship was the most extraordinary of his major triumphs. That victory – on one leg – took place at Torrey Pines, in the suburbs of San Diego. It was a Herculean effort that added significantly to his already substantial legend.

Since that win, though, Woods' aura had diminished. It wasn't just the epic downfall of his personal life, which was chronicled in such detail by the tabloid press, it was also his presence as a golfer. In fact, you could chart it from the summer of 2009. He missed the cut in a bad-tempered display at the Open at Turnberry, and then lost the PGA Championship at Hazeltine to South Korea's unheralded Y. E. Yang. It was the first time Woods had been beaten in a major having led going into the final round.

Later that year, he suffered the car crash that prompted the revelations of his serial adultery. This led to rehab, to treat a form of sex addiction, and ultimately to divorce from his wife Elin, the mother of their two children. Thereafter, it has been a constant struggle for Woods to reassert his reputation.

There was nothing special about his return to Torrey Pines at the start of 2014. Rounds of 72 and 71 were followed by a miserable 79 and he missed the third-round cut. From California he flew to the Middle East, where he was reportedly paid $3 million to appear in the Dubai Desert Classic.

'Yeah, I definitely feel fit,' he claimed. 'There's no doubt about that.' He was less buoyant about his form, though: 'My game was nowhere near as sharp as I would have liked last week.'

Nevertheless, he was ready to talk up his chances for the year, after remodelling his swing under the tutelage of coach

Sean Foley. 'I've always played my best with a shorter position,' he said. 'If you look at my younger days on tour, it was even shorter than it is now. Only difference is that I can't wheel on it like I used to – just snapping at the end to get power and rotation. If I did that now, I'd destroy the knee just like I did before, which is why I had so many operations on it.'

Still the biggest draw in the game, he was taking on a strong European Tour field, with the organisers inviting back all the past champions from its 25-year history, apart from the late Seve Ballesteros. Woods, though, struggled for inspiration. He shot 68 and 73 in the first two rounds, accompanied by eventual champion Stephen Gallacher who defended the title from the previous year. Over the weekend Woods shot 70 and 71 to finish in a share of 41st place. His start to the year could be described, at best, as mediocre. He felt sure he had found something to bolster his long game by tweaking his grip, but knew his short game was still rusty.

That certainly wasn't the case for Walker who had remained in the US. As Woods headed home, fretting over his long-range putting and chipping out of rye grass, his Texas-based compatriot was looking to maintain momentum at the AT&T Pebble Beach Pro-Am. It is a pro-celebrity event but serious business for the pros, with a purse of $6.6 million.

Walker was on a roll. Going into the final round he had accumulated a six-stroke cushion and he was still five ahead with nine holes to play. Then Walker's touch on the greens began to falter. Commenting in the television announcers' booth, veteran Hollywood legend Clint Eastwood said the tournament would be decided by 'whoever chokes this tournament away, or doesn't choke this tournament away'.

The lead was down to two with two holes to go and reduced to a single shot by the last. It meant that when Walker arrived on the final green he had two putts to secure his third victory in eight tournaments. Despite those two previous wins, there was little guarantee Walker would be able to perform what should have been a routine job of closing out the tournament. Especially when he charged the first putt five feet past the hole.

Walker needed to make the return to avoid a play-off against Dustin Johnson and Jim Renner. Johnson, a two-times winner of the event, had closed with a brilliant 66.

Failing to capitalise on such a healthy lead might have been catastrophic for Walker's confidence. 'I hate three-putting,' he said. 'I had two of them back there, and definitely didn't want another one on the last.' Somehow he summoned the nerve to make the winning blow. 'It's drama, man,' Walker said on the 18th green. 'It was too much for me.'

It was enough, though, for yet another win and he had holed a clutch putt to secure it. 'I've always felt like I could win out here, and I think that's what you have to believe to be out here, that you belong and that you can win. And finally it happened. And it's cool that it's happened a couple more times. Quickly.' In the past 20 years on the PGA Tour, only Woods, Mickelson and former number one David Duval had won so often so early in a season.

This was only early February and the Ryder Cup was still some 229 days away, but it was clear that this previously little-known player would almost certainly make his debut at Gleneagles. Furthermore, he was convinced that he had what it takes to be an asset to his country's cause. That five-foot putt on the final green at Pebble Beach told him all he needed to know. 'I'll take a lot from today, I think, into that,' Walker said of the Ryder Cup implications, before adding: 'I don't remember this much talk about the Ryder Cup in the last couple of years. I don't know if it's because I haven't been on the radar screen or what, but it seems like it's a very big pressing thing.'

This was how the Ryder Cup qualifying table looked after

Walker's blistering start to the season:

1. Jimmy Walker (3,605.833)
2. Dustin Johnson (2,593.212)
3. Phil Mickelson (2,446.755)
4. Jason Dufner (2,261.279)
5. Zach Johnson (2,196.277)
6. Harris English (2,106.940)
7. Ryan Moore (1,986.201)
8. Webb Simpson (1,982.898)
9. Chris Kirk (1,819.570)
10. Kevin Stadler (1,511.197)
11. Patrick Reed (1,334.152)
12. Brian Stuard (1,228.108)

The top nine golfers would qualify automatically. Players were awarded one point for every $1,000 earned on the PGA Tour, with two points given for every $1,000 won at the four majors in 2014. They also received a point for every $1,000 won in the majors played in 2013, but performances during the season that began with Walker's win at the Frys.com tournament were the ones that really mattered.

Extraordinarily, he had all but guaranteed his place before any of the majors had been played. In 2012, Hunter Mahan finished in ninth spot (for that match, there were four captain's picks, so he didn't qualify) with a total of 4,082.228 points. Walker was already only 400-odd points shy of that total, with the majority of the season still to play.

Two days after his triumph he was the talk of a news conference given by Watson to announce fellow veteran Ray Floyd as his second vice captain. Andy North, US Open champion in 1978 and 1985, had already been appointed. Watson highlighted the gutsy way in which the AT&T had been won the previous Sunday, saying: 'What Jimmy Walker did this last week is what I'm looking for. He knocked it from 25 feet, he knocked it five feet by and he holed the putt coming back. That's not an easy putt to make because that putt doesn't break. It just doesn't.' Watson, who had won his US Open on that same Pebble Beach green back in 1982, continued: 'You can play it right edge and it just hangs on that right edge. It doesn't break and he made it. That's what I'm looking for, the guy that's going to make that five-footer to win or tie. That's what I'm looking for, the guts it takes to do that.'

One of Watson's hallmarks in his prime was his fearless return-putting, which meant that he would often strike the ball aggressively with his first attempt. But his points in common with Walker were not restricted to golf. 'Studied him a little bit,' Watson admitted. 'He's 35 years old. He has an interest in astronomy, which I do. The first book I read was *All About Astronomy*. If he makes the Ryder Cup team, maybe we'll have some common things to talk about.'

But what of golf's biggest star?

Woods was pacing himself. He wasn't at the Riviera Country Club for the Northern Trust Open, where Watson's news conference had taken place. Woods also opted out of the WGC Accenture Matchplay at Dove Mountain in Arizona. He has never enjoyed the course and preferred to rest rather than subject himself to the hazards of sudden-death 18-hole knock-out matchplay. His return to action came the following week at The Honda Classic, staged at the PGA National at Palm Beach Gardens.

A glamorous event, it heralds the start of the 'Florida Swing' which forms a big part of the build-up to the Masters in the second week of April. 'When we get to Florida, I think we are all thinking about our way to Augusta,' Woods acknowledged.

By the Saturday evening, Woods was full of optimism. It seemed the rust of an off-season, during which he had spent more time rehabilitating his body than practising his golf, had finally been shaken off. After opening rounds of 71 and 69, he fired his lowest score of the year, a brilliant 65, putting him firmly in the mix for the title. Clad in his familiar final-day red shirt and black trousers, he headed to the range, seemingly full of confidence. His purposeful stride suggested he was once again the man to beat.

The body language was misleading. As he warmed up, his back felt tight. He had no freedom of movement and he was starting to feel a sense of dread. 'You never know when it's going to happen,' said PGA Tour stalwart Ryan Palmer, observing the nature of back injuries. 'You go 25 weeks a year, 10 straight years and then you throw in the amount of time you practise without playing the tournaments; your body, the explosion your body has on the golf swing, it takes a toll.'

Out on the course, Woods' play was ragged. He bogeyed the second, double-bogeyed the third and dropped another shot at the fourth. He birdied the seventh but dropped another as he went to the turn. Rubbing his back he made his way to the spectator ropes to chat with his girlfriend, Lindsey Vonn. The US international skier, no stranger to injuries herself having missed the Winter Olympics with knee trouble, looked concerned.

Woods soldiered on but, after making his par at the 13th, he turned to his playing partner Luke Guthrie and shook hands. Woods' round was over.

He climbed into a white van and was driven off to the players' car park where he met Vonn and his two children, Sam and Charlie. 'Hey, Daddy can handle pain,' Woods told his young daughter but he was at a loss on how to explain why he was no longer playing.

'I just couldn't move out there,' Woods said. 'I got to the point where I couldn't twist. So try to explain to your six-year-old daughter why you quit.'

The back spasms that had hit him at the Barclays tournament during the previous year's play-offs had returned and he had no idea whether he would be able to play the following week at the WGC Cadillac Championship at Doral.

Once again, Woods was making headlines for all the wrong reasons. Speculation was rife over the cause of his problems. Could it be the new swing that had evolved from his still-young relationship with his coach Foley? 'That change of action might well have contributed to his current problems,' said leading sports physiotherapist Linda Stevenson. 'The only way to get long-lasting relief might be to go back to the drawing board.

'Typical golfing posture does not help. The increased curvature caused by the stance puts more weight through the facet joints. This causes more compression, they get more wear and become inflamed and the back goes into spasm. Eighty per cent of the weight should be going through the discs instead. They are the part of the back designed to have more weight on them.

'The situation is then made worse by the dynamic action that goes into hitting the ball,' Stevenson added. 'Tiger's core strength will be amazing but he has relied on his back for many years and now it would seem it has come to find him out. Around 10 years ago I was at a conference of physios which looked at Tiger Woods' action and we agreed then that he was likely to end up suffering back problems.'

The five victories in 2013 now seemed a distant memory. Woods was frail and fallible as he arrived at another of his favourite courses. The Doral resort is located close to Miami's international airport. It was built on 2,400 acres of swampland bought by Polish migrants Alfred and Doris Kaskel for $49,000 in the late 1950s. The venue's name originated from combining the Christian names of the married couple and they developed a resort famed for its Blue Monster course. Four times, Woods had recorded victories here, at one of the staple stops on the PGA Tour. In 2012 it was bought by Donald Trump for

$150 million and two years later it was a re-designed layout that staged the World Golf Championships event, where the 38-year-old was determined to prove his fitness.

Woods had continual treatment from the moment he departed the Honda Classic. 'I feel better; how about that?' he said. 'I feel good.' His positivity then manifested itself in an uncharacteristically open account of the fitness challenges he was facing. 'You have repetitive injuries, and most of my injuries are that. So that's the nature of why we lift, why we work out. It is to try to prevent a lot of these things and keep us healthy.

'The will to win hasn't changed. It's physically am I able to do it? A bad back is something that is no joke.'

Woods went on to explain why his current problems had different implications compared with the injuries he'd suffered earlier in his career. 'When I've had injuries in the past, it has always been after impact. So it's fine; the ball has gone. It's going to hurt like hell but the ball has gone.

'But, with the back, it is a totally different deal. There are certain movements you just can't do. That's one of the things I've started to learn about this type of injury, it's very different.'

At World Golf Championships tournaments there is no halfway cut. It was just as well as far as Woods was concerned. His poorest start to a golfing year continued with opening rounds of 76 and 73. With those scores, there would have been no weekend action for him at a regular tour event or a major. But, taking advantage of this reprieve, he went out early on the Saturday and hit form with an excellent 66.

It proved a temporary respite, though. By the final day his back was starting to hurt again. He winced his way to a closing 78. On the sixth hole he had a downhill lie in a bunker and tried to hit an eight-iron approach. 'That's what started it off,' Woods admitted. Thereafter he was battling spasms while completing the round.

Already his preparations for the Masters appeared in tatters. He was due to play the Arnold Palmer Invitational at Bay Hill on 20 March in his last competitive outing before heading to Augusta. Then came word that he wouldn't be fit to play Arnie's tournament. It was another big blow, especially since he had won at Bay Hill on eight occasions. By now, though, it was clear he was going to have to take out time to cure his back problems. Woods' career would be over if radical action wasn't taken.

The diagnosis was a damaged disc that was pinching a nerve in his spine. This was prompting the back spasms and shooting pains down his right leg when he swung the golf club. To alleviate the condition, Woods needed a 'microdiscectomy' – minimally invasive surgery aimed at relieving the pressure and pain caused by a herniated disc by removing small disc fragments pressing against spinal nerves. The surgery was carried out on 31 March in Park City, Utah, by neurosurgeon Charles Rich.

All hope of the world number one making it to Augusta had gone. 'I'd like to express my disappointment to the Augusta National membership, staff, volunteers and patrons that I will not be at the Masters,' Woods said.

'It's a week that's very special to me. It also looks like I'll be forced to miss several upcoming tournaments to focus on my rehabilitation and getting healthy. This is frustrating, but it's something my doctors advised me to do for my immediate and long-term health.

'It's tough right now, but I'm absolutely optimistic about the future,' he added.

Doctors' orders included no twisting or bending. Woods struggled to get out of bed and, although the procedure brought instant relief, the discomfort from the incision took a while to clear. A self-confessed insomniac, Woods found sleeping even harder, and although still officially the world's best golfer, he couldn't even pick up his own children, never mind swing a club.

Sleeping wasn't easy either for the player who had produced the best golf of the year so far. Walker had travelled down the Interstate 20 ready for his Masters debut. Watson had arranged for them to play a practice round together. Walker was going to be playing the hallowed Augusta National course with the great Tom Watson! Of course he couldn't sleep – the drive down Magnolia Lane was so close and his heart was racing: 'I was lying in bed. I was saying to myself: "Man, it's just across the street, it really is,"' Walker recalled. 'It's excitement. I think if you don't have that anymore, you need to do something else.'

This was April 2014. The golfing year was about to really take off, with the most glamorous event of the year. The excitement would then gradually build through to the Ryder Cup showdown between Europe and the Unites States.

For Walker, apart from his astro-photography, there was little else to do other than go and play good golf. For Woods, there was little on offer beyond a diet of video games. Walker's season was mapped out and was going to reach its climax at Gleneagles. Who knew whether Woods would make it to Scotland? America's captain had no idea. Nor did the player himself.

CHAPTER 7

Spieth and Dubuisson

*'If he wants to go putt, he will go and putt, even
if it's eight o'clock in the evening. And if he does
not feel like practising at all, he will spend the day
in front of the TV and not do anything. So, with
Victor, you have to let him do his own stuff.'*

Thomas Levet on Victor Dubuisson

On a typically hectic day for the young Spieth family, Shawn and his wife Chris were out shopping for baby supplies with newborn Steven and his 18-month-old brother Jordan. Passing through the mall, Shawn spotted a set of plastic golf clubs and figured they might help occupy his energetic toddler.

He was right. When they returned to their North Dallas home, Jordan was straight out into the back yard to swing away with his newest toy. 'We had to yank him in at 11 o'clock that night,' said Shawn.

His recollection of the timings may be rather apocryphal, but the episode certainly suggested how life might turn out for Jordan. As Shawn recalled: 'Maybe it was a precursor to going out and spending hours on the range.' It was the first golfing experience for the player who, twenty years later, became the youngest member of the American Ryder Cup team at Gleneagles.

The Spieths were an athletic family. Chris was a fine basketball player, while baseball was Shawn's game. He also played golf to a seven handicap and his father, Donald, had shown enough promise to be offered a scholarship. His preference, though, had been music and he went on to become a leading conductor.

When Jordan was eight, the family joined Brookhaven Country Club. The facility, in Farmers Branch on the outskirts of North Dallas, had three golf courses, but that wasn't the motivation for joining. Mum Chris liked the friendly atmosphere and wanted an athletic outlet for her two boys. She thought the swimming team would provide the ideal opportunity. For the first summer Jordan was in and out of the pool but would wistfully stare in the direction of the range and the first tee. That's where he really wanted to be.

'When he was nine, he would come in and wake me up on a Saturday morning, fully dressed and ready to go to the course,' Chris said.

At this stage Spieth was self-taught and, by the time he was 12, felt ready to be taking on 18-year-olds in junior competitions. 'The biggest sport, obviously, when you are growing up in Texas is football. And baseball is kind of second,' he explained. 'And I love basketball too, and that's what most of my friends chose the path of. I fell in love with golf with some of my other buddies at the club when I was real young. I ended up being better at it at an early age than I was at any other sports. I like controlling my own destiny.'

Spieth collected three straight high-school titles and caught the eye of coach Cameron McCormick. On one occasion they were out playing nine holes and the teacher decided to issue his young pupil with a challenge. For the last half-dozen holes, he would place three balls around the green. Spieth had to try to get up and down in two shots from each spot. McCormick said that he would buy his pupil a golf cap if he could complete the task in three over par or better. When they reached the final hole Spieth needed to sink one of his three chips. He proceeded to hole two of them and get the other one up and down. As the adage goes: 'If you want to get ahead, get a hat.' Spieth got the hat.

'He's the last person I have to ask to do more,' McCormick told Associated Press golf correspondent Doug Ferguson. 'Jordan always tries really hard to play his best golf, regardless of whether his game is there that day.'

Although there are plenty of sporting options, it's not overly surprising that a young sports enthusiast would choose golf as his or her athletic pursuit when growing up in the Dallas area. Texas is one of the great golfing heartlands of the US. Two of the game's most famous names, Ben Hogan and Byron Nelson, grew up in Fort Worth; six-times major winner Lee Trevino was born in Dallas; and double Masters champion Ben Crenshaw hails from Austin. Courses like Whispering Pines, the Dallas National, Colonial Country Club, Redstone near Houston and Oak Hills in San Antonio head a long list of facilities of the highest quality, including the Brookhaven club favoured by the Spieths.

The golfing heritage of France is less rich. The country has produced only one major winner – Arnaud Massy, who became the first overseas winner of the Open in 1907. He took up the game after becoming a caddie at the Biarritz Golf Club and beat the great J. H. Taylor by two strokes to claim his title.

Jean van de Velde came desperately close to matching Massy's feat in 1999. The genial Frenchman, however, contrived to take seven strokes down the final hole at Carnoustie when six would have sufficed to claim the Claret Jug. He infamously found the Barry Burn, which runs in front of the home green, and contemplated playing from the hazard. Van de Velde became a figure of fun as he rolled up his trouser legs to paddle into the stream and size up his fourth stroke. Eventually the man from Mont-de-Marsan, in the south-west of France, holed an eight-footer to force his way into a play-off with eventual champion Paul Lawrie and Texan Justin Leonard.

Three years later, the Parisian Thomas Levet also made an Open play-off along with Australians Stuart Appleby and Steve Elkington as well as champion Ernie Els. Levet had shot 66 in the final round at Muirfield to take his place in the four-hole shootout. He tied with Els to take it to sudden death before falling to the South African, who claimed his third major. Levet went on to play in the victorious 2004 European Ryder Cup team while van de Velde made it into the 1999 side that lost at Brookline. These two were the only French players to compete in the match until Victor Dubuisson came along, taking the early qualifying period for the 2014 match by storm.

Aged 24, Dubuisson was the European equivalent of Spieth – the baby of the team. And, like Spieth, he forced his way into the side with some of the most exciting golf witnessed during the qualifying period. The two men differ greatly in terms of public persona, though. Spieth is open, articulate and clearly comfortable in the limelight. Dubuisson is much more a man of mystery. He says little and is happy to leave observers guessing. Asked about his childhood, he told reporters: 'I didn't really have a family, so I just did what I wanted to do.'

And while Spieth followed a conventional route into the game, taking full advantage of the sporting opportunities made available to him from the moment he could walk, his French contemporary was a self-starter who discovered the game for himself. Tiger Woods was his inspiration.

In 1997, Woods stunned the golfing world with his 12-stroke victory at the Masters. Dubuisson was just about to celebrate his seventh birthday. At the time, he played a bit of tennis and basketball. He enjoyed his sports, although he didn't like to be reliant on teammates when it came to basketball. 'I prefer to be on my own and control what I do,' he said.

At home in Cannes, Dubuisson saw how an individual can dominate a sporting event when he watched Woods' first major triumph on television. Woods made an awful start on the first morning, reaching the turn in 40, before coming home in 30 and eventually ran away with the green jacket. It was his first Masters as a professional and the game of golf had never seen the likes of his triumph before.

Dubuisson was mesmerised and inspired in equal measure. 'He had a very bad start,' the Frenchman explained. 'He was four over par after nine holes. Everybody was saying: "Okay, Tiger has made a good start as a pro, but now that it is an important tournament, his first major (in the paid ranks), he's not going to do very well, maybe because of the pressure." And then he just completely broke the course and broke the record.'

Woods finished 18 under par with rounds of 70–66–65–69. His total of 270 was the lowest score in tournament history and his winning margin the biggest in a major since Old Tom Morris's 13-shot triumph in the 1862 Open. The watching child back in France couldn't get enough of this imperious display. 'Just every shot, every fantastic shot he hit in the tournament and the way he was,' Dubuisson said. 'I was very impressed by just the way he was hitting the driver. It was Tiger, I mean, I could not explain everything I felt during this Masters. I was not a golfer at this time, so yeah, I started to dream.'

Like Spieth, Dubuisson discovered a natural affinity with the sport. Aside from Levet and van de Velde, there were other French players on the European Tour – the likes of 2007 Scottish Open winner Grégory Havret and the elegant Raphaël Jacquelin – providing evidence that a good living could be made from the game. Dubuisson was naturally athletic. He had no time for study. All he now wanted to do was play golf. He claims he left school at the age of 11, although that is as hard to verify as Shawn Spieth's claim that he allowed his 18-month-old son to stay out until 11 p.m., swishing his new plastic clubs.

'Victor was going to school but he was on the golf course at school and he didn't go to school after he was 15, something like that,' explained Levet, who has become a mentor to his younger compatriot. 'He was learning only the things that were going to be helpful for his golf career – speaking English, things like that. He was always golf-oriented.

'He's very, very quiet. He's very shy. He doesn't like to talk about himself, so he makes the job of the media quite difficult. He is opening up slowly. He has learned to give a little bit about himself. He has a tendency not to do the things he doesn't like. So if he doesn't like talking about himself, it is very difficult to make him talk. The higher he goes in the rankings, the more questions are going to be asked about him.'

Dubuisson enjoyed a very successful amateur career, and soon leading figures in the French game, Levet among them, were taking note. 'I first heard of him about nine years ago,' Levet told me during the 2014 US Open. 'It was a name that kept coming back from French Championships and French teams. He was only 14 or 15 at the time and people were already talking about him like a top amateur. So you think: "Wow, maybe we have a talent here!" As an amateur he was not winning all the time, but he was winning a few things and always in the top of the rankings.

'Then I got to play with him a few times in practice and tournaments as well and saw the guy had a lot of potential. Then I got to meet him on tour and played with him a lot more. His long shots are quite impressive. He doesn't miss too many fairways, he doesn't miss too many long irons and he's very, very accurate. He thinks he can put any shot in the hole, or very close. That's a big quality.'

By the age of 19, Dubuisson had become the top-ranked amateur in the world. That year he won the 2009 European Amateur title when he birdied the 71st hole to beat Scotland's Ross Kellett by a stroke at Chantilly Golf Club, just north of Paris. He had already won the 2006 French Amateur and the Mexican equivalent in 2008 and the following year, with rounds of 66, 69 and 71, he won the prestigious Trophée Des Régions to go to the top of the amateur world rankings.

Dubuisson's victory in the European Amateur gave him his first taste of major championship golf with a place in the 2010 Open at St Andrews. He still had a lot to learn, as indicated by rounds of 80 and 73, and missed the cut by seven strokes. Nevertheless, he was well on the way to fulfilling his dream of becoming a professional. Still in the unpaid ranks, he played the Open de Lyon on the Challenge Tour – the feeder circuit for the main European Tour – and finished third. He was getting a strong sense that he was ready to step up and, later that year, he emerged from the tortuous six rounds of Qualifying School. The Frenchman finished 11th to claim precious playing privileges.

In the US, there was an even more spectacular route being taken to the riches of tour golf by the prodigiously talented Spieth. Unlike Dubuisson, the young American didn't totally neglect his classes but he shared the Frenchman's all-consuming passion for the game. A pupil at the Jesuit Preparatory School of Dallas, he was travelling the length and breadth of the US, picking up trophies almost every step of the way. He joined Woods in becoming the only multiple winner of the US Junior Amateur Championship with victories in 2009 and 2011 and was ranked number one junior in his country as well as Player of the Year in 2009. He was selected for two Junior Ryder Cups, on both occasions winning all three of his matches. The 2010 event was played at Gleneagles and the US won 13½–10½. The putter head cover he used on that occasion accompanied him to the same course for the Ryder Cup.

As a callow 16-year-old, he accepted an invitation to play the Byron Nelson Championship at the TPC Four Seasons Resort Club, Las Colinas in Irving, Texas. He had been going to the course to watch this PGA Tour event since he was five. Spieth's inclusion was big news locally. Classrooms were abandoned as fellow pupils flocked to see their contemporary do battle with some of the best players in the world. 'There are a lot from my school,' Spieth said. 'I don't think they are shutting [the school] down, but they might as well.'

Despite his tender years and lack of experience, the teenager was undaunted. He played a practice round with Justin Leonard, who pointed out where the youngster should be aiming. Professional golf is as much about knowing where to miss a shot as where to hit it. Which is the safe play? How can you best avoid a big number going on to your scorecard? How should you plot your way round a massive course full of hazards and lightning-quick greens?

'Obviously I know the percentage chances of me winning an event like this right now, but anything can happen,' Spieth told reporters. 'When I'm out there, I don't think of myself as a 16-year-old. I think of myself as a competitor in this tournament.' He wasn't being cocky – he was clearly just imbued with the fearlessness of youth, as well as plenty of golfing talent. With that, his pre-tournament press conference concluded and he proceeded to do something that would never have crossed Dubuisson's mind at the same age. Spieth headed back to school. There were classes in English, Spanish and Physics to attend, and his finals were only a week away.

Before that, though, there was an examination that was much more relevant to the youngster's future career. The Byron Nelson was there to be played – a historic and prestigious championship, named after one of the legendary figures of Texas golf.

Spieth passed the test in the most impressive of styles. He opened with a two-under-par 68 and added a second-round 69. He had three birdies and two bogeys and said: 'I'm in shock right now. I feel like I played better than my score showed.' At halfway he was three under par, on one of the most demanding courses used for professional golf in the US.

He became the sixth youngest player to make the cut in PGA Tour history.

This was his first taste of the big time and Spieth seemed to have the golfing attributes and attitude to succeed. 'I'm a pretty aggressive person when I have a golf club in my hand,' he said. He was whisked off to the television tower to share his thoughts with the Golf Channel. This fresh-faced figure sat alongside six-times major champion Sir Nick Faldo and long-time presenter Kelly Tilghman and revelled in his moment in the spotlight. 'It was awesome,' he said. 'I can't wait to watch it back tonight if I get the chance. I watch Golf Channel all the time.'

Spieth was fully justifying becoming the first amateur exemption in the tournament for 15 years. His third-round 67 took him into a share of seventh place and a day later he carded a 72 to finish the week at four under. 'I ended up enjoying it, of course, after the rounds. But during the round I was intense. I was trying to win,' he said.

Spieth had tied for 16th place alongside major winner Elkington, veteran Kenny Perry and Ryder Cup player Chris Riley, each of whom banked $94,250. As an amateur, Spieth had to forego the prize money, although that was of little concern to him.

'You really had to pay attention to realise that the kid was, well, a kid,' wrote Richard Durrett for ESPN Dallas.com. 'He didn't talk like someone who was merely happy to be playing with golfers that he idolised growing up. He said he wanted to win and he didn't really come off as being brash. Why? Because he had the game to back it up.'

Spieth headed to the University of Texas to continue his education and reap the benefits of playing on the 'Longhorns' team. This prodigiously talented teenager also had a healthy dose of perspective because he and his basketball-playing brother Steven have a younger sister Ellie, who has special needs through delayed cognitive and neurological development. Spieth has often helped out at his sister's Vanguard Preparatory School. 'A lot of them are much smarter at certain subjects than we were at their age and, you know, they just have some things that they don't do quite as well,' Spieth said. 'But it's a lot of fun to be able to help. That's what I look forward to doing for years down the road, getting involved with special needs kids.'

His mother also saw the benefits of her eldest son's relationship with his sister. She said: 'I still think he wants to be the best at what he does, but I think it calmed him down a little bit and made him realise there's more in the world.'

At the University of Texas, head coach John Fields already knew about the talent heading his way. He had first seen him as a 13-year-old. 'You could just kind of tell he was different,' Fields said. 'He just looked professional at that age. He was polished.'

In a stunning freshman year, Spieth won three times, led the team scoring average and helped them win the NCAA Championship. 'I have a lot more time to practise than I did at high school,' he said. 'We get out of class at 12.30 and I have the rest of the day to practise, which is nice. Really, everything has been more consistent. Everything is more refined, the kind of tightening up to how it needs to be.'

He was named in the honorary 'All-American' team and caught the eye of the selectors for the Walker Cup – the amateur equivalent of the Ryder Cup.

It was a very strong US team that travelled to Royal Aberdeen to defend the trophy against Great Britain and Ireland in 2011. Spieth was joined by the likes of Harris English and Russell Henley, now both firmly established on the PGA Tour, Peter Uihlein, who was Rookie of the Year in Europe in 2013, and stand-out amateurs Patrick Rodgers and Patrick Cantlay. 'Any time you can represent your country, for me, it's the biggest honour I've had,' Spieth said.

In often atrocious conditions on a fearsome Scottish links, the unbeaten Spieth was a shining light in an American team that fell to a shock defeat. He partnered Rodgers to a four-somes half against Tom Lewis and Michael Stewart, before winning both his singles clashes against Jack Senior and Andy Sullivan by the same margin, 3 and 2. Spieth's contribution wasn't enough to save the Americans from a 14–12 loss as the home team coped better with the high winds and side-ways rain.

Nevertheless, the experience only served to stoke further the 18-year-old's appetite for representing his country. He said: 'The crowds and the emotions are higher. The format is different. Peter [Uihlein] and I both hope that we can play on a Ryder Cup some day. I think this is a great step towards it.'

An even bigger-stride came as a result of the decision Spieth took after his first year at university. Following his encouraging start as a 16-year-old at the Byron Nelson, he had continued to be offered places in PGA Tour events. In the 2011 running of that event, he was within three strokes of the lead on the final day but then he played the last four holes in six over par to finish 32nd. On that occasion he played alongside the champion Keegan Bradley. 'I saw what it took to win a tour event,' Spieth said. 'In all these tour events, not only am I just measuring my own game against them but I'm trying to learn stuff from them.'

And he had now learned that he was ready. He made the cut six times in the eight professional events he played as an amateur. He would have netted in excess of $150,000 had he been eligible to claim prize money. 'Being out there and feeling what it is like to compete with some of the best players in the world, that made a huge impact on my decision. That gave me the confidence that I could do this. These guys are really good but at the same time, some of the top amateurs are not too far off. And it just shows how the game is getting younger. If you can play as many PGA Tour events as an amateur as you can, then that's a huge advantage.'

It was December 2012 and, aged 19 and midway through his sophomore year, it was time to cash in. It was time to join the professional ranks. Spieth quit the University of Texas. 'The hardest part of my decision was telling my teammates,' he revealed. 'It's bittersweet, but they understand. This is my lifelong dream.'

He departed the collegiate and amateur scene with a glowing reference from Longhorns coach John Fields. 'Jordan Spieth is a remarkable young man,' he said. 'He has left a positive, indelible mark on our programme. Jordan is first class as a student, first class as a teammate.' Just the qualities Tom Watson was looking for at Gleneagles.

Despite such a spectacular junior, amateur and collegiate career, there were few guarantees. He signed with the Forefront Sports Group and agent Jay Danz announced: 'This is a rising star who will be an elite player for years to come.' There have been many managers who have expressed such sentiments about a new signing but they are not always correct.

Spieth had failed to make it to the second stage of PGA Tour Qualifying School and thus had no official status in the professional game. He was reliant on sponsor's invites (of which he would only be allowed to accept seven) and the lottery of Monday qualifying to get into events on the main tour or the Web.com feeder circuit. Indeed, Spieth's first round as a professional was a Thursday qualifier to get into the Monday qualifying tournament for the Torrey Pines event in January 2013.

'There are quite a few ways to earn a card, but the bottom line is I have to earn one,' Spieth told the *Dallas Morning News*.

No status, no world ranking – just the reputation of being one of America's best junior and amateur players. That's all

Spieth had as he embarked on his first full year in the harsh world of professional golf. It turned into one of the most spectacular debut seasons the game has ever seen.

He finished 10th on the US money list and laid the foundations for becoming the youngest US Ryder Cup player since Horton Smith in 1929. During 2013 he rose from 810th to 22nd in the world rankings, and was a runaway winner of the Rookie of the Year title.

His season began relatively quietly. He missed the halfway cut by two strokes in the Farmers Insurance Open at Torrey Pines. From there, he headed to the AT&T National pro-am where he finished in a share of 22nd place, earning $65,000, his first cheque as a professional. Spieth looked at home, rubbing shoulders with the top names on the PGA Tour and the rich and famous who provide the amateur section to this event. But he still lacked the playing credentials to make him a regular on the world's most lucrative circuit.

As a result, he headed to the rather more humble golfing environs of South America. Spieth finished seventh in Panama, then grabbed a share of fourth in Colombia. These were Web. com events. But the next stop in Puerto Rico, to which he had been invited, counted on the main tour.

That March week proved pivotal in his fledgling career. He had a hole in one during the third round and carded scores of 69–66–67–67 on the Trump International course to finish 19 under par. Only Scott Brown beat that mark, by a single stroke. Spieth took home $308,000, sharing the runner-up berth with Fabian Gomez. More significantly, it earned him a spot in the Tampa Bay tournament the following week where, once again, his name figured on the leaderboard.

In every event he has played, Spieth's aim has been to win and this Florida competition was no different. If he couldn't win, the next priority was to finish in the top-10. By doing that, he would amass more dollars than the player who finished

150th on tour the previous season and thereby become eligible for special temporary membership of the PGA Tour.

In short, he could become a Tour player within three months of turning professional.

His Tampa performance resembled the episode when, as a junior, he had won the hat from his coach, all those years ago. It took some inspired short-game play to get the job done. Spieth chipped in on the 71st green, then holed out from seven feet at the last to claim a share of seventh place. In four events he had earned $521,892, as well as the right to accept unlimited sponsor invitations from that point on. 'To go four weeks, four different countries and play well, it's a big confidence boost,' he said.

Had he not holed the flop shot from the rough on the 17th, he would have fallen $195 short of the figure he needed to gain his new status. Spieth said: 'That would have been brutal, that would have hurt. That was one of the coolest shots I've ever hit.' The watching galleries knew they were watching something special and didn't hold back with their acclaim. 'That was as loud as it gets, the hair on the back of your neck stands up.'

An even more significant chip-in followed later in the season, but only after a succession of impressive returns as Spieth grew ever more comfortable on tour. He collected top-10 finishes at the RBC Heritage event, at Colonial and then in the AT&T National in early June. He was rocketing up the world and FedEx Cup standings, and many observers were now speculating that he might be worth a wildcard pick for the American Presidents Cup team in the autumn. Such chatter grew louder in mid-July after the John Deere Classic at TPC Deere Run in Silvis, Illinois.

Throughout the tournament, Spieth was in the thick of the action at the sharp end of the leaderboard. He started the final round six strokes behind third-round leader Daniel Summerhays and bogeyed the first to fall seven back.

Thereafter he played brilliant golf, but it looked as though he would probably come up just shy of victory. Former Masters winner Zach Johnson, a couple of groups behind, seemed more likely to claim the win.

When Spieth arrived at the final hole late on Sunday evening it was flat calm. The water to the left of the green provided vivid, perfect reflections of the trees on the other side of the pond. To the right of the putting surface lay a pure white bunker which had swallowed up the young Texan's ball from his approach to the green.

As he addressed his escape from the hazard, the crowds that had gathered on the banking short-right of the green were contemplating yet another high finish for the newest talent on tour. Victory appeared to be just beyond his reach, though, especially when Spieth's sand wedge caught the ball a fraction clean and it flew forward much faster than he would have wanted. The water on the opposite side of the green looked set to drown his chances as the ball careered on its way. It landed just short of the hole without much control and hopped right, but the second bounce never happened. The ball ricocheted off the flag and wedged itself into the cup. Birdie. His third in a row. A third successive round of 65. Nineteen under par. The clubhouse lead. The lad clad in white cap, green shirt and grey trousers emerged from the trap hands aloft, punching the air in delight. The challenge had been set for Johnson and David Hearn of Canada. They were two holes behind and also on that 19-under-par mark.

'The shot on 18 was the luckiest shot I ever hit in my life,' the 19-year-old conceded. 'The fact that it bounced right and hit the pin and dropped down in the cup, it's just extremely fortunate.'

There are some days where everything falls into place. Johnson managed to get to 20 under, so a par at the last would have been enough for victory but he bogeyed. And so

Spieth found himself in a three-way sudden-death play-off with Johnson and Hearn. All three parred the first four extra holes before the teenager held his nerve to par the next as well, which neither of his opponents could match. 'Congrats to Jordan. He's going to have an amazing career,' said Hearn. 'He's an incredible talent, to come on tour at this age and have as much success as quickly as he has.'

Spieth became the first teenager in 82 years to win on the PGA Tour and only the fourth youngest to ever achieve the feat. He moved to 59th in the world rankings and was now eligible for the majors that, under the American system, provide the platform for Ryder Cup qualification. That night he was on a charter plane to Scotland for his first Open Championship. The only concern was the fact that he hadn't packed anything other than short-sleeved shirts. 'I didn't think it would happen this early. I had a plan. I guess the plan got exceeded,' Spieth admitted. 'I just got so lucky. That's what it is, but right now I'm extremely pleased.'

At Muirfield he finished in a share of 44th place as Mickelson became Open Champion in the major thought most likely to evade the left-hander. Spieth missed the cut in his first PGA Championship the following month but then embarked on a spectacular end to a stunning first season. He finished second at the Wyndham Championship after losing a play-off to his brash fellow Gleneagles rookie Patrick Reed. Then he fired a closing 62 to finish fourth in the second of the FedEx Cup play-off events, the Deutsche Bank Championship. This astonishing closing round prompted Mickelson to text Presidents Cup captain Fred Couples. The message was simple: 'Dude, you've got to pick this guy.'

Couples heeded the message and the 20-year-old found himself in the team as a wildcard to play the Internationals at Jack Nicklaus's Muirfield Village in Dublin, Ohio. Spieth took his place in the side after finishing second to a rampaging

Henrik Stenson in the Tour Championship at East Lake in Atlanta. That win netted the Swede a $10 million jackpot for winning the FedEx Cup and in the first month of qualifying for the European team he garnered a significant chunk of the world ranking points that earned him his return to Paul McGinley's team.

At the Presidents Cup, Spieth was the kid of the team but commanded huge respect. Couples paired him with the experienced Steve Stricker, who went on to become a vice captain to Watson at Gleneagles. Although they lost their opening fourball match, one down to Ernie Els and Brendon De Jonge, it proved a successful partnership. Youth and experience combined to beat Brandon Grace and Richard Sterne in the Friday foursomes and then Jason Day and Graham DeLaet in the Saturday morning better-balls. Spieth was then rested until the Sunday singles when he beat DeLaet by one hole as the US completed a victory of 18½–15½.

Spieth had established himself in his country's top dozen players. He was firmly on Watson's radar, although it took his performances at the Masters and Players Championship in the following spring to secure his Ryder Cup place. The momentum came from the brilliant start to his professional career in 2013.

While Spieth was making his name, Dubuisson began his charge into the European reckoning.

More than three years older than the American rookie, Dubuisson's start to professional life had been considerably less spectacular. In his first two seasons on the European Tour, Dubuisson had one top-three finish and just seven top-10s. He finished 106th on the money list in 2011 and a year later was 52nd in the Race to Dubai standings. It was still, however, a decent rate of progress for someone who only turned 23 in April 2013, and this would be the year of his breakthrough.

There were promising results from his early season

globe-trotting; ninth in Qatar, ninth at the Avantha Masters in Delhi, fourth in the Maybank Malaysian Open and third at the Volvo China Open. As the tour headed back through Europe, Dubuisson's performances dipped a little until he arrived at the glorious Crans-sur-Sierre course in the Swiss Alps for the Omega European Masters.

The qualifying process for the European team had begun a week earlier at the ISPS Handa Wales Open, where Dubuisson withdrew after an opening 75. He appeared an unlikely candidate to force his way into the top-four money-winners on the Tour in the coming 12 months or the top-five Europeans in the world rankings. These would be the nine automatic qualifiers for McGinley's team, supplemented by three wildcards.

First indications that he might force his way into the reckoning, however, came in Switzerland, where he put together rounds of 68–65–66–66. He fell one stroke short of making the play-off, won by Thomas Bjørn against Scotland's Craig Lee. Bjørn's victory set him on the way to qualifying for the European Team for the first time since 2002. Dubuisson's finish took him to 101st in the world.

The Frenchman played only a couple more tournaments before a November date with destiny at the Turkish Airlines Open, on the Montgomerie Course at the Maxx Royal resort in Belek. This was the third of four tournaments that comprised the European Tour's newly re-branded 'Final Series'. It was a controversial concept that required the continent's leading players to compete in two of the first three events to be eligible for the concluding DP World Tour Championship in Dubai. The first two in the series were in Shanghai – the BMW Masters and the HSBC WGC Champions. Some players complained that it was unfair to stipulate how many of these events they should enter, among them Sergio García and Ernie Els. They did not comply and so became ineligible for the season finale in the Middle East.

These were big-money tournaments, each boasting a prize fund of at least $7 million, and they counted towards Ryder Cup qualification. It meant that anyone who had a decent spell of form over the closing month of the season would be putting at least one arm into the sleeve of a European team blazer for the following September.

Dubuisson began the Final Series inauspiciously, with a tie for 44th place at the BMW Masters. He finished well, though, with a closing 67. He didn't play the second of the Shanghai dates before heading to Turkey where he arrived as a largely anonymous figure.

All the talk surrounded Woods, who had stopped traffic on the Bosphorus Bridge in Istanbul at the start of the week. The publicity stunt of hitting a ball from Europe to Asia was an obligation, part of the deal included in a $3 million appearance fee. Woods headed a strong field that included Race to Dubai leader Stenson and his closest rival, Ian Poulter. These two had a private bet that would have involved Stenson acting as waiter to the flamboyant Englishman if he managed to overtake the Swede in the standings. Reigning US Open Champion Justin Rose was also competing in a tournament that was delayed three hours by a violent thunderstorm on the first morning.

Stenson and Bjørn were the early pacesetters, with opening rounds of 64, and Dubuisson found himself three strokes back. Woods had started quietly with a two-under-par 70 before hitting the headlines with a brilliant second round 63. The world number one's performance overshadowed Dubuisson's fine 65, which had been good enough to earn him the lead.

'It feels great, especially as I didn't feel that I played that well at the BMW Masters,' Dubuisson said. 'I have worked very hard at my game and my putting over the last few weeks so it's been a good month. There are very good players in this tournament, the top of the world, and Tiger is playing another game, a different sport. It's also a good feeling that I can lead a big tournament like this.'

Dubuisson knew the real hard work was still to come and his prodigious driving served him well in a third round where he carded a nine-under-par 63. 'Sometimes I can be very long under pressure,' he said. 'With the adrenaline, I can hit the ball very long. This week, though, it's all about my short game. I have really improved that in the last few months.' Even though he held a commanding lead, most attention still surrounded the chasing pack. Woods, Rose, Stenson and Poulter were all within touching distance.

That made Dubuisson's closing 68 all the more credit-worthy. Jamie Donaldson fired a closing 63 that included a hole-in-one at the 16th, Woods was round in 67, Rose 65 and Poulter 69. None of the big names backed off but the man who began the week 106th in the world held firm to finish a remarkable 24 under par, two shots clear of Donaldson and four ahead of Woods and Rose. The champion took home a cheque for €848,930 as well as enough ranking points to move into the top-40 in the world. He could now look forward to making his Masters debut at the same Augusta venue where Woods had inspired him to take up the game.

'I didn't know, but if I'm in the Masters it is a dream come true,' he said. 'Winning this tournament is already a dream come true. I didn't realise I won such a big tournament. Tiger, Stenson, Justin Rose, they were all in contention with me today. I'm really proud of what I did because this is the toughest day of my golfing life.'

The Andorra-based 23-year-old had announced himself to the golfing world. All the promise he had shown as an amateur was starting to come to fruition. Dubuisson headed to Dubai for the final event of the European Tour season and, thanks largely to a third-round 64, he quietly added another €384,345 to his bank account (and Ryder Cup qualifying tally) by finishing third in the DP World Tour Championship. Stenson won that event in emphatic style, beating Poulter into second place to add the Race to Dubai to his FedEx Cup title. The Swede had effectively already booked his place in the Gleneagles team.

Dubuisson wasn't far off either, even though the Ryder Cup was still more than nine months away. His stunning fortnight had propelled him into the game's elite top-30 and he could plan a schedule that included all of the majors and World Golf Championships events.

The following February, at the first of these WGC tournaments, he sealed his place in McGinley's team. In the process, the quiet Frenchman established his reputation with American fans, becoming an instant YouTube hit in the process. The WGC Accenture Matchplay is a popular break from the normal diet of 72-hole strokeplay. The top 64 players in the world competed in a straight knock-out format amid the rugged beauty of Dove Mountain near Tucson in Arizona. With his flowing brown hair and carefully tended beard, Dubuisson looked every bit a sporting superstar when the fates chose this week for him to step into the global limelight.

It can be argued that this tournament is easier to win than most because you only have to beat six opponents, rather than 155 others as is the case in a full-field tour event. The flip side is that you have to keep on winning – there are no second chances if you lose. Dubuisson marched through the field, demonstrating the qualities that would be so vital in the head-to-head combat of a Ryder Cup. He began with a 5 and 4 thrashing of American Kevin Streelman, then beat Sweden's Peter Hanson 3 and 1. Thereafter the victories were much harder won. He beat Bubba Watson one up and then, in the quarter-finals, took out Graeme McDowell on the final green before going the distance with Els in the Sunday morning semis. McDowell commented: 'He has such a strong game, I'd love to be his partner in a Ryder Cup.'

Dubuisson was so stuck in the moment after completing his tense win over the South African that he had no idea who he would meet in the final. Reporters informed him it was the young Australian, Jason Day. Amid the desert cacti, this youthful pairing shared the best final the event had witnessed in its 15-year history. Day was never behind and held a three-hole lead with six to go. Dubuisson birdied the par-5 13th to reduce the arrears and needed another at the 15th to remain only two down. The Frenchman was still two down with two to play. His brilliant birdie from a fairway bunker at the 17th kept the match alive before his opponent bogeyed the last to take the final into extra time.

It was at this point that Dubuisson started to cause a real stir, with the kind of escapology synonymous with the late, great Seve Ballesteros. An indication of what might follow had come on the final hole of regulation play. He imaginatively spun his bunker shot to the contours that allowed his ball to trundle down to within three feet of the hole. It was a shot of the utmost delicacy, but nothing to what occurred at the second extra hole. Dubuisson's approach flew through the green and nestled in a clingy desert bush. Somehow he needed to get up and down to keep the final alive. With the minimum of fuss, he produced a downward chop with a wedge that propelled the ball forward to within four feet of the hole, cut on an elevated green. Day looked on in utter disbelief and the final continued to its third extra hole.

The enraptured fans then witnessed yet another miraculous escape. This time, Dubuisson found his ball trapped under a wiry, stick-like branch in a bush to the back left of the putting surface. Addressing the ball with the bush between his legs, he again produced a chopping pitch that enabled him to escape with a par that denied Day victory. 'Golden hands!' cried the commentators on television. 'Oh my goodness!' yelled an astonished Sir Nick Faldo into his microphone, while on-course announcer David Feherty wondered: 'Is his middle name Houdini?'

YouTube replays of these shots have generated hundreds of thousands of hits. Dubuisson had shown golfing flair of the rarest kind and skill that transcended the game and excited sports fans of all persuasions. 'Those two chips, they could have stayed in the rocks or the bush, it was 50/50,' he later admitted.

Ultimately, Day birdied the fifth extra hole to deny Dubuisson victory but this was an occasion that proved more about the loser than the winner. The runner-up's cheque for $906,000 provided plenty of consolation because the Frenchman now knew what he would be doing, come late September. 'I'm very excited about the Ryder Cup,' he said. 'It was a big goal for me this year. And this event was a good preparation for me. I now know what I have to work on for the Ryder Cup.

'I haven't had the chance to talk with Paul McGinley,' he added. 'But that's probably because I have changed my mobile phone. Maybe he sent me a text or something, but I haven't received it. I have great support from my friend Thomas Levet, who has been on a winning Ryder Cup team, and he will give me good advice.'

Dubuisson may have been the baby of the European team but he took his place in the side in a very grown-up fashion. He suffered shoulder problems mid-season but bounced back through the summer months to take advantage of his new status in the game. He lost a three-way play-off, which also included Stephen Gallacher, to Thailand's Thongchai Jaidee at the Nordea Masters in early June and then recorded top-10 finishes at the Open and US PGA to confirm his readiness for Gleneagles.

'He loves matchplay,' Levet observed. 'He loves competition between two people. For matchplay, it's pretty nice. He's fearless and he makes a lot of birdies so, for a competition like the Ryder Cup, it's nice to have that guy in the team.

'In the team environment he will be shy at first, because he won't know the players that well. If the guys go towards him he will respond. He will not be the guy who goes towards people that easily. He's going to be quiet in the team room, but he's going to listen and learn.

'There won't be too many problems with him, I hope. The only problem with Victor is he goes with the flow and if he doesn't feel like practising he will not practise. If he feels like practising, he will practise for hours. So it could be interesting.

'I spoke with Paul McGinley and told him to try to be closer with Victor because he will have the problem of not knowing people otherwise. And he went and saw him already and has been talking with him a lot, just to make sure there aren't any problems because he's so shy. If he wants to go putt, he will go and putt, even if it's like eight o'clock in the evening. And if he does not feel like practising at all, he will spend the day in front of the TV and not do anything. So, with Victor, you have to let him do his own stuff. And it's working. It can't be wrong if it's working.'

By the time the Ryder Cup had come around, Dubuisson was established as one of Europe's leading professionals. He had done it in style, taking full advantage of the big-money tournaments early in the qualifying period. For the Americans, the emphasis is much more on the majors. Play well in those and you will be on the team. For Spieth, therefore, the challenge was to carry the form that earned him a Presidents Cup debut in the autumn of 2013 into his first Masters tournament the following spring.

CHAPTER 8

The Masters

'I'm sorry to say that I have not won a Ryder
Cup yet and I would like to. That's the next
big tournament I would like to win.'
Bubba Watson

In the coming decades, golfing historians are likely to point to 2014 as a year of accelerated transition; a period that marked the end of the Tiger Woods era and a time when a group of new names became regular challengers for the biggest titles. This was a vibe that started to be felt in the weeks leading up to the first major of the year, the Masters at Augusta.

The calendar in men's golf provides four occasions each season when competitors can make their individual mark on the history of the game. Players may be remembered for Ryder Cup heroics, but it is the majors that define careers. This is why the PGA of America attach so much importance to them and award double points for performances in the big four championships in their Ryder Cup qualifying tables.

There is always a summer rush, as the US Open, Open and PGA Championship follow one after the other in a hectic eight-week spell. The first of the majors, however, manages to stand alone in the second week of April. 'It's always the highest-rated and most anticipated golf tournament of the year,' says the Chairman of CBS Sports, Sean McManus. Played at and run by the ultra-exclusive Augusta National Golf Club in Georgia, the Masters is a unique tournament and the only major to be played at the same venue every year.

News that Woods required back surgery and would miss his 2014 trip to Augusta was a big blow. He had played every Masters since his debut as an amateur in 1995. Jim Nantz, CBS's lead announcer, said Woods' absence was 'the story that dwarfs all others'. The seasoned broadcaster's comments summed up the mood of many observers. But he added: 'We will miss Tiger for sure, but that tournament is never about one player. I can't wait to see what the next script is to be written.'

Whatever the story, it needed to be a good one. The game was struggling to maintain its position in the sporting marketplace. Although the likes of Spieth and Dubuisson had made impressive breakthroughs, and Patrick Reed had established himself as a multiple winner, golf was lacking an 'X factor'. The Ryder Cup was still too far away to excite attention and it seemed that every week produced a different winner. There were no easily identifiable champions; too much parity, not enough clarity. The Florida Swing of tournaments that constitute the early spring build-up to the Masters had been won by a largely anonymous bunch: Russell Henley, Reed, John Senden and Matt Every. All were ranked outside the top-40 in the world. Die-hard golf fans knew these players, but none was going to excite more transient sports fans.

Henley won the Honda Classic at the start of the PGA Tour's month-long stay in the sunshine state only after a shambolic final round and a four-way play-off with Rory McIlroy, Russell Knox and Ryan Palmer. It should have been a McIlroy procession, the sort of win that great champions knock off with consummate ease. Instead, the Northern Irishman, seeking a wire-to-wire victory, came home in an ugly 38 that included a double bogey and two more dropped shots.

At the final hole, he almost rescued the situation with a stunning 245-yard five wood that only he could hit. McIlroy fired it with an extraordinarily high trajectory to produce the soft landing that carved out an eagle chance. The putt that followed, sadly, lacked the majesty of the approach. It missed on the low side and the former world number one was sucked into a play-off.

None of the contenders had covered themselves in glory. NBC commentator Johnny Miller described it as 'a group of players basically just flailing', and it felt a blessed mercy when Henley eventually prevailed to end the proceedings in extra time.

A similar malaise struck reigning Masters champion Adam Scott a couple of weeks later at the Arnold Palmer Invitational at Bay Hill. The Australian was eyeing the possibility of succeeding Woods at the top of the rankings and began the tournament in fitting style. He fired an opening 62 and followed it up with a 67 to lead by seven. Over the weekend, though, his game fell apart and miserable rounds of 71 and 76 left him in third place behind Every, who climbed to the dizzy heights of 44 in the world. It would have been unthinkable for Woods in his pomp to throw away such opportunities for victory.

The final event before the Masters was the Shell Houston Open. On the Tuesday of that week, Woods released the news that he wouldn't be playing at Augusta.

A day later, McIlroy was fine-tuning his game during the pre-event pro-am in Texas. He was happy to chat when I met him on the seventh tee. First he wanted to discuss the prospects of his beloved Ulster rugby union team but inevitably the conversation turned to the game that he plays for a living. 'We're not cutting through,' he admitted. 'Too many different players are winning; we don't seem to have the champion players. What golf really needed was me to win the Honda Classic and for Adam to have taken the Bay Hill title. That would have excited fans and got people talking about golf. There's a void that needs to be filled and it's tough because there are so many potential winners every week.'

McIlroy accepted that Woods' absence was a shame. 'Golf is always better when Tiger is in the conversation,' he said. 'It's almost like we are waiting for someone to stamp their authority on the game and be that dominant player. A few guys need to put their hand up and break away. I hope it's me.'

The 23-year-old Reed, who became the youngest winner of a World Golf Championships event during the Florida Swing, was clearly in the mood to step up. His victory at the WGC Cadillac Championship, on a revamped Trump Doral course, was as impressive as any seen in the early part of 2014. He held off Bubba Watson and Welshman Jamie Donaldson and could afford to two-putt for a bogey at the last to secure his third tour victory. Donaldson's runner-up finish was a big step towards his Ryder Cup debut, while Reed's win was also a significant stride towards a place in the US team.

Like Spieth, Reed hails from Texas. The San Antonio native generated a reputation for being brash and aloof after a successful college career at Augusta State. He is often a lone figure on the range, earphones in place as he strikes ball after ball. It is as though he puts up a subliminal 'do not disturb' sign. His confidence and bravado is reflected in his tendency to wear the red shirt and black trouser ensemble that has long been Woods' preserve on the final day of tournaments. Reed believes he is entitled and good enough to ape the greatest player of the modern era.

In the wake of his Doral victory, which followed successes in the Wyndham Championship in August 2013 (when he beat Spieth in a play-off) and the Humana Challenge in January, Reed came out with one of the quotes of the year. He claimed he was among the top-five players in the world, even though the rankings at the time insisted this status belonged to Woods, Scott, Henrik Stenson, Jason Day and Phil Mickelson.

In fairness to Reed, he had just joined an exclusive club made up of Woods, McIlroy, Mickelson and Sergio García as the only recent winners of three PGA Tour events before their 24th birthday. The 'I'm in the world's top-five' quote, however, was repeatedly taken out of context by his critics and used as a stick with which to beat him. Many regarded Reed as someone who had grown too big for his golf shoes. The taunts were evident in the run-up to the Masters and well beyond.

Here, in full, is what the American, who had been ranked 584 in the world at the start of 2013, said as he celebrated his Doral victory: 'I've worked so hard. I've won a lot in my junior career, did great things in my amateur career, was 6–0 in match play at the NCAAs, won the NCAAs two years in a row and was third individually one year. Now I have three wins out here on the PGA Tour. I just don't see a lot of guys that have done that besides Tiger Woods, of course, and all the other legends of the game. It's just one of those things that I believe in myself, especially after how hard I've worked, that I'm one of the top-five players in the world. To come out of a field like this and to hold on, wire-to-wire like that, I feel like I've proven myself.'

Reed had certainly beaten a field filled with the best players in the world. It was a very big win – only a major or a Players' Championship could feel bigger. Reed was entitled to his comments, even if they lacked humility.

He had also caught the eye of Tom Watson, who arranged to play nine holes of practice with the Texan on the Monday of Masters week. This was an important opportunity for the skipper to acquaint himself with a member of the younger generation. 'He was a complete stranger to Patrick Reed, so we made sure we played a practice round at Augusta,' recalled Watson's caddie Neil Oxman. 'And you really get the chance to talk to a guy much more in a practice round rather than a tournament, when everyone is so much more pre-occupied.'

Scott was the defending champion at the 2014 Masters, but while he took his fair share of the headlines, he also had to share the limelight with McIlroy, Reed and Spieth, who were grouped together for the first two rounds.

Since his dramatic breakthrough the previous year, Spieth had continued to make excellent progress. He hadn't added to his victory at the John Deere Classic but did enough, with three top-fives, in the early months of the year to climb to 13th in the world rankings.

History suggested debutants couldn't win at Augusta; Fuzzy Zoeller had been the last, 35 years earlier. But professional golf was changing, and there were no fewer than 24 players making their Masters debuts that week. The chances of someone emulating Zoeller had never been higher.

With Woods out of action, Spieth was relishing the prospect of trying to make history. He said: 'Whether he is here or not, we are trying to win week in, week out. We don't change that because he's not playing. I never played against Tiger in his prime, so maybe that helps me, but it's not something I think much about.

'I have contended in World Golf Championships, so why should a major be any different? I have certain goals and they are definitely focused on the majors this year. The plan we picked, in the gym, with my swing, everything, was gearing to peak at certain weeks to coincide with the majors.'

Ever since his John Deere win, he had known he would be at Augusta in April 2014 and he had made reconnaissance visits in October and March. 'It was nice to get the awe factor out of the way so I can get right to work,' he said.

Reed was equally bullish. He had visited the revered Georgia course on three occasions during his student days at Augusta State. It didn't fully prepare him for his first journey down Magnolia Lane as a Masters competitor, though. 'It was amazing,' he said. 'I wanted to reverse and do it again. Every time, driving down, you get a big smile on your face and this time it's different because the first three times I did it was as an amateur. Now I'm doing it as a professional, playing in the Masters.'

Players who command most interest are brought to the interview room in the Augusta media centre, a 20-year-old building that resembles a large university lecture theatre. It had accommodated the media world's move into the digital age, but was now nearing the end of its working life, with a replacement centre scheduled for 2016.

The interview room is on the ground floor, to the side of the main, tiered work area. Competitors emerge through a cream-coloured door onto a raised desk and sit alongside an Augusta member who, clad in the club's famous green jacket, acts as a moderator for the press conferences. On the walls, electronic screens display photographs that capture the full beauty and glory of the course. Sitting in that room, there is no mistaking the feeling that you are at the most exclusive and beautiful golf course in the world.

Augusta members are known simply as 'green jackets' because of their attire during Masters week. The idea is to make them easily identifiable and available to offer assistance to spectators, known as 'patrons', at this very prim-and-proper tournament.

On the grounds, no one is allowed to run, lying down on the ground would result in a security guard giving the offender a polite order to move on, and woe betide anyone caught in possession of a mobile phone. This would lead to instant ejection, and a probable life ban. Proceedings on and off the course are kept as civilised as possible, but the rules are rigorously enforced. That is the way of things at the Augusta National.

So when a brash young player addresses the world in such a strikingly positive way as Reed did in his pre-tournament news conference, it is bound to cause a stir. 'I'm very confident,' he said. 'I try to treat it like it's just another event. I did it at

Doral. I just kept my mindset on it being just another golf tournament. Go out and play your game.'

Inevitably, reporters were keen to discuss the player's contention that he was one of the top-five golfers in the world. The 23-year-old wasn't about to back down, now that he had arrived on the biggest stage of his career. 'I believe in my comments,' he said. 'Michael Jordan had nothing bad to say about it, Gary Player and Henrik Stenson the same. You know, you have to feel and believe in yourself to be successful and that's all it is. I believe in myself. You can't let doubt get in your way.'

With so much attention elsewhere, the champion of two years earlier was happy to be going about his business largely unnoticed. Bubba Watson's game was in good shape. He had played well to miss out by a single stroke when Reed won at Doral and he had won at Riviera earlier in the season. There was none of the fuss of 12 months before when he had been defending champion. 'For me, it was overwhelming,' Watson admitted. 'The Champions Dinner, everybody still congratulating you, so I just never got the focus. I'm back with the take that I want the jacket again. I'm coming back with a different mindset, full of energy.'

What's more, he had a disciplined game plan. It was simple. Just hit the greens with his approach shots and don't try anything clever. This was an interesting approach for a self-taught and instinctive golfer. The left-hander is anything but conventional, after all. He had hooked a wedge with 40 yards of swerve at the second extra hole of a play-off against Louis Oosthuizen to win the 2012 Masters. It was an astonishing stroke to which television pictures couldn't do justice. The morning after that victory, I visited the spot from where he had hit his ball. It was in the trees and bushes to the right of the 10th fairway, and it was clear his shot was way beyond a mere hacker's understanding of how so much sideways motion could be intentionally imparted on a golf ball.

That amazing stroke brought Watson his first major title but, having just become the father of an adopted son, Watson struggled for more than a year to cope with the attention that accompanies such triumphs. By the time he returned in 2014, Watson appeared much more at ease with himself. And the conservative game plan worked well on a difficult first day.

It is often said that the Augusta committee know what scores they want the world's best professionals to post and they set up the course accordingly. Conditions were perfect. The skies were bright and clear and the course had recovered magnificently from the damage inflicted by severe ice storms that had ripped through Augusta during the winter. These adverse climactic conditions demolished the famous Eisenhower tree on the 17th. The 65-foot loblolly pine had been named after the former American president because of the number of times his drives had tangled with its branches. Eisenhower had even urged the club's chairman, Clifford Roberts, to get rid of it. But the tree had remained until Mother Nature did the job in the late winter of 2014.

Typically, the course was presented in immaculate condition. The greens were firm, the grass on the fairways (which is longer than you might imagine) was mown back towards the tees to reduce run and make it play every inch of its 7,435 yards. The committee chose challenging pin positions that made the par of 72 a fine opening score.

Bubba Watson's 69 was one of only four rounds to break 70. He stuck to his plan and hit 16 of the 18 greens in regulation. The two that he missed found the fringes and he was putting anyway. The only moment of stress came on the final hole where, after hitting into a fairway bunker, he left himself a demanding 50 feet to negotiate with two putts to save par. He didn't know how good the round was, because he was largely oblivious to the rest of the field. 'I'm trying not to look at leaderboards,' he said. 'I don't want to give my secret, but

I'm trying just to hit greens. I'm trying to get the green jacket again.' By close of play, Watson trailed first-round leader Bill Haas by one.

Spieth started well alongside McIlroy and Reed. He recalled his opening drive: 'I kind of had a smile on my face. I just soaked it in; it was really cool.' Aged just 24, McIlroy was the old man of the threesome and, despite struggling on the undulating greens, he matched Spieth's one-under-par 71. Reed bogeyed the last four holes to squander a promising start and shot 73. He was frustrated by his driving, uncomfortable with a swing he felt he couldn't let rip. He was guiding the ball into play, rather than smashing it off the tee, and he was conceding 20 yards to his big-hitting playing partners. That didn't sit well with the Reed ego.

Jimmy Walker's debut round also went pretty well. He shot 70 and seemed to be growing in stature. Like Reed, he had practised with Tom Watson and had taken the chance to pick one of the most experienced brains in the game. It also meant he was on the American skipper's Ryder Cup radar and that was a confidence-building place to be. 'He's a wonderful player,' said Watson

Yet Walker had failed to take full advantage of his length, settling for pars on the par-5 second and eighth holes and, after tangling with a tree, he ran up a damaging bogey six at the 13th. In that context, he was happy enough with a two-under-par start. 'It was cool,' he said. 'I definitely felt a few jitters on the first green. I had a long putt up the hill. I thought it was uphill, not sure. Hit a good putt and settled in.

'This is a tournament you have watched your whole career on TV. You feel like you've played it quite a few times, just from all the tournaments you have watched.'

It was a congested leaderboard, heading into the second round, and it was going to take something special to create some separation.

Left-handers have prospered at Augusta in recent years. Canada's Mike Weir set the trend when he won in 2003 and Mickelson followed up with his victories in 2004, 2006 and 2010. Then came Watson, two years later. Part of the reason is the shaping of the majority of the holes, which move from right to left. For a right-hander, manoeuvring the ball with a draw can be beneficial on such layouts, but it is not as controlled a shot as a fade. For left-handers, controlled fades are perfect at Augusta, especially if they are allied to the prodigious power generated by Bubba Watson's homespun swing.

Watson reeled off five straight back-nine birdies to take the tournament by the scruff of the neck. His 68 put him three clear of the field. It was one of those days when everything fell into place. On the 14th, where the massive, undulating green seems to have been imported directly from St Andrews, Watson was surveying a devilishly difficult 40-foot birdie putt. First, though, playing partner Sergio García had to chip and the Spaniard's ball happened to travel over Watson's marker to give the ideal indication of the line the American should take. As a result, he was able to slot home the monster putt for yet another birdie. 'Without Sergio's chip, I would probably have three-putted,' Watson said.

Consecutive rounds in the 60s took Watson to seven under par. Big names, meanwhile, buckled. Mickelson suffered two triple bogeys as he missed the cut, while Reed imploded with a 79 to bring his first Masters to an early end.

Spieth was the shining light among the trio of young guns, because McIlroy was struggling as well. He would be grateful that the cut had been moved from the top-44 and ties to the top-50. He needed to par the last five holes to survive, after suffering bouts of misjudgement and bad luck.

At the long par-three fourth he pulled his tee shot long and left, into an unplayable position close to the fifth tee. McIlroy had to return to the tee to reload. At the 13th, his approach bounced on a sprinkler head and careered into the azaleas to the back left of the green. He was then able to par the last five holes for a 77, which meant he made the cut on the mark at four over.

Spieth, meanwhile, played with a maturity beyond his 20 years. He followed up his opening 71 with a two-under-par 70 to leave him within four strokes of the leader. 'Bubba is tearing it up, so we have to go get him,' Spieth commented.

It was with that intent that the Texan set about his third round. Behind him, Watson struggled to an unconvincing 74. He seemed haunted by his career statistics, which showed a poor record for converting halfway leads. On Sky Sports Colin Montgomerie told viewers there was no way that Watson could go on and collect a second green jacket.

By contrast, Spieth continued in a similar vein to his first two rounds. His free and aggressive swing looked tailor-made for the demands of the Augusta National. 'He's very good,' the American former European Tour professional Jay Townsend told BBC 5Live listeners. 'The only reservation I have surrounds his footwork. On the follow-through his right foot is lifted at an angle and that suggests a lack of balance that could lead to some inconsistency when the pressure is on.'

Spieth's 2.25 p.m. tee time was the third-from-last pairing and he played alongside defending champion Scott. In the group ahead was veteran Fred Couples, the man who had picked Spieth as a wildcard rookie for the previous year's Presidents Cup. 'For a 20-year-old, he's pretty savvy. Not much bothers him,' Couples said.

And so it proved as Spieth's momentum showed no sign of slowing. He moved to five under par with an excellent 70 and finished the day at the top of the leaderboard, tied with Watson. 'Today was moving day,' Spieth said. 'I'm very confident in the way things are going.' He seemed on schedule to smash Woods' record as the youngest winner of the Masters.

He had already become the first rookie in almost 20 years to make it into the last group on the final day.

One of the most striking aspects of Augusta is its intimacy. There are some grandstands on the course, but few compared with other major venues. Around the first tee, it is standing room only. Spectators assemble five or six deep in close proximity when the biggest names begin their rounds. It is a claustrophobic environment and both sides of the fairway, which plunges downhill before climbing steeply, are lined by expectant fans. In 2011 McIlroy began his final round with a four-stroke advantage but the rarified atmosphere sucked the certainty from his game. He eventually capitulated to a final-round 80, tumbling down the leaderboard to finish 15th.

Spieth seemed to revel in the situation. His body language appeared certain, he moved smoothly and positively. Watson, in contrast, is a more jumpy character and often appears to be battling his emotions. While Spieth was happy to make eye contact with the crowds, his rival stared into the middle distance, where no one could catch his eye and invade his concentration. A perfunctory wave to acknowledge the applause for a good shot appeared largely emotionless – polite yet detached. It was the ideal response, one that might be invaluable in a Ryder Cup. Watson maintained his focus on hitting greens.

His younger opponent was inspired but less convincing in his play. Fortuitously, he made the first jump up the leaderboard. At the fourth, he missed the green but played an inspired bunker shot that disappeared into the hole. It seemed the force was with him to claim a record-breaking debut win. Both contenders made brilliant birdies at the par-3 sixth and, at the seventh, Spieth drained a delicate birdie putt to go two clear. It was a thrilling duel, and the younger man was winning it.

But then came the mammoth uphill par-5 eighth and it all changed.

Watson dispatched a massive drive that seemed to unsettle Spieth. His uncertainty was compounded by a sloppy third to the green. Watson got up and down for a birdie and suddenly Spieth was under pressure. He three-putted and bogeyed, his first six in a previously immaculate week. The lead was gone.

At the next he made an error commensurate with his rookie status. He landed his approach to the dogleg par-4 short of the hole, which is always cut at the very front of the green on the last day. Gravity did the rest. His ball rolled back off the front of the putting surface. The 35-year-old Watson had the experience to play the perfect approach and made a routine birdie that proved decisive, even with nine holes still to play. 'Two two-stroke swings is difficult on this course to come back from,' Spieth said. 'Eight and nine were the turning points.'

His game was no longer the same. He became tetchy and displayed outward signs of annoyance. He went on to find water at the short 12th and couldn't create makeable birdie chances.

Spieth's caddie Michael Greller, a former school teacher, had already hinted that his boss could be prone to losing composure. 'A lot of monologue, a lot of dialogue. He can be pretty hard on himself,' he said.

Watson had two more moves to ensure he donned the green jacket for the second time. At the par-five 13th he took an ambitious line down the left side, cutting the corner on a hole that dramatically swings from right to left. His booming drive clipped the top of a tree and still sailed 366 yards into the ideal spot in the fairway. 'His drive on 13, I will never forget,' said Spieth. 'I thought it was out of bounds, 70 yards left. And it was perfect.' Watson had a mere sand wedge to the green and two putts later he collected his final birdie of the tournament. Then, at the 15th, he conjured a daring approach through trees to a green surrounded by water. It was a shot of the utmost imagination, nervelessly executed.

From there, it was a cruise to the title for the man from Bagdad, a largely anonymous town in the north-western corner of Florida's panhandle. He completed the final round in 69 strokes and had broken 70 three times in a Masters where no other player had recorded more than one circuit in the 60s. His total of 280 was eight under par, three better than Spieth and Jonas Blixt who shared second place. Spieth, despite his tender years and having surpassed expectations for a Masters rookie, was bitterly disappointed. 'I've worked my whole life to lead Augusta on a Sunday and, although I feel like it's very early in my career and I'll have more chances, it's a stinger.'

Blixt had joined the European Tour to become eligible for the Ryder Cup and appeared to have made a significant move towards a debut at Gleneagles with rounds of 70–71–71–71. 'It's clear that he is a man for the big occasion,' commented McGinley. 'It looks like Victor Dubuisson and Jamie Donaldson are nailed on as rookies, and maybe Blixt as well.'

Dubuisson had missed the cut with rounds of 74 and 75 and joined the likes of García, Donald and McDowell in making an early Augusta exit. Indeed, it was a largely disappointing Masters for the Europeans. Blixt offered the most encouragement to the continental captain.

'His short game was special, but it wasn't just a short-game exhibition. This guy has a lot of heart and a lot of game,' McGinley said. But the Swede had shown false promise. Thereafter in the qualifying period he missed seven cuts and recorded a best finish of 16th, at the BMW PGA Championship in May.

The other Europeans to shine in the first of the four majors were 50-year-old Miguel Ángel Jiménez, who carded the lowest round of the week, a Saturday 66, to finish fourth, and Lee Westwood, who was seventh before going on to win in Malaysia the following week.

There was much more to excite the Americans. They had

the winner in an emotional Bubba Watson, while Spieth had acquitted himself superbly in his first Masters. Another youthful star, Rickie Fowler, finished in a share of fifth with US compatriot Matt Kuchar, while Walker shot level par for eighth spot, and seemed very much at home in golf's big time.

For McIlroy, there was the consolation of a closing 69, rounding off a weekend that had started with the ignominy of being sent out first on Saturday morning with Augusta member Jeff Knox to mark his card. Knox, a fine golfer in his own right who holds the course record of 61 from the Augusta members' tees, performs this duty when an odd number of players make the cut, and McIlroy was in joint-last position heading into the final two rounds. Extraordinarily, the amateur outscored the much-vaunted man from Holywood in Northern Ireland, in the third round by carding a 70 to McIlroy's 71.

'I thought he was going to be nice and three-putt the last, but he beat me by one,' McIlroy smiled. His three-under final round enabled him to finish alongside Walker at level par. Statistically, it was McIlroy's best Masters but the second round had proved ruinous. It was not a performance to suggest he was ready to fill the Tiger Woods-sized hole that was besetting the game.

In Woods' absence, viewing figures were down, and although the action was always compelling, it wouldn't be remembered as one of the great Masters. That was of little concern to the new champion. 'Small-town guy called Bubba now has two green jackets. It's pretty wild,' he said. He blinked back tears as he added, in his trademark machine-gun speaking style: 'It's overwhelming. As a kid, all you want to do is make the PGA Tour. Nine years on Tour now. Somehow six wins, two of them have green jackets wrapped around them. It's something I could never dream of.

'I play golf because I love it, I love the game, I want to grow the game. The game has brought me everything that I've ever owned in my life. The first one [Masters title] for me was almost like I lucked into it. This one was a lot of hard work, dedication and I got back here.'

With his victory, Watson had jumped to the top of America's Ryder Cup qualifying table and as he spoke his phone buzzed continually with congratulatory texts. One of them read: 'See you on the plane to Gleneagles.' It came from his namesake skipper.

Tom Watson was delighted with how the Masters had played out. The man himself had carded miserable rounds of 78 and 81, but it was hard to imagine better scores on such a brute of a course for a 64-year-old veteran. 'That course is just too big for him these days,' admitted his caddie. And the Ryder Cup picture was much more significant to the skipper. The players he wanted on the trip to Scotland had taken advantage of the double qualifying points. Spieth, Walker, Fowler and Kuchar were just the sort of characters he wanted in his team.

Watson told readers of his blog on the PGA of America's website: 'I tuned in for the entire final round on TV and I liked what I saw from Bubba Watson, especially that low cut shot on the par-five 15th that he intentionally hit through the trees and over the water. I don't know if I would have recommended he take that risk as a captain, in his situation, being three shots ahead. But what I do know is that he pulled it off – what a gutsy shot!

'It was an all-round impressive win for Bubba Watson and he's our first lock for the US Ryder Cup team. He is an unusual player, in that he curves every shot, left to right or right to left, and that makes him very interesting to watch. He wants to block out one side or the other and he can do it big time. I like somebody who can control the ball that way.

'I was also very impressed by the play of Jordan Spieth. He had his opportunities and made some mistakes, but I thought the up-and-down he made for bogey on the par-three 12th showed true grit. Another yard further with his tee shot there and he would have been just fine. Instead, the ball hit the bank, like it has for so many others before Jordan through the years, and it rolled back down the steep embankment into Rae's Creek. Instead of getting down on himself, Jordan pulled it together and got up and down after the penalty drop to keep himself in the tournament.'

The 2014 Masters suggested it was advantage America in this Ryder Cup year, and Tom Watson would also have been thrilled to hear that, amid euphoric scenes late on that April Sunday night, the Masters champion was already turning his thoughts towards Scotland in September. 'I figure that I have made the team,' Bubba Watson said. 'I'm sorry to say that I have not won a Ryder Cup yet and I would like to. That's the next big tournament I would like to win.'

CHAPTER 9

Kaymer and the Players' Championship

*'In Germany we always look for perfection. You
are the best in the world, so why didn't you win?'*
Martin Kaymer

It was not until mid-May that Europe could celebrate a
victory on the PGA Tour. That week, Sergio García was
asked if he was surprised about the continent's dearth of
success on American soil. 'I didn't even think about it, but
yeah, I guess so,' the Spaniard said. 'It is such a thin line
between winning and finishing second or third. Hopefully it
will happen soon.'

Captain Paul McGinley shared those sentiments. He was
in a phase of the campaign where he felt it was important to
give his leading players encouraging nudges. They wouldn't
be short of individual motivation to succeed, but he wanted to
remind them that Gleneagles was fast approaching.

The 2014 season had a different feel, compared with recent
years. Rory McIlroy, Luke Donald, Justin Rose, Henrik Stenson
and García had previously been racking up overseas victories
in Uncle Sam's backyard, but this year they were collecting
hard-luck stories instead of wins.

McIlroy was bemoaning the one destructive round per tournament that was costing him any chance of contending. Donald
was still bedding in swing changes. Rose was rediscovering his
game after a shoulder injury. Lee Westwood, meanwhile, was

trying to find his old swing after the failure of his relationship with Rose and Tiger Woods' coach, Sean Foley. García, with his ever-impressive ball striking, was threatening a victory but remained short of the extra ingredient required to get over the line.

McGinley travelled to TPC Sawgrass at Florida's Ponte Vedra Beach keen to see European success. The Players' Championship is the biggest tournament outside the four majors. The course is famous for its short par-three island-green 17th hole. It is not, strictly speaking, an island, more a peninsula, but the putting surface is almost entirely surrounded by water. 'If it was just rough and bunkers around the green we'd hit it all day long. Just a simple wedge or nine iron,' commented Graeme McDowell ahead of the tournament.

Forty-six of the world's top-50 players were competing. Woods was still recovering following back surgery, Victor Dubuisson was nursing a troublesome shoulder and the veteran Miguel Ángel Jiménez was getting married. Australian Jason Day was the only other top-50 player missing as he continued to nurse a hand injury. There was a top prize of $1.8 million, but just as important were the 80 world ranking points available to the winner. McGinley was working as a commentator for Sky Sports and wanted those points to land in the hands of a big name from Europe. They would count in the qualifying process for his team.

He flew into Orlando on the Tuesday evening and drove 150 miles to Ponte Vedra Beach that night. This gave him a clear day before the tournament began to scout the course and see as many of his prospective team as possible. On the ninth hole he caught up with García's practice round. The Spaniard was in stunning form. Off the tee on that par five he struck two drives – one with a controlled fade, the next with a raking draw that propelled the ball 40 yards further down the fairway. He then fired a 288-yard three wood from the fairway into the heart of a tiny green. 'It was one of the best shots I have ever seen,' McGinley said.

Stenson was on the range and locating the centre of the club face with every shot. His coach Pete Cowen, a straight-talking Yorkshireman not prone to hyperbole, said it was the best ball striking he had encountered. 'If he could get the putter going he could be very dangerous this week,' he said. Stenson was one of four players, along with Adam Scott, Bubba Watson and Matt Kuchar, with the chance of being promoted to world number one by the end of the tournament (Scott, in fact, took over from Woods the following week).

Stenson, meanwhile, had made himself the main man of Europe after his sensational return to form in 2013. It had been some turnaround – until he rediscovered the consistency to land the PGA Tour's lucrative FedEx Cup and Europe's Race to Dubai, he had been a largely forgotten figure. The Swede hadn't played a Ryder Cup since 2008.

It was a similar scenario for Martin Kaymer. The German had been the hero at Medinah when he holed the putt that retained the trophy, but that had been a rare moment of joy. The 2012 match coincided with a slump in form for a player who had topped the world rankings the previous season. 'I didn't play well at all going to the Ryder Cup. I almost thought I shouldn't play because I was thinking: "I'm not really helping right now,"' Kaymer revealed.

'That's why it was okay for me to play only one foursome out of four. It was completely fine with me. But then in the end, when you play singles, it doesn't matter how bad you play. Through playing with your heart and playing with passion, you can just get it done somehow. Fortunately I could make that last putt.'

Kaymer had won the US PGA Championship for his maiden major title in 2010. It was one of four victories he enjoyed that year. The next February he had become officially the best player in the world. That was fine. Better than fine – it was great. But – and it was a big but – how was it possible to assume such a mantle with what he felt was an incomplete game?

Kaymer could fade the ball left to right at will but moving it in the opposite direction with any dependability was beyond him. 'I wanted to become a better player and I didn't feel like I was the best golfer in the world,' the 29-year-old reflected. 'So that's why I needed to change, to become more happy that I can do anything. I wanted to be able to say whatever I need on the golf course, I can hit it. That's why I wanted to change. It was very necessary.'

But it wasn't easy, particularly with outsiders questioning his need to change a game that had made him, statistically at least, the best player in the world. 'I think it's because of where I'm from,' Kaymer said. 'In Germany, we always look for perfection. You are the best in the world, so why didn't you win? It's very difficult to deal with all those things. If you win or not, people tell you their opinion and it's very difficult to deal with all that. I didn't really know how to handle it in the past.'

When he arrived at the Players' Championship, Kaymer had fallen to 61st in the rankings. He was an also-ran in the Ryder Cup qualifying tables and his share of 18th at the Quail Hollow tournament the previous week had been the best return of a modest season. He looked like a player unlikely to retain his place in the side – the fallen hero of Medinah.

But McGinley knew that Kaymer, having played the two previous Ryder Cups, warranted some consideration. The skipper walked a few holes of the German's practice round on the eve of the tournament. 'We had a very nice chat, and I think he will be a brilliant captain because as a person, the way he talks to you, he's a very respectful man,' Kaymer said. 'He really listens to you and he wants to help. He's not a selfish player and not a selfish captain; he wants us to feel as comfortable as possible, and hopefully I can make the team.'

The conversation wasn't as out of place as it might have seemed. Kaymer knew a corner was being turned. 'He played well at Houston the week before the Masters but missed the cut because he couldn't putt,' remembered his caddie Craig Connelly. 'He has worked extremely hard. His hands can be in some state. You know, they can bleed. Hours on the range when he's away from tournament play, when he's back in Phoenix at Whisper Rock and then when he's back in Germany with his coach Günter Kessler.

'He was probably at his lowest towards the end of last year,' Connelly added. 'He was really struggling because he still had the really bad shot going left, which he hates. He just stripped it down and went back to basics with Günter. He now knows he can draw the ball when he has to and that's what he's going to do.'

And where better to do it than at the home of the American circuit's flagship tournament? The Stadium Course at TPC Sawgrass is a penal layout that will punish errant strokes and poor positional play. But the Pete Dye-designed course also rewards brave, aggressive and well-executed strokes. And Kaymer was feeling brave.

The build-up to the 2014 Players' was not straightforward. A cold, wet winter left the greens in poor condition. Ground staff had also misapplied a treatment to the putting surfaces and three of the greens couldn't be opened for play until the eve of the tournament. Recent rain meant the course was softer than usual so by the time Thursday rolled around there was a real prospect of low scoring.

Kaymer duly obliged, with a record equalling 63. 'Ballstriking-wise, that's one of the best rounds I've ever played,' he said. He'd really got started at the tenth hole and then covered his closing nine holes, the outward half of the course, in only

29 blows. It was the first time any player had gone sub-30 on either half of this famed stretch of golfing real estate. 'Well, I stopped thinking. That's pretty much the bottom line,' Kaymer told reporters. 'I thought a lot the last two years about swing changes, what I did wrong, what I did right. Then a couple weeks before the Masters I worked a little with my coach. He came to Phoenix, and then I went to Germany the week before, and we had a good session. And then it just clicked. I thought, okay, I know I can hit pretty much every shot when I need to hit it. If it's a draw, if it's a fade, low or high, I know that I can do it.'

At close of play Kaymer was two strokes clear of American Russell Henley. There had been a rash of low scores and Englishmen Westwood and Rose both carded 67s, alongside American Spieth. They were four strokes off the pace but the impressive Spieth was to take a big chunk out of that advantage on the second day. He had completed the first round without dropping a shot. This became the talking point on the Friday. How long could the 20-year-old maintain his remarkable run? This, after all, is a course where an abundance of water, trees and small tight greens means a bogey is never far away. Spieth seemed oblivious to such fears. Relentlessly, he went blemish-free again, this time carding a 66 in much tougher afternoon conditions. Kaymer had been happy enough with his 69, which was posted early. At one point he had been five strokes clear but, by the time Spieth had finished, the advantage was down to a single stroke.

In true Ryder Cup-style the American and German played the next 36 holes together in a memorable shoot-out. On the Saturday, Spieth again produced immaculate golf and the players competed in a remarkable spirit. When the American missed a short birdie putt on the 10th, Kaymer made a point of consoling his opponent as they walked down the next hole. 'Don't worry about it, you're here to have fun, this is where you want to be,' he told him.

Spieth acknowledged the magnitude of the gesture. 'It was really cool for him to come up and say that at the time,' he said. 'Something that I can look at and see as a role model is the way that he approaches the game. He was out there truly having fun.'

Even though Spieth's putter had gone relatively cold, it was only later in the day that his long game started to waver as well, and his remarkable run of avoiding a dropped shot came under serious threat. Each time, though, he found a way to escape with par and move on.

Kaymer continued to hold his own and remained one stroke ahead when the players reached the 18th tee. With water stretching all the way down the left side of the par four, the temptation is to let the ball drift right. But too far in that direction will leave a second shot obscured by trees. Both players fell into the trap.

Spieth could only bunt his second shot under the branches, leaving a 50-yard up-and-down to save par. Kaymer was more ambitious. He took the aerial route but the ball flew too far and settled on the downslope of a swale at the back of the green. Spieth's chip-and-run looked good, but trundled 12 feet past and nestled just off the back of the green.

Kaymer knew a par would be enough to maintain the lead going into the final round. He attempted a delicate pitch but it was a fraction shy. It came to rest nine feet short, on a similar line to Spieth's ball.

The young American had now gone 53 holes without dropping a shot and the Saturday crowd around the 18th collectively held its breath. The lad from Dallas settled over the putt, aiming at the left edge of the hole. His stroke held admirably firm and the left half of the hole duly grabbed the ball, which disappeared for a spectacular par save. 'I was struggling to really find that stroke,' Spieth admitted. 'And with a bogey-free streak on the line and the nerves of the

18th hole, it was really big for me to put a good stroke on it and see it roll true and go in.'

Now the pressure was on Kaymer and he buckled. He pulled the putt left and his ball never threatened to drop. It was a bogey five and a level-par round of 72. Spieth had bettered him by one and was now tied for the lead. Some of the galleries cheered the miss 'which I wish didn't happen', said Spieth. Kaymer seemed oblivious. Gracefully he removed his cap and acknowledged the spectators.

As the players marched off in the evening sunshine, the young Texan could hear his name being elongated by raucous, beer-infused fans. 'Spieeeeeth!', they were yelling. There was little support for Kaymer but that was to be expected in deepest Florida. 'It had a bit of a Ryder Cup feel about it,' the German later commented.

Spieth, meanwhile, was determined to make up for the disappointment of failing to convert a similar position at the Masters a month earlier. 'I'm very excited. This is a position I wanted to get into in another big tournament. Augusta left me feeling a little hungry for it again,' he said. Spieth was also delighted he would be playing with Kaymer again on the final day. 'Great guy, a class act,' was how he described his rival, who he had only met for the first time during the third round.

The atmosphere generated by their transatlantic battle left Spieth rather in two minds. 'To be honest with you, with how great of a guy Martin is, I wish it didn't feel as much like a Ryder Cup. And that's really kind of what it felt like out there, which is great. I think that's only going to help me to have momentum, with the crowd behind me.'

Kaymer knew he was on the threshold of escaping the golfing doldrums. He was also more than aware that Spieth posed a serious threat. 'Seems like he doesn't make many mistakes,' Kaymer commented. Equally, former champion Sergio García might mount a charge from three strokes back, or there was a host of other players five and six strokes behind, any of whom might make a charge and deny him his first title for 19 months.

Kaymer also knew that he had the experience of winning a play-off to clinch a major and of holding his nerve to secure a Ryder Cup defence. 'A lot of people ask me what was more important to you, or what was more exciting, winning the Ryder Cup or winning the PGA,' he said. 'But really, you can't really compare those things.

'You realise afterwards how much pressure there really is playing the Ryder Cup, and you can use it a lot for the next few tournaments. As a person, you grow a lot and you get to know yourself a lot better. So all those things, when you add them up, I'm sure will help me one way or the other tomorrow. It's tough to put into words, but it's very, very important that I have that experience.'

Throughout the week at Sawgrass, Kaymer had talked about the need for bravery. Little did he know just how much courage he would have to summon on an extended final day.

Both he and Spieth made excellent starts. Again, the crowds were firmly on the side of the young American. He had come close to becoming the youngest winner of the Masters a month earlier. Now he was trying to become the youngest to win the prestigious Players' title.

Since joining the PGA Tour in 2013, he had repeatedly given himself chances to win events. Only once had he converted one of those opportunities into victory, but if he added this Players' title he would have achieved his second win at a younger age than Tiger Woods had managed, which would be a very impressive statistic.

Spieth matched Kaymer's birdie at the second and they remained locked together at the top of the leaderboard, now at 13 under par. The Texan then took on the tucked pin on the fourth. Like a veteran, he exploited the contours of the green to perfection to set up a short birdie putt on the par 4. When his ball duly disappeared, Spieth assumed the lead for the first time. It was the only occasion Kaymer had been knocked from the top spot since his opening 63.

Spieth still hadn't dropped a shot and Greg Norman's 20-year mark of 66 blemish-free holes at Sawgrass was coming into his sights. His hopes of rewriting the record books, however, were soon dashed. Moments after taking the outright lead, his first bogey came at the fifth hole and was followed by a second just three holes later.

Now Kaymer was back out in front. He was playing par golf until collecting his second par-five birdie at the ninth. He appeared unflappable and was now two strokes clear, heading into the back nine.

Further down the leaderboard, local resident Jim Furyk was mounting a charge, Sergio García was keeping his name prominent and Westwood was flickering. But it was Kaymer who was in control.

Lightning flashes could be seen in the distance and rumbles of thunder were starting to grow louder. Weather warning signs were posted on the scoreboards and there were increasing concerns that the event would suffer its first interruption of the week.

Spieth bogeyed the 10th. He had gone 58 holes without dropping a stroke and now three had slipped away in the space of six holes. Kaymer made a routine birdie at the par-five 11th and was now four clear of his playing partner and seemed to be cruising towards the title. It was no longer the young pretender who was the German's biggest threat but the grizzled veteran Furyk. He had moved to 12 under with two holes to play and remained on that mark coming up the last, while Kaymer headed down the 14th at 15 under.

Furyk had just missed a decent birdie chance and was surveying a three-foot par putt on the home green for a 66 when a loud crack of thunder was heard. Seconds later, horns sounded to herald the suspension of play. It was hot and muggy, rain was on its way and the players headed for the clubhouse.

For a little over 90 minutes, Kaymer had to brood over his three-stroke advantage. There was a lot to take in, and a lot that might mess with his mind. The significance of this day could not be overestimated. This was someone whose previously stellar career had been stuck in reverse for most of the last three years.

Yet to this point he had been playing faultlessly. It was exemplary front-running golf that had seen off Spieth's challenge. Now the only question was whether he could finish the job that night or would have to return next morning to complete his victory. Kaymer thought he would probably have to sleep on it. He couldn't envisage there being enough time – or light – for the tournament to be completed that night. But he was wrong on both counts.

Word came through that play would resume at 7.10 p.m. The remaining players had a brief warm-up before climbing into the white vans that would take them back to the 14th green. Rain was still falling as Furyk wandered back to the putting surface at the 18th. Typically, Furyk stood over his three-footer and took repeated practice swings before the hooter heralded the resumption. He had already hit 20 three-footers on the practice green. 'I think I missed only one of them, so that still kept me on a little edge,' Furyk said. 'But I feel like I got the one miss out of the way. That is what I was telling myself. I had a lot of confidence over there.' When play resumed, he went through the routine one more time and tapped in for the clubhouse lead at 12 under par.

Kaymer completed his par at the 14th, and then the drama began. His tee shot on the tough par-four 15th went straight left. It's the shot that he hates most, a destructive blow that undermines his confidence to steer clear of trouble. From the trees he was fortunate to have a shot at the green but then hooked his ball left of his target. Short-sided, he had no green to work with, as well as an unpredictable wet, fluffy lie. His pitch landed meekly in the bunker that lay between him and the hole. The escape from the trap flew long and two putts later he was writing a six on his scorecard.

'Wow, that went quickly,' Kaymer said to his caddie Craig Connelly. 'A three-shot lead down to one in the blink of an eye.'

'Don't worry, we're still in front,' the Scottish bagman countered, knowing his man needed a positive response. 'That's the position we would have taken at this stage.'

The par-five 16th lay ahead. The German had birdied the first three long holes and completing the set would help settle nerves, heading to the treacherous 17th. Kaymer missed the green in two and betrayed signs of nerves when he chose to putt rather than chip his third shot. 'It was the wrong decision,' he admitted.

He left the ball woefully short and it was a well-judged two-putt that secured him a par to maintain his slender advantage. In the clubhouse, the 44-year-old Furyk sat with his wife Tabitha, intently watching the action unfold.

For the first time, a three-hole play-off rather than sudden death would be implemented if there was a tie. That would have to wait until the morning, because darkness was rapidly falling.

Kaymer peered through the gloom at the 17th green. Should he hit a soft wedge, or a hard gap wedge? The latter option, with more loft and a shorter shaft, would need to be hit harder, making for a more certain swing but with more spin. In theory, this would make it easier to find the middle of the green. Pumping adrenaline would also add a couple of yards to the shot.

Kaymer opted for the gap wedge. The pin was located in its usual Sunday back-right position. Hit it over the bunker

Above: Would he or wouldn't he? One of the biggest questions of 2014 was whether Tiger Woods would play at Gleneagles after undergoing back surgery in March.

Opposite (top): Martin Kaymer lines up a putt on the 15th hole in the final round of the 114th US Open at Pinehurst on 15 June 2014. Kaymer went on to win with a score of 9 under par and a four-day total of 271.

Opposite (bottom): Bubba Watson has the victor's green jacket put on by Adam Scott, the winner of the 2013 Masters, after Watson won the Masters for the second time at Augusta on 13 April 2014.

Above: Rory McIlroy with the Claret Jug after winning the 2014 Open Championship at Royal Liverpool Golf Club, Hoylake. Three weeks later he also celebrated landing the PGA Championship at Valhalla.

Opposite (top): Phil Mickelson after missing from short range on the 4th during his Friday foursomes at Gleneagles. Despite pleading to play, the ensuing defeat cost him his place in the US team the following day.

Opposite (bottom): Europe's Graeme McDowell, left, and Victor Dubuisson pose after victory in the afternoon foursomes match against USA's Jimmy Walker and Rickie Fowler on the second day of the tournament.

Above: Texan twins; America's big success story was the pairing of their two youngest players, Patrick Reed (crouching) and Jordan Spieth.

Above: Europe's Rory McIlroy, left, and Ian Poulter line up a putt on the 13th green during the fourball match on the second day.

Opposite (top): US Captain Tom Watson, left, surveys a worrying scoreboard on the final day alongside the man who appointed him, PGA President Ted Bishop.

Opposite (bottom): Europe's Martin Kaymer plays onto the 6th green from an awkward lie during the fourball match on the second day.

Above: Mission accomplished – Europe's captain Paul McGinley celebrates with his triumphant team.

and the ball should gravitate towards the hole. Tug it a fraction left and it would take the wrong side of a central spine and move away from the hole to leave a devilishly difficult approach putt.

Kaymer hit what he thought was a good shot, but one that was just a couple of yards short of what he needed. The ball bounced off the back of the lone bunker, kicking left away from the flag. Then the spin took an unexpectedly potent hold. It had a slingshot effect, sending the ball racing across the green before it caught up in the rough on the fringe. Without that collar of longer grass, it would have dropped into the water.

This was seriously shaky stuff. The giant scoreboard was offering the only illumination, and it helped show the stress etched all over the 29-year-old's face. Connelly, known as the 'Wee Man', was trying to maintain a confident body language, but his unblinking eyes told the opposite story.

Kaymer's heels were almost overhanging the wooden walls of the green. A momentary loss of balance would have had him swimming with turtles and alligators. But his biggest concern was whether his mind would fall prey to the demons of doubt. The first half of the chip across the green was uphill, the rest of the journey was a rapid descent.

Furyk looked on. He knew how tough this shot would be and stared at the screen. He saw Kaymer's ball hop in the air, lacking any purpose, to reach the downhill section. It limped towards the summit but came to rest 28 feet short of the hole.

This left a putt that Kaymer had practised before, but never in near-darkness. He had a feel for the line, but pace would be the key ingredient. It was downhill, down-grain and downright difficult. Forget the fact that it had to go in to preserve a one-shot lead, with one hole to play, because reminding himself of the enormity of his next shot would only make it more difficult. He needed to be brave. He needed to remember he had holed a putt to save a Ryder Cup. He had also holed a tough one to earn the play-off against Bubba Watson that yielded the 2010 US PGA title.

Settling over his putt after deciding a line around five feet left of the hole, he made the perfect backswing. The club-head accelerated through the ball. Smoothly, it headed off in a direction that didn't look remotely like it would lead to the cup. Then the ball began to turn from left to right. Kaymer watched, willing it to remain on course. It did, swinging all the time towards the hole. Spectators peered through the gloom. They blinked in disbelief. The little white sphere disappeared, diving into the hole, its destiny certain thanks to the guts and determination of the man who had set it on its journey.

'Obviously, a left-to-right, downhill putt with the grain and the darkness, it's not that easy. There's always a little bit of luck involved. But it was a good putt,' was how Kaymer summed it up. 'It was a very strange way to make a three.'

Connelly wheeled away, giving the air a celebratory upper-cut. In the clubhouse, Furyk just nodded, a rueful smile on his face. He knew the television cameras were on him and his reaction equated to a tip of the hat to the German. The American has seen most things in golf, including a lot of Ryder Cup heartache, and he knew something very special had just happened. He also knew Kaymer now only had to par the final hole to end all hopes of a home win.

Kaymer nailed his drive. Sending it up the waterline down the left side of the hole, he watched his controlled fade take the ball away from danger and into the centre of the fairway. When he reached it, he judged it was a mere eight iron to the flag. He was almost there.

But he caught his approach heavy and the ball came to rest a couple of paces short of the green. Should he chip or putt? It was the same dilemma that he had faced at the 16th. Then, he had had three shots available. This time, he could only afford two. Any more and he would be back in the morning for a play-off with Furyk.

This time, the first putt was more positive. It shaved the edge of the hole and ran three feet by. It wasn't a 'gimme' but it was manageable. Kaymer dropped the putt into the hole. He had won. It was an exhausting, tortuous and ultimately courageous victory, easily the equal of his one major, the 2010 US PGA. This one probably meant even more. It confirmed he was back in the big time. The changes and all the hard work had been worth it and the tangible reward was much more than his $1.8 million winner's cheque.

'There's no major behind the tournament here but, at the end of the day, for all of us it's a major,' Kaymer said. 'It's the biggest field. It's a tough golf course, a very tough week, and very difficult to beat all of those guys. Pressure-wise, I can compare it to the PGA Championship.

'The last few holes weren't about how good I play or how bad I play, but about how much I wanted that win. You can hit good golf shots, but everybody hits some bad golf shots. How bad are the bad ones? And how much do you want to bring it home the last three, four holes? I didn't show much of it the first two; I know that. But 17 and 18, I really, really wanted it, and it gives me a lot of satisfaction.'

McGinley was satisfied too. He had watched one of Europe's classiest golfing acts see off two Americans from either end of the age spectrum. The young superstar, Spieth, finished fourth, three shots behind, after a closing 74. Furyk, one of the US's oldest campaigners, had been left frustrated, not for the first time. He had, though, given his own Ryder Cup chances a serious shot in the arm.

McGinley's nudge of encouragement on the Wednesday, when he walked those few holes with Kaymer, had proved time very well spent. Kaymer's win catapulted him into the reckoning for Gleneagles and jeopardised Ian Poulter's chances of an automatic berth. More significantly, Kaymer had hit top form with excellent timing. Three majors would hove into view very quickly and he was well positioned to capitalise.

As Connelly observed: 'I shouldn't say he's back to the old Martin, because he is obviously a much-improved golfer. The mindset is the old Martin, the golfer is better.'

CHAPTER 10

McIlroy and Wentworth

'I didn't know what was going to happen, to be honest.'
Rory McIlroy

Martin Kaymer's victory at Sawgrass swung the golfing focus back towards Europe and two of the continent's biggest stars ensured the momentum was maintained. Miguel Ángel Jiménez and Rory McIlroy come from opposite ends of the age spectrum but share an uncanny knack for making headlines. Jiménez is the pony-tailed, mustachioed, happy-go-lucky veteran with a penchant for the best cigars and Rioja of the finest quality. He has also developed an unconventional, baseball-style swing that has endured through to senior status. McIlroy is half the Spaniard's age, much more athletically minded and even more impossible to ignore.

McIlroy left Sawgrass with another top-10 under his belt but knowing that a chance to win had been squandered by substandard front-nines. He had made birdies galore – no fewer than 25 in 72 holes – but still only managed a share of sixth place. He knew a win wasn't far away. He could feel the form that had made him the world number one in 2012, and he was optimistic.

'I just need to eradicate the misses, the bad shots,' McIlroy said. 'It's more mental, making bad decisions, going for pins where you don't need to. Missing fairways on the wrong side, just things like that. I don't think it's anything technical, because if it was I don't think I'd be able to make birdies as easily as I'm making them.'

Next on his agenda was to spend some time in Europe with his fiancée, the tennis star Caroline Wozniacki. Both were facing busy spells, during which they would struggle to make their calendars coincide.

It was time to send out the invitations for their November wedding. The fact that Wozniacki was due to play in the French Open at the end of May was enough to persuade McIlroy to add the BMW PGA Championship to his schedule. It might be the European Tour's flagship event, but McIlroy hates the West Course. He had seriously considered skipping a tournament that might hamper his preparations for the US Open in June. But by playing he would, at least, be on the same continent as the woman he was going to marry.

Jiménez was also juggling matrimonial matters. He didn't play at Sawgrass because he had a date at his own golf complex in Torremolinos. It was there that he married his long-term girlfriend Susanna Styblo in a ceremony attended, among others, by José María Olazábal.

Life could not have been any better for Jiménez. He had finished fourth in the Masters and, having just turned 50, he promptly won his first event on the Champions Tour in the US. As ESPN's Rick Reilly observed: 'He's been a high-school drop-out, a caddie, a soldier and a car mechanic. Now he's a millionaire. His swing is smooth, his life smoother.'

The Jiménez philosophy is simple. The good things in life should not be passed by: 'When you rush, you cannot enjoy the food, the wine, the cigars, no?' And it was with this attitude that he entered the Spanish Open, the 626th European Tour competition of his career, the following week.

As with McIlroy and the PGA at Wentworth, this event had never treated Jiménez particularly well. It would be his 27th attempt to win a home championship. His previous best was as runner-up in 1999. Outside the elusive majors, it was the title he coveted most.

Rounds of 69, 73 and 69 over the tough stadium course at the PGA Catalunya resort in Girona left the home favourite firmly in touch heading into the final day. Early in the concluding 18 holes he held a two-stroke lead, only to squander it. He carded a closing 69 to finish at four under par, a mark matched only by the experienced Australian Richard Green and 22-year-old Belgian Thomas Pieters.

As they headed back down the 18th for a sudden-death play-off, it was clear who the home crowd were supporting. The normally laid-back Jiménez still appeared relaxed, but there was little doubt that he was feeling the nerves. The same applied to his opponents. Green, a tall, elegant left-hander, hadn't won on the European Tour since the 2010 Portugal Masters, while the even taller Pieters was playing only his 15th Tour event.

The barrel-chested Jiménez held his nerve to get up and down from the back of the green for a tournament-winning par at the first extra hole. 'There's no words to describe what it means to me, you need to be in my skin but I'm not going to let you!' he said.

'It's amazing. It's my 21st victory on the European Tour and 27 times I played the Spanish Open. I have been close a couple of times. Today, it was very tough out there but I got it in the end. All the victories are special, all are unique, some of them give you more money, some less, but all of them are important. You play to win and when you make it, you have to appreciate it. I don't know if I felt nerves, but you do feel tension, you feel the pressure.'

Asked the secret to his longevity, Jiménez added: 'There is no secret. Good food, good wine, good cigars and some exercise!'

But on a more serious note, his thoughts inevitably turned to September. 'I would love to make the Ryder Cup team, I would break all the records at 50. I hope I can make the team and defend the European colours in Scotland.'

Two days later, Jiménez prompted the biggest cheers of the night at the lavish European Tour Awards Dinner in the Sofitel Hotel at Heathrow Airport. As he was announced to the audience it was clear he had achieved one of the most popular wins of the year.

Earlier that evening, McGinley appeared on BBC 5Live's golf programme being broadcast from the function. 'It's extra-ordinary,' he said of Jiménez. 'He is more young at heart than he is young in age. He's really, really determined to make the team and I wish him the very best of luck. He's shown a lot of form in recent weeks, a real purple patch. You can trace it back to the EurAsia Cup in March. Even though he was our captain there, he was the stand-out player. For Miguel, the important thing now is to keep that form up over the summer period and solidify his place on the team.'

At that point, the Spaniard was just outside the top nine automatic spots in the qualifying tables, occupied by Victor Dubuisson, Jamie Donaldson, Thomas Bjørn, Henrik Stenson, Sergio García, McIlroy, Justin Rose, Kaymer and Luke Donald. McGinley's implication was clear. Jiménez would need to play his way into the team rather than rely on being one of the captain's three wildcard picks.

That Tuesday evening function was the traditional curtain-raiser to the BMW PGA Championship week. This is the continental equivalent of the Players' Championship and the biggest 72-hole tournament organised by the European Tour. Attracting a fitting field is one of the Tour's biggest challenges, because most of their stars live in the US. Staying stateside to play the Crowne Plaza Colonial tournament in Fort Worth, Texas, would be a much easier option. There has to be a good reason to decamp to the west of London, especially with the US Open just three weeks away.

There were plenty of reasons to head to Wentworth, how-ever. Firstly, there is considerable loyalty to the Tour from players who grew up on the circuit. The likes of Rose, Lee Westwood, Poulter and McIlroy cut their teeth on the European Tour. They all live in Florida now and are predominantly PGA Tour players but, to remain eligible for the Ryder Cup, they are required to play 13 counting events on the European schedule. For the English players, there is also the 'home Open' rule, which requires them to play the PGA because it is regarded as their native tournament. For the likes of McIlroy and Padraig Harrington, the Irish Open fulfils that role.

Only one of the dozen heroes from Medinah was absent. Graeme McDowell decided to stay at home at Lake Nona in Florida with his pregnant wife. Her due date was in August and she would soon be unable to travel with him. In golfing terms, McDowell was taking a big risk, because he was already trailing in the Gleneagles qualifying tables. There was big money as well as 64 world-ranking points on offer for the PGA title, and he was sacrificing a week that could put him on track to retain his Ryder Cup place.

Tour bosses were understanding. 'I very much appreciated Graeme taking the time to phone me personally to tell me he wouldn't be at Wentworth,' said Chief Executive, George O'Grady. 'The fact that he wants to spend time with Kristin, who will not be able to travel for the next three months, is entirely understandable.'

O'Grady was otherwise thrilled with the turnout. Several of the biggest names attended the Heathrow dinner where Stenson was honoured as the Players' Player of the Year for his 2013 exploits. Poulter presented the Swede with his trophy. There was a celebratory mood as Rose took to the stage to relive his US Open win at Merion and McGinley was joined by Ryder Cup vice captains Sam Torrance and Des Smyth.

Stenson had told the audience that the multiple millions he had won by taking the FedEx Cup and Race to Dubai spoils had not changed his outlook on life, to which Torrance retorted: 'If that money doesn't make a difference to Henrik, he can send it over to me!'

The question-and-answer session with Europe's captain and his assistants was chaired by American broadcaster Steve Sands. It would be hard to imagine a golf function of such stature being dominated by Ryder Cup fever in the same way if it had been staged in the US. The Gleneagles contest, after all, was still four months away.

In the States, the American challenge for the biennial matches is organised by the PGA of America, a body that principally looks after club professionals. The PGA Tour has no say in the Ryder Cup, so wouldn't be looking to celebrate the match at any of its functions. The top professional players wouldn't ordinarily attend events put on for their club brethren. As Paul Azinger, the victorious US captain in 2008, observed: 'We are different about the Ryder Cup over here than they are in Europe. They have more of a chip on their shoulder. Their tour supports it and it's much more a big team effort. It certainly seems a lot more personal to the Europeans than it does to the Americans.'

The Ryder Cup props up the European Tour with the money it generates. Culturally, the continent's players grow up with the match as a focal point. It drives the calendar and their schedules. It is only natural for it to be at the forefront of everyone's mind at such functions.

McGinley used it to provide a rallying call. 'I want Gleneagles to be the loudest Ryder Cup ever,' he said. 'I don't want us to be on the wrong side of the line, but I want the crowds to be really loud and passionate.'

The captain's enthusiasm was infectious. You could tell he was revelling in his role. On the one hand, he couldn't wait for the matches to start, to become embroiled in the tactics of picking pairings and working out the order in which he would send out his players. On the other, he didn't want his captaincy to come to an end. He had embraced every aspect of the job and was having the time of his life.

He also knew that there was no point in getting ahead of himself. Events would dictate three-quarters of his team. 'I have a lot of faith in that system and it is going to produce nine players who form a strong side,' he said. 'It's constantly shifting sands. There's no point in getting caught up with it at the moment.'

Little did he know the seismic shifts that lay just around the corner.

The following day, the pre-tournament pro-am was staged – a gathering of the leading professionals in the championship, partnered by famous names from the worlds of entertainment and sport. The biggest golfers in the event would also attend news conferences to give their thoughts on the four days ahead.

McIlroy hadn't been at the dinner the night before and was scheduled to be interviewed at 11.30 a.m. At around 9.30, his PR team released a statement no one had been expecting. The sporting world's most high-profile relationship was over. His wedding with Wozniacki was off.

The statement read: 'There is no right way to end a relationship that has been so important to two people. The problem is mine. The wedding invitations issued at the weekend made me realise that I wasn't ready for all that marriage entails. I wish Caroline all the happiness she deserves and thank her for the great times we've had. I will not be saying anything more about our relationship in any setting.'

The relationship had seemingly been ended during a three-minute phone call. McIlroy and Wozniacki had become engaged on New Year's Eve, amid the fireworks in Sydney Harbour that heralded the arrival of 2014. Subsequently, they had managed their conflicting golf and tennis schedules in order to see as much of each other as possible. Four days earlier, the golfer had tweeted a photo, captioned: 'Nice view for dinner with @CaroWozniacki at Nobu Monte Carlo.'

The Danish former world number one tennis player had not been shy about her desire to settle down to married life. She had even indicated that she was ready to give up her career. 'I want to be a relatively young mother, and I do not see it as being too far in the future. I have always been like that,' she said.

McIlroy kept his date with the press on the morning of his bombshell announcement. He look shattered. Few could believe he would put himself through public scrutiny, having made such a personal announcement. Earlier Mark Steinberg, who manages Tiger Woods, expressed utter disbelief. 'He's not still going to do his press conference, is he?' the agent whispered while another of his clients, Justin Rose, talked to reporters. Woods hates talking to the media at the best of times, and Steinberg has earned the nickname 'Dr No' for the number of times he has turned down requests for interviews with his players. It was little wonder that he struggled to comprehend the Northern Irishman's PR strategy.

McIlroy, though, rarely shies away from questions, cameras and microphones. 'Our relationship was played out so much in the public eye, it seemed the right thing to do,' he later explained when asked why he had been prepared to talk so openly.

His press conference was kept short, though. A little over six minutes. He appeared close to tears; haunted, embarrassed and humble. The last thing he looked like was a prospective Wentworth champion. The only moment of levity came when the *Telegraph*'s James Corrigan ventured, with a degree of mischief: 'At least you're at a golf course that you love?'

Even McIlroy couldn't stop himself from laughing. He had missed the cut on his two previous visits to the West Course and readily admitted that it didn't suit his eye.

The split with Wozniacki was front-page news. Tabloids live-blogged his press conference, marriage experts and wedding planners gave their views to radio phone-ins and speculation was rife as to why sport's golden couple had separated.

McIlroy immersed himself in his golf. His phone remained switched off and he gave away his laptop computer. He wanted no part in the furore being played out all over the media. He played the pro-am in the company of former members of the Manchester United team that he has supported from the moment he realised his dad was a City fan (McIlroy can be contrary like that).

There was no doubt that he enjoyed spending time with Peter Schmeichel, Teddy Sheringham and Phil Neville. But he readily admitted that concentrating on his game during the BMW PGA Championship would not be easy. 'I'm not going to lie. It's going to be very difficult,' he said. 'But you know, at least when I get inside the ropes, I can just try and concentrate on the shot at hand.'

McIlroy was probably grateful to another Dane for stealing the first-round headlines. Bjørn fired a course-record 62 to set a blistering pace on the rain-softened layout. The 25-year-old McIlroy acquitted himself well enough, but lay six strokes back. The highlights had been eagles at the par-four seventh and the par-five 12th. The first of those came from a 130-yard wedge that spun back 30 feet down a slope before taking the borrow to perfection and falling in the hole. At the 12th, he opted for a seven-iron second that finished within tap-in range.

As expected, though, concentration had been a problem. 'I think it's only natural,' he said. 'I don't think you would be a human being if it wasn't tough, especially when it's a little slow out there and we were walking in between shots. But once I had my mind focused on the task in hand, it made it a little easier.'

'Honestly, I'd just be delighted to make it to the weekend because I haven't done that here for a couple of years,' he said, before adding that he felt capable of shooting a similar score in the second round.

That appeared less likely after dropping shots on the second and third holes the next morning. Then came a double-bogey six at the seventh, and he went to the turn in a three-over-par 38. There was every chance that he would miss the cut for the third year running. McIlroy, however, steadied the ship. Another eagle at the 12th set up an inward half of 33 – three under par – and a second-round 71 meant that he was comfortably in the field for the weekend.

His mood afterwards remained subdued but not to the extent of the two previous days. 'I was apprehensive going out yesterday,' McIlroy said. 'I didn't know what was going to happen but at least today I knew what to expect.'

As for his performance over the first 36 holes, he had pleasantly surprised himself. 'I've exceeded my expectations so far, I think. I don't know if wildly, but reasonably, yeah. I didn't know what was going to happen and didn't know how I was going to feel. So to be in there with a chance at the weekend is good.'

His third round began with a double-bogey six but McIlroy showed admirable composure to recover from his potentially ruinous start. He carded a three-under-par 69 but found himself trailing Bjørn by a formidable seven strokes. This time it was the Dane who was doing the separating. The 44-year-old, who lay third in the Ryder Cup points list, fired seven birdies in his last eight holes, including six in a row from the 11th for an inward half of 30. His 67 took him to 15 under par, five strokes clear of his nearest challenger.

Bjørn seemed destined for the biggest win of his career while McIlroy was chasing his best Wentworth finish. The title looked beyond him but he wasn't yet ready to concede defeat.

'Look, I've had big leads and let them slip and I've come from behind and won,' he said. 'Eighteen holes of golf is still a

long way to go, but I'm going to need something very special.'
He had in mind something similar to Bjørn's opening round
of 62. 'If the conditions are favourable, then you never know
what can happen.'

That final day at the European Tour's headquarters, the
weather could not have been more pleasant. The golf could not
have been more unpredictable. It turned into one of the most
compelling days the event had ever produced.

Bjørn began with a confident, jaunty stride. His birdie at
the par-five fourth was routine; it also gave him a six-stroke
lead. Then he dropped a shot at the next and made a dreadful
error of judgement at the sixth. Having driven into a fairway
bunker, he tried to advance his ball down the fairway. His ball
belted into the substantial lip of the hazard and bounced back
at his feet, plugging into the sand for good measure. From
there he could only splash out with his third shot. With his
fourth, he tugged the ball into a greenside trap and failed to
get up and down. It was a miserable seven. Four strokes had
been dropped in two holes. He was back to 12 under par and
his advantage had disappeared.

The Danish star was now locked at the top of the leaderboard with Shane Lowry. His only consolation was that Donald,
his playing partner and two-times champion, had also contrived to rack up a triple bogey.

McIlroy, meanwhile, had earlier enjoyed a moment of good
fortune when his eagle putt on the fourth sat on the edge of
the hole for a good five seconds. It was only as the player began
to advance to complete his tap-in that it dropped into the cup.
But the benefits of that eagle were soon handed back with
bogeys at the sixth and ninth holes. He went to the turn in 34,
one under par, and nine under for the tournament. Something
special was still needed and it didn't look like coming when he
missed the green on the short par-three 10th.

After hitting his tee shot, McIlroy leant to the left, as if wishing to guide his ball back to the target, but it resolutely hung out to the right. When it landed it clung to the bank just to the side of the green. At this point he found his golden touch. The chip headed straight for the hole. Birdie. Two more followed at the 12th and 13th. McIlroy was applying scoreboard pressure. Bjørn was wilting. Donald was fighting back. Lowry was powering on.

The Irishman had grown up with McIlroy. When the Golfing Union of Ireland invited coach Pete Cowen to have a look at the 15-year-old McIlroy during a squad session, another player caught his eye as well. 'You've got another one there. The fat guy with the glasses,' Cowen said.

Lowry has since shed the spectacles while playing golf but is still a burly figure. As an amateur, he won a play-off against Robert Rock to claim the Irish Open. It was a remarkable triumph for someone not yet in the paid ranks. Three years later he edged out another Englishman, Ross Fisher, to win the Portugal Masters and in the 2013 WGC Matchplay in Arizona he beat McIlroy head-to-head in the first round.

Now 27, the professional from Clara in County Offaly had the scent of the most significant title of his career in his nostrils. From the 10th he birdied three holes in a row. He was still keeping the charging McIlroy at arm's length until he drove into the trees down the left side of the sweeping dogleg 13th. The hole swings from right to left. Lowry had to take a penalty drop for an unplayable lie and proceeded to accumulate a double-bogey six. Now the Championship was back in the balance, but Lowry responded immediately with a birdie.

McIlroy got up and down after spinning off the green at the 16th before collecting single-putt birdies on the last two par-five holes. Crucially, Lowry bogeyed the 15th. This meant McIlroy's four on the penultimate green put him in the lead for the first time. At the last, he hit an immaculate drive before pushing his approach into a greenside bunker. His escape was beautifully judged, leaving a five-footer to move him to 14 under par.

The two-times major champion made no mistake, his putt all but assuring him of the title. He clenched his fist. There was no smile, though, following a painful, extraordinary week. He threw the ball to the crowd. The exuberance of that action was as close as he got to a celebration, although he would later spray champagne over cheering spectators.

As his final putt dropped, he wasn't sure he had won. Spectacular finishes from Bjørn, Lowry or Donald could have forced a play-off. So he sat waiting in the recorder's area, chatting with European Tour media director Scott Crockett. In search of a neutral topic, they discussed Colin Montgomerie's fine performance in the Seniors' PGA that was underway in Michigan. McIlroy's mind was elsewhere though. He didn't know how to feel. As a golfer, there was immense satisfaction. As a person, it was still a hard week.

'I wasn't expecting to win like this, this week,' he would tell BBC Radio after his victory was confirmed. He agreed it had been the most extraordinary win in a career that has never been short of headlines. 'It's sort of surreal in some ways, but it ranks up there. This is the flagship event on the European Tour and it's 18 months since I won on the European Tour, so it's been a long time coming,' he said. It was, in fact, his first win as a professional on European soil.

'I was just happy to be out on the golf course, able to do what I do best. It was nice. I was really thankful for the time I had on the golf course because my mind was solely on the task in hand.'

He admitted his celebrations had been deliberately muted. ' They were. It was mixed emotions, I didn't know how to feel. To feel happy? To feel sad? I didn't know what to do,' he said.

'I'd played well, I got the win but when someone asked me to describe how I'm feeling I had to tell them I didn't know. I'm very happy that I won but there's a few other things that went on in my life this week that have been very difficult.'

Tellingly, in golfing terms, he was aware this had been very significant: 'Knowing I'm playing well going into the second major of the year, I couldn't be happier with that.' In terms of Ryder Cup qualification, McIlroy jumped to second on the world ranking points list behind Stenson, who finished seventh.

McIlroy had spent half an hour chatting with McGinley on Saturday morning at Wentworth. 'He was really excited about the Ryder Cup and the summer coming up,' McGinley said. It later emerged that this was the moment McIlroy had suggested a potential Ryder Cup partnership with García. Given the split with Wozniacki, the captain made an ironic choice of phrase when adding: 'I couldn't have more engagement from Rory as Ryder Cup captain. He is really up for it. He wanted to know a lot of the ideas and the lines I am thinking on and I didn't want to give him too much information.

'I want him to stay focused on his own career and to try and win majors. He is really engaged and I couldn't ask more for him at this stage. I am sure, come September, he will be even more engaged and ready to fulfil a big role. He will obviously play in the team.'

In his champion's news conference, McIlroy gave his take on the conversation. He said: 'We were just talking about pairings and what he's thinking. Even without this win it sounded like I was going to be on the team,' McIlroy smiled.

'I'm looking forward to it. We don't get a chance to come back and play in the UK and Ireland very often. It's going to be great. I think I'm pretty much cemented on the team now and looking forward to that.'

McGinley was thrilled to see the Ulsterman return to winning ways. 'In terms of his personal stuff, maybe it was a weight off his shoulders,' he told the Irish broadcaster RTE. 'I don't know. We will never know. Only Rory can answer that question. It certainly gave him a sense of clarity and he went on and played well. He was either going to miss the cut or he was going to win and, fortunately for everybody, he won.'

McGinley went on to make a comparison with how Woods had performed at the height of his powers. 'I think we are seeing a more mature Rory, and certainly one for the better. And maybe a little into the "Tiger-esque" way of consistency, week after week after week, because he's done it this year.'

Bjørn's tie for third place with Donald strengthened both players' qualification hopes. Indeed, the Dane was now assured of his place. But at what cost? Squandering a six-stroke advantage can damage anyone's psyche when handling pressure situations. He headed to the following week's Nordea Masters, muttering about taking the positives from Wentworth and using them as building blocks for the rest of the season. They were the usual sort of platitudes expressed by someone trying to salve the pain of bitter defeat.

McIlroy flew to Belfast to see his mum. Then it was off to Jack Nicklaus' Memorial Tournament. Once again, he was a single bloke. Once again, he was a winner.

CHAPTER 11

The US Open

'You can't control too many things.
That's what I have been trying to do, these
last three years. Now I just play.'
Martin Kaymer

The victories for Rory McIlroy and Martin Kaymer in the two flagship events of the PGA and European Tours set the tone for the big championships that followed in quick succession. Both players produced landmark performances to add to their major tallies. McIlroy had to wait until the Open Championship at Royal Liverpool, while Kaymer produced a truly great display to claim the US Open at Pinehurst in June. It meant that Europe was able to boast the two dominant players from the most important tournaments of the preceding summer in their Gleneagles line-up.

After McIlroy's Wentworth victory he headed to Jack Nicklaus's tournament, the Memorial, at Muirfield Village in Dublin, Ohio. He was supposed to dine with the Nicklaus family early in the week but was unable to keep the date. 'I blew him off,' McIlroy joked. Instead, he called Nicklaus's secretary to schedule a lunchtime meeting. The two men share huge mutual respect and have developed a strong bond. McIlroy is always keen to pick the brains of a man who won a record 18 majors and set the benchmark for success in the game.

Nicklaus was curious to know why McIlroy was struggling to back up excellent opening-day starts, producing destructive second rounds like the 77 he shot on the Friday at Augusta.

McIlroy was at a loss to explain and wanted tips on how to grind out wins in championships like the US Open. 'He had some advice for me that I hope I can use to good effect at Pinehurst,' said McIlroy, who had turned 25 a month earlier.

True to form, he began the Memorial in stunning style with a 63 only to follow it with a typically inexplicable 78 that cost him the chance of back-to-back wins. He finished 15th, behind the young Japanese Hideki Matsuyama, who won a play-off against the American-qualified Korean Kevin Na.

Kaymer took two weeks off after sharing 12th spot at Wentworth to recharge batteries that were running low in the wake of his start-to-finish victory at the Players' Championship. Like most competitors, he arrived at Pinehurst wondering how the famous Number 2 course would play. It was vastly different to any US Open test they had faced before. The second major of the year is always regarded as the toughest set-up in golf. Level par is usually a winning score on courses that traditionally have ribbon-thin fairways, thick penal rough and concrete greens. The USGA say they want to test every aspect of a golfer's game with these extremely difficult courses.

That remained the objective at the 2014 US Open but the course, which sits in the North Carolina Sandhills and in a resort known as 'the cradle of American golf', was radically different from the one that had hosted the Championship there in 1999 and 2005. Since then, Pinehurst had undergone massive alterations.

Architects Bill Coore and Ben Crenshaw were contracted and their aim was to take the Number 2 course back to the way it was intended to be played when it was originally laid out by the revered Scottish designer Donald Ross. Coore and Crenshaw studied aerial photographs of the course taken in 1943. The fairways were comparatively wide and there was no rough. Instead, there were just sandy wastes that led into wooded areas populated by tall pine trees.

Construction staff set about clearing more than 40 acres of Bermuda grass that had provided the rough and then leaving those areas to nature's own devices. This enabled the wasteland to return and wire grass bushes to grow. These could provide a severe penalty if found by errant tee shots. Equally, players could be fortunate and find positions from which they could advance the ball. The element of luck and chance is an integral part of the game and Coore and Crenshaw wanted it to come to the fore with their new design. The upturned saucer greens, designed to repel approaches that lacked precision, remained to maintain one of the signature features of this outstanding course.

The headline news, though, was that the USGA were putting on a US Open with no rough, which represented a massive break from tradition. Officials were thrilled with what they found when they arrived. 'It's awesome,' commented USGA Executive Director Mike Davis. 'I wouldn't call this an inland links, but it's got character. It looks like it's been here for a long time.' The layout was reminiscent of Royal Melbourne, regarded among the very finest championship courses in the world. The youthful Jordan Spieth said: 'I've never played anything like it.'

A more experienced professional, the 2006 US Open winner Geoff Ogilvy, also liked what he saw. The Australian, one of the more cerebral figures on tour, stated: 'These are Melbourne fairways. This is the kind of way grass is supposed to be. In summer it browns up and in winter it's green. To my eye, this is what golf courses are supposed to look like. Hopefully this sets a precedent.'

Each fairway has a line of sprinklers down the middle, leaving the centre portions more lush and accommodating. The edges receive less water and are firmer and harder to hold, making it more likely for an inaccurate ball to run into trouble. It creates a strategic test, as do the run-off areas from the greens where players can choose to pitch, chip or even bunt a three wood or hybrid. Another choice is to putt from the fringes of the greens – Kaymer's favoured method throughout the four-day championship. So the course demanded a variety of techniques and shots which was a refreshing change from the usual one-dimensional diet of US Open golf, where players are left with the one option of gouging the ball out of clinging rough.

These were popular design changes, and ones with the potential to act as a template for other courses where the modern trend of heavy and expensive irrigation produces lush, manicured layouts. Here was another aspect of 2014 that contributed to the feeling of change within the game.

A player who had been a significant part of golf's outgoing era commanded most attention in the build-up to this US Open. Phil Mickelson, who won five majors between 2004 and 2013, was returning to the scene of the first of his six runner-up finishes in America's national championship. In 1999 he was beaten by the flamboyant Payne Stewart, who never had the chance to defend his US Open after losing his life in a plane crash later that year.

Following Mickelson's victory in the 2013 Open at Muirfield, the US Open was now the only major missing from his resumé. Where better for him to complete a career grand slam than at Pinehurst?

The left-hander's recent form had been poor, though. He had been runner-up in his first event of the year in Abu Dhabi but thereafter hadn't posted a top-10 finish on the PGA Tour. He had also had to deal with off-course distractions. The FBI investigated him as part of an enquiry into insider trading on the American stock market. 'I've done nothing wrong,' Mickelson insisted, and the investigation was soon dropped. But it still provided an unsettling backdrop to his quest to complete a career grand slam.

Not that you would have guessed it, given his bullish mood heading into the tournament. 'I hate to put all the pressure on one Open,' he said. 'But Pinehurst is the perfect set-up for me, so I have to think I have a phenomenal chance this year. Kind of reminds me of Muirfield. Touch and chipping and the ability to save par are going to be critical. That's my strength and why I'm excited.'

McIlroy, who had climbed from 11th to sixth in the world rankings during a promising spring, was equally confident. He was reminded of his claim in an earlier BBC interview that he felt winning two majors in the year was within his compass. He was more than happy to stand by those comments. 'I think it's definitely a reasonable goal,' he said on the eve of the championship. 'It doesn't happen that often, but I feel that my game is in a good enough place where I can definitely give myself a chance to do that. I've got three majors left and I do feel like I can contend in all of them.'

It was an upbeat message from a player who had emerged from the trauma of his split with Caroline Wozniacki a month earlier. No longer pre-occupied with wedding plans, he had only one dominant theme in his life. 'Just really enjoying my golf right now,' he said. 'I just want to concentrate on being the best player I can be. I just want to focus on golf. It has been a nice release for me, these past few weeks.'

As it turned out, he wasn't quite ready to take the game by storm. That would come soon enough, though.

Around Pinehurst, McIlroy carded rounds of 71-68-74-73. At least there was no 'Freaky Friday' meltdown in the second round – indeed, it was his best day of the week, but he could only finish on six over par and in a share of 23rd place.

At no time did he contend with the blistering pace set by Kaymer. During the practice days, the par-70 course played fast and firm and the German thought that a score of eight over par might be good enough to win. The USGA, though, feared the course might play too hard. They also had to make sure it didn't burn out, because they were staging the Women's US Open there the following week.

As a result, water was applied to the greens on the eve of the tournament. The greens became a lot more accommodating, the hitting targets more generous and there were more birdie chances. Kaymer, so confident in the swing changes that had brought him the Players' title, needed no second invitation. Just as he did at Sawgrass, he rose to the top of the leaderboard from the outset and was never caught.

In the first round he shot a five-under-par 65. 'Winning the Players' was a big, big relief that now I can start playing good golf again and not have to think too much,' he said. Even so, Kaymer admitted he had surpassed his own expectations on the first day: 'I would never have expected myself to shoot such a low round at Pinehurst.'

Spieth, the youngster who had pushed Kaymer so hard at the Players' Championship, was less surprised. 'I always liked his game. He just plays that high fade and doesn't make many mistakes and he works really hard,' Spieth said. 'He's here early, he's here late and he's been obviously grinding to get back. And he's such a nice guy and such a classy guy; somebody who has offered advice to me and put his arm around me when things weren't necessarily going well at the Players'. You can only root for the guy.'

Spieth's comments came at the end of the second round. By then Kaymer had taken advantage of overnight rain, which had meant the course was again softer and more receptive than expected, and shot a second successive 65. In those 36 holes the German had amassed 11 birdies and just one bogey to move to an imposing 10 under par. Spieth, who opened with creditable scores of 69 and 70 to lie one under, added: 'I've always been a fan of his game, he's back on top right now and playing incredible. I never played on tour when Tiger was doing this, leading by six, seven, eight shots, but I imagine this is what it was like, the way Martin's playing this week.'

Defending champion Justin Rose, who was at one over par after rounds of 72 and 69, added to the praise being heaped on Kaymer's shoulders. 'I've been watching him play and listening to him. He seems very clear and comfortable with what he's doing. So obviously the next two days will really test him and find out how just how comfortable he is, but right now he looks great.'

The odds on the result sought by the vast crowds that tramped through Pinehurst's sandy wastes were lengthening by the moment. Mickelson struggled to a second-round 73 and, at three over par, trailed by a massive 13 strokes. 'I feel like I'm playing well enough to win the US Open, except for putting,' said the American, who was about to celebrate his 44th birthday. 'After I've three-putted three or four times, I kind of lose my focus on the other stuff. It really affects my ability to concentrate. It's a frustrating time, because I feel like the other parts of my game are there.'

Compounding Mickelson's frustration was the fact that he knew there was the opportunity for low scoring. 'Because the greens were receptive, the surface area is double what it would be if they were firm. So we have seen a lot of low scores because of that. But certainly Martin's game is on, he's putting incredibly well, driving it very well, and playing great.'

Kaymer's pair of 65s was arguably the best stretch of 36 holes played by anyone during the 2014 season. Yes, the course was more receptive than expected, but it was still a fearsome test. 'I played with Martin the first two days; he's playing so good,' said Keegan Bradley who shot a pair of 69s. 'I played well, but it was fun watching him hit every fairway, every green and make every putt – it was pretty awesome.'

Kaymer was rather less complimentary of Bradley's idiosyncratic pre-shot routine. In comments that could easily have sparked controversy had they been made in the febrile atmosphere of a Ryder Cup, he said: 'It's not easy to play with Keegan, I must admit that. Because sometimes he takes a little bit more time and sometimes he takes a little bit less time, so it's quite difficult to adjust. But we know that. I've played with Keegan the last few years many times, so we know that his pre-shot routine can change.'

Masters champion Bubba Watson, meanwhile, succumbed to the challenge of the US Open set-up and missed the cut. So did two Englishmen in desperate need of Ryder Cup qualifying points, Luke Donald and Lee Westwood.

Kaymer had set the lowest 36-hole total in US Open history and was six strokes clear of his closest rival, Brendon Todd of the United States. McIlroy, as the runaway winner of the US Open in 2011, advocated a positive mindset for the leader: 'If I was Martin, I would be thinking about how to get seven ahead and then how to get eight ahead and then how to get nine ahead – you've just got to keep the foot to the floor and just keep it going.'

By Saturday, the USGA had clearly had enough of their US Open being ripped apart by such inspired golf. They were helped by the drying conditions, which made the greens harder to hit. But, just to be sure, the pins were tucked away to cut down on the number of birdie opportunities.

As the leader, Kaymer teed off last. Scoring conditions were at their most difficult and he put together a two-over-par 72 which finished with a timely birdie at the last. 'I didn't play as good as the first two days, but I kept it very well together,' Kaymer told TV viewers after emerging from the recorder's hut. 'I felt like, today, if you have 25 feet or 30 feet on every green, you've done well. The USGA put the pins in very, very tough positions. On 18 it was probably the easiest pin today and, fortunately, I could take care of it.'

There were only two sub-par rounds, and they came from

Rickie Fowler and the extraordinary Erik Compton. They both shot 67 and it was inevitable that Compton, the recipient of two heart transplants, stole the headlines. He was an inspirational figure who had come through qualifying. Ahead of claiming his place in the US Open, Compton played the Memorial tournament where he was another of Jack Nicklaus's lunch companions.

'There's different characters of the game that I feel like I've gained strength from and it's nice to have the greats take an interest in me because of my story,' Compton said. 'It just goes to show you what great characters we have in the game. They know that people's backgrounds and life stories are more important than just golf. Jack, at Muirfield, he had a look in his eye and you know how he is; he sometimes is very dry. He said that if I got here, I would have a special week. So maybe it's just kind of a self-fulfilling thing that I brought on myself. But I felt like I was going to have a great week.'

Compton and Fowler moved into a share of second place at three under par, but still five strokes behind.

Kaymer had watched the film *The Legend of Bagger Vance* the night before. The player found a way to draw on the message of the Robert Redford-directed movie. It is a story of a down-and-out golfer's attempt to recover both his game and his life with the help of a mystical caddie. 'I watched Bagger Vance and he said: "At the end of the day, we're playing a game." And that is what we're doing. We can't control a lot of things that happen on the golf course. You have to play the game.'

Kaymer admitted that, for someone who is instinctively a control freak – 'I think a lot of Germans are' – such a mindset doesn't come easy. 'You have to create that feel, and trust your skill and all the work. And today, when I was standing on 18, that's a tough tee shot. It's very difficult to see any fairway from the back tee. So you stand there and, for me, it was such an enjoyable shot, because I knew exactly where I wanted to aim and I thought: "What a great position this is now." '

'You are seven under par at the US Open, playing your third round. It's the final hole, it would be nice to finish it off with a birdie. If I hit the fairway, it's a tougher shot to play. But if you can pull it off, you gain some confidence. So it was a very, very nice thing. And it's about that feel, that touch, that you play with your heart, that you can't control too many things and that's what I was trying to do the last three years. Now I just play.

'Obviously, the way I play golf right now, I shouldn't think too much about technique. I'm very happy the way I hit the ball. I can hit any shot whenever I need it. So it would only be distracting myself from focusing on the main thing if I focus too much on the technique.'

There was no doubt that he was reaping the rewards of his dedicated practice regime – and of his new way of thinking. Kaymer was 18 holes away from collecting his second major title. 'I don't need to set any goals,' he said. 'If you set goals, then you're adding a little pressure again because you try to reach them instead of going out there and being neutral. Just play.'

In the way that Nicklaus has acted as a mentor for Compton and McIlroy, so Bernhard Langer provides guidance and inspiration to his younger compatriot. The 57-year-old two-times Masters champion finished in a remarkable share of eighth place at Augusta and when he won the British Senior's Open later in 2014 by 13 strokes, the veteran even provoked talk of earning a wildcard pick for Gleneagles. McGinley quickly dispelled that notion, however, saying he should and would only pick players from the main tours. But Langer was still an influential figure, and never more so than during the week of his young protégé's US Open victory.

'Bernhard sent me very nice texts. He's following the golf, even though he's not playing this week,' Kaymer revealed. 'I think he's on a family vacation. So just hearing something from him, obviously it gives you a lot of confidence and it's really nice of him. He doesn't have to do that, but he takes the time to send out a text and it does push me a little bit.

'I want to achieve similar things that he has achieved in his career, even though it's very difficult to win at Augusta, to be the Ryder Cup captain, to play the Ryder Cup a few times. But it's nice if somebody is trying to help and he's obviously always there. If I need something, if I struggle with certain things, I can always call him.'

The next communication between the two Germans would be a simple but hearty congratulations. Kaymer completed a brilliant week with a 69 to finish at nine under par. Compton and Fowler were round in 72s and shared second place, eight strokes behind. They were the only other players to break par in a championship utterly dominated by the 29-year-old from Düsseldorf.

His national football team kicked off their World Cup campaign the following day. Kaymer is a big soccer fan and had been exchanging texts with members of the German squad. The golfer had set an inspirational tone with his Pinehurst performance. A month later, Germany's footballers duly lifted the World Cup in Rio de Janeiro.

Kaymer's total of 271 was the second-lowest in US Open history, beaten only by McIlroy's 268 at Congressional in 2011. His margin of victory was the fourth largest in the 129-year history of the championship. He was only the eighth man to win the tournament leading from start to finish. And all this within a month of doing the same at the Players' Championship, which he admitted had provided valuable experience to help him claim his second major title.

'It's very, very exhausting. It's very tiring because you have to speak a lot. You have to do a lot of interviews,' he said. 'You have to answer a lot of questions. And people bring thoughts into your head. So it's very difficult to handle all that from the first day. Sometimes, on moving day, when you move forward and you're in the lead, then you start answering those questions. But I needed to do that at the Players' on the Thursday and this week on the first day as well. The main thing is that you always try to stay calm and really try to challenge yourself and play against the golf course and not too much against the other players.'

It was one of the greatest performances seen in major championship history, and one that he could trace back to the Ryder Cup at Medinah.

In 2012, he had been seriously out of form. He played poorly with Rose to lose 3 and 2 to Dustin Johnson and Matt Kuchar in the Friday afternoon fourballs, redoubling Kaymer's determination to make a contribution in the singles. At the end of the contest, he found himself holing the putt that retained the trophy for Europe.

For Kaymer, it was hugely significant, that victory and that one moment representing so much more than it may have seemed. 'People don't realise that a moment like that can change a career,' Kaymer said. 'If I'd have missed, it could have broken me as an athlete. I didn't think about that as I stood over that putt but I think it is now important to understand both sides. I experienced a positive but what would have happened if I had experienced a negative? Medinah made a very big difference to me in terms of confidence and knowing that I could make these important putts when it really mattered.'

The outcome at Pinehurst made it 1–1 between Europe and the Americans in terms of majors won in 2014. Stenson finished in a share of fourth place at one over par on a leaderboard that was otherwise dominated by US players.

Compton's share of second was the big news, given his back-story of how he had received new hearts, at the age of nine and then again in 2008 when he drove himself to hospital after suffering a heart attack. 'I told everybody I would be a Major League baseball player at age eight. And I was serious about it,' said the 34-year-old from Miami. 'Even when I got wheeled out of the operating room, and they have it on camera, I said I would still be a professional baseball player. My parents have always done a really great job of pushing me to be a normal kid and a normal child. Sports was something that I lived for and something that they pushed me to do.

'My mom summed it up pretty well. She said Erik's a golfer with two transplants, not a transplant recipient that plays golf,' Compton added. 'I'm just so thrilled to be here and playing at this level. I finally had that feeling of putting myself on the map. And now I've just got to keep going out and trying my best. But I don't have anything to really prove to anybody anymore. If I never played golf again for the rest of my life, I think that I have made my mark in this game.'

For Fowler, who made his Ryder Cup debut as a 21-year-old wildcard at Celtic Manor in 2010, playing in the final pairing on a Sunday at a major for the first time was a big step forward. He was showing significant signs that his game is made for the big occasion. 'The goals going into the year were to get ready for Augusta and then contend at majors,' Fowler said. 'Finishing tied for fifth and tied second in the first two majors of the year, I'm definitely pleased about that and looking forward to the next two.

'I felt really comfortable, which is a very good thing. The more experience you can get in the final groups, and especially in majors and in contention at majors, it definitely helps out for down the road.'

The result propelled Fowler towards a return to the US Ryder Cup team. Bradley, meanwhile, expressed what qualifying for the side means to this generation of Americans. He was in the group sharing fourth place. 'You know that a major is double points. I know that I've got to make a move,' he said. 'I know that Captain Watson is watching. This is big for me, because I want to be on that team, first and foremost.'

Bradley added: 'I was so nervous coming down the stretch because there were so many Ryder Cup points on the line. I was thinking about it and it was a battle for me because of how badly I want to be on that team. I wasn't worried about the money or the placing. All that mattered were those Ryder Cup points.'

Europe, in the shape of the magnificent Kaymer, had won America's national championship. But several of their stalwarts failed to make much of a mark. Ten of the top-16 finishers were from the United States. Meanwhile Poulter, Westwood and McDowell remained outside the top nine automatic qualifiers.

'I have talked a lot over the last few years of form being important and that now begins in earnest,' noted McGinley. 'It probably started at the BMW PGA Championship at Wentworth and will run until the FedEx Cup, on the PGA Tour, and the Italian Open, on the European. This is the window where I will consider "form" and the opportunities are there for the players.'

Kaymer had already taken that chance with two massive wins, but even his achievements were about to be dwarfed by a fellow European, who was on the verge of lighting up that window with a brilliance that stunned the golfing world.

CHAPTER 12

The Open

'If Phil and Tiger don't make it in the mix there, I've got some real thinking to do. Everybody is thinking that I'm going to pick them automatically. I can assure you that I'm not going to pick them automatically.'

Tom Watson

R ory McIlroy's time was about to come. It was almost the moment for him to become the world's dominant golfer. With two majors played in 2014, that role still belonged to Tiger Woods, even though he hadn't taken part in either the Masters or US Open. This all-time great might have been toppled from the pinnacle of the world rankings, but he was still the man who generated the biggest buzz.

Golf witnessed command performances in the first two majors from Bubba Watson and Martin Kaymer, yet they were seen by relatively few people – television audiences had plummeted in the US and UK because of Woods' absence. Now, though, he was on the comeback trail. The general sports enthusiast was interested in golf once more, intrigued by the big questions posed by Woods' return. What would it mean for the remaining majors – the Open and the PGA Championship – and what were the implications for the American Ryder Cup team?

Recovery had been a slow and painful process. For Woods, this was the worst of many injury problems in 18 years as a professional. 'I wasn't able to function,' he revealed. 'I couldn't get out of bed. I just couldn't do any normal activities. When I blew out my knee and even had my Achilles problems, I could still do things. I would still be able to function. This was different.

'Anyone that's had any kind of nerve impingement, it's no joke. That part was relieved as soon as I got out of the surgery. The pain that I was feeling going down my leg was gone. I've heard numerous people talk about it, and I've had people come up to me and say they had the same procedure and got their life back. That's basically how I felt. I was able to do things, and do things that I had previously taken for granted.'

Hitting full golf shots was still some way off following his 31 March operation, but Woods was allowed to putt almost as soon as the anaesthetic had worn off. He took a novel approach in the back yard of his mansion in Jupiter, Florida, by filling the holes on his putting green with sand: 'I wasn't allowed to bend over and pick the balls out of the holes,' he said. 'So I knew if the putt went in or not, but I never had to bend over. We did that for a couple of months. Then it was chipping and pitching. And then we added, basically about 10 yards every day or two, depending on how I felt and how much inflammation was in the area.

'That's how it went, to the point where I was out there hitting drivers a couple weeks ago,' Woods told reporters on 24 June, a couple of days ahead of his comeback event, the Quicken Loans National at Congressional, near Washington DC.

'And then I started playing golf. I wanted to knock off a little bit of rust on the range before I actually went out there and tried not to embarrass myself on the golf course, and I was able to do that. Got some holes in. Started feeling comfortable doing that. I think anyone who has had this procedure knows that probably the worst thing you can do is sit, and sitting in a golf cart wasn't the most ideal circumstance.

'So sometimes I would ride on the back of a cart like Freddie [Couples, who has a history of back trouble] does sometimes. I was able to do that a few times, and I was able to get in more holes because of that.'

Woods' charitable foundation supports the National tournament, so he had an extra incentive to make his return at Congressional. 'I'm actually a bit ahead of schedule,' Woods said. 'I've had great trainers and physios help me every day with soft tissue work; the cold baths were no fun but you've got to do it. When you get treatment all the time, it's amazing what you can do. Also, nutritionally, making sure I eat perfect – anti-inflammatory meals, all the different things I needed to do to get back.'

Woods is fascinated by athletes from other sports, and this helped him cope with the demands of a speedy recovery. 'It's a normality in other sports,' he said. 'If you play football or hockey or any other sport, this is just common. But I think in the golfing world, looking at most of the physiques, it's not really that common. But having friends who are in other sports, it does help, what they have done and what their protocols are for their teams.'

The golfer he could relate to most was PGA Tour player Graham DeLaet, who had undergone a similar procedure in 2011. The Canadian tried to come back after six months' recuperation and stopped playing again after only two tournaments because he lacked the power and strength required to escape from rough or hit from difficult lies. 'I thought I would be out for three months and in the end it took almost a year,' said DeLaet.

The 38-year-old Woods returned to competitive action within 87 days of going under the knife. It was a remarkably speedy comeback – one that could either add to his aura or wreck his hopes of making the US Ryder Cup team.

Rounds of 74 and 75 revealed a predictable level of rust and it was no surprise that he found himself three strokes on the wrong side of the cut-line in Washington. The good news was that he suffered no adverse reaction and would take his place in the field at the Open Championship, at the Royal Liverpool club in Hoylake, the following month.

By that time, Justin Rose had recorded back-to-back victories. The Englishman, who had waited just over a year since his last win, at the 2013 US Open, edged home in a play-off against Texan Shawn Stefani at Woods' National event. Rose then claimed the Aberdeen Asset Management Scottish Open title at Royal Aberdeen.

He was delighted with the resulting boost to his Ryder Cup qualifying points, commenting: 'It probably takes that off my mind. So yeah, it's a really nice time of year to have a victory and allows me to focus on the exciting challenges now ahead.'

The first of those was to try to make it a hat-trick of victories by claiming the Open. 'I don't feel these wins have taken a lot out of me in the last couple of weeks,' Rose said, while clutching the latest trophy to add to an ever more impressive collection. 'I will enjoy this moment and then, as of tomorrow, my mind will be on the job in hand.'

As it turned out, his bid for a first Open and a second major foundered through the misfortune of being on the wrong side of the draw at Hoylake. He and world number one Adam Scott were sent out on a breezy Thursday afternoon and then a tricky Friday morning, and both struggled to keep pace with those who benefited from more favourable tee times. Rose managed rounds of 72 and 70, including chip-ins at the ninth and 10th holes, while Scott went 68 and 73.

Woods was in the luckier half and it was a big week for him; his first major in almost a year. With just 36 competitive holes played since his surgery, logic suggested it was unrealistic for him to challenge for the title. He would do well to make the cut. Woods had other ideas, though. They were fuelled by his need to preserve his old aura of invincibility. So he set about shifting the dynamics during his pre-championship news conference, two days before tee off.

This was typical Woods, trying to recreate the vibe that was always so apparent when he dominated the game. This sense of invincibility had been generated by his record-breaking rampage through the game as he collected 14 majors between 1997 and 2008. Since then, though, he has been revealed as a serial adulterer, been to rehab, divorced by the mother of his two children and suffered a string of debilitating injuries. He had split with coach Hank Haney, who guided him to his last six major titles, as well as Steve Williams, the caddie who was his faithful assistant for all but the first of his successes in the majors.

None of this is referenced by Woods these days. He is like a politician who studiously avoids talk of failed, abandoned policies. He carefully selects his facts to present the most positive spin, presumably in the hope that it intimidates the opposition. It worked when he had the game to fuel the words. As veteran commentator Johnny Miller once said: 'If you are in the final group with Tiger Woods, it doesn't matter how big a lead you might have, he is the sun and you are butter.' Those days were gone.

Woods' press conferences can be tedious affairs. He talks in the jargon of a golfing geek and skilfully avoids subjects with which he doesn't want to engage. Nevertheless, he always attracts the biggest audiences. There is an ongoing fascination with someone who remains one of the most significant sporting figures of the 21st century.

On the Tuesday morning before the Open Championship at Royal Liverpool, it was standing room only in the interview tent annexed to the vast media centre marquee. Somehow Woods put forward a persuasive argument that he had a decent chance of winning at the same venue where he claimed his most recent Open, back in 2006.

When I asked whether he had considered that the Open Championship had gone around its full rota of venues without him winning again, he batted away the question. 'Not until now,' he smiled, encouraging an ever-willing audience of hacks to laugh with him at the impudence of the suggestion.

'So what do you think?' I asked.

'What do I think? I wish I could have added a few more. I'm at three and hopefully I will get more.'

It was classic Woods, trying to generate a positive thought to deflect a negative fact. Moments before, he had an exchange with the *Mirror*'s Neil McLeman.

McLeman: 'Given your limited preparation coming in here, what would be an acceptable finish for you this weekend?'
Woods: 'First.'

People laughed, but Woods didn't. He just stared at his questioner.

McLeman: 'Anything less than that would be unacceptable?'
Woods: 'Yeah.'

Only Woods could say such a thing. Was he trying to dupe the media or was he just deluding himself? He was certainly trying to send the message that Tiger Woods was back and ready to win again. He added: 'I've been in circumstances like this before. If you remember in 2008 I had knee surgery right after the Masters. I teed it up at the US Open and won a US Open. I didn't play more than nine holes and the Sunday before the US Open I didn't break 50 for nine holes and I was still able to win it in a play-off, with a torn ACL [anterior cruciate ligament] and a broken leg. I've proven I can do it, it's just a matter of putting my game together and giving myself the best chances this week.'

Tom Watson had been asked about Woods' chances of making his Gleneagles team. 'If he's playing well and he's healthy, I will pick him,' the US captain said. 'I'll be watching Tiger and I want him on the team. I do. He's a tough competitor and he'd be great in the team room. Wouldn't you want him on your team?'

In a BBC Radio interview, Watson expanded on this, saying that he was hopeful Woods would do enough at the Open, the WGC Bridgestone Invitational and PGA to make it into the FedEx Cup play-offs. 'That would allow him to play four more tournaments,' Watson told me. 'You know, after being off for three months, you want to get back playing in competition and I fully expect him to play well enough to get into the FedEx Cup. That would help me a lot in being able to pick Tiger.'

Watson seemed oblivious to the fact that Woods had only been on one winning Ryder Cup team, way back in 1999. He'd been injured the last time America won the trophy in 2008. When this was pointed out, Watson simply reiterated: 'As I say, who wouldn't want him on the team? I don't know any Americans who wouldn't want him on the team.' And so, without a ball being struck, the legend of Tiger Woods was being revived ahead of the Open.

McIlroy, meanwhile, was wondering if he could finally convert his promising golf into actual silverware. Twelve months earlier, the Northern Irishman had been a lost soul. He had crashed out at the halfway stage of the Muirfield Open, apparently confused by his new Nike equipment and overwhelmed by legal difficulties following an acrimonious split from his management company. He said he felt 'brain dead' as he slunk away from the Scottish links. A year on, he was a different person.

'Jeez, a lot's happened in 12 months, that's for sure,' he said. 'Coming away from this championship last year wasn't one of my best weeks on the course and I was just really disappointed because it was the first time I hadn't played the weekend of an Open. That hurt. That really did hurt and I'll try not to be in the same position this year.

'I'm happy to be at Hoylake, it's a fantastic golf course and a really good set-up. I don't think it will be as much of a grind as some Opens are. It gives you opportunities to make birdies so hopefully I can go out there and make a few.'

The big question was how he would fare on the Friday. Those days had continued in their 'freaky' vein at the Scottish Open, where he shot a 78 to follow his opening 64. At Memorial, he had gone 63–78, The Players 70–74, Quail Hollow 69–76 and the Masters 71–77.

'The elephant in the room?' McIlroy laughed. 'Look, it's something that's just been made bigger than it is and I think I've made it bigger than what it actually is. Fingers crossed, I get off to a good start and then I want to go out on Friday and try and keep the momentum going.' It was evident, though, that the malaise of failing to back up fine starts was preying on his mind: 'You know, it's almost at the point now where I'd like to have an average first day and then I can sort of back it up with a better second day, but if I go out and shoot a good score on Thursday morning, I will be trying to go out on Friday and do the same thing.'

And that is precisely what he did: 18 July 2014 officially marked the end of 'Freaky Fridays' from the McIlroy CV. The scene seemed set for a repeat after a brilliant 66 on the first morning of the championship, but McIlroy held firm this time, sticking to the two key words he had vowed to focus on all week – 'process' and 'spot'. The 'process' of a good golf swing and the 'spot' he would seek to roll his putts over, en route to the hole.

After that excellent start, McIlroy had Thursday afternoon and Friday morning to brood over a second round that was certain to come under intense scrutiny, not just from the media but from the player himself. And the omens weren't promising when he bogeyed the first. He looked much more settled, however after birdies at the fifth, sixth, and the eighth hole, where a pheasant crossed his path wandering across the green. Birdies of all persuasions were populating McIlroy's performance. Making the most of the calmest conditions of the day, he added four more to his scorecard on the inward half, including a pair at the closing two holes for a second successive 66.

At the halfway stage he was four clear of Dustin Johnson, who fired a second-round 65.

'I saw that it was a little trickier today with the wind being up,' McIlroy said. 'It seemed like the guys out earlier were struggling to make many birdies. Starting off, I was just trying to keep steady and solid and I knew I would have some chances on the par fives. So, even though I started a little shaky with that bogey on the first, I was still pretty confident.'

And he had at last curtailed the media's obsession with his Friday failures. 'It's understandable. People ask you. My second rounds this year have been terrible. And there isn't really any explanation. But hopefully I put it to bed today.'

By contrast, Woods failed to prove that he was ready to compete at the highest level. He began encouragingly, recovering from early bogeys to card a first-round 69, but on the Friday afternoon he was poor. His round started double bogey, bogey and he went out of bounds on 17 en route to a 77. Woods needed to hole a seven-footer to birdie the par-five last and make the cut on the mark at two over par.

Change was in the air. It felt as though the tectonic plates of the game were making a significant shift from the US superstar to his European successor. In apparent empathy with this re-ordering of world golf, officials from the R&A were meeting to decide an unprecedented move of their own. Violent, intense storms were forecast for the third round. Chief Executive Peter Dawson and Executive Director of Championships Johnnie Cole-Hamilton were determined that the Open should not overrun. So, for the first time, they decided to send off the players from two tees.

'Play will be in groups of three and we will utilise a two-tee start, using the first and 10th tees,' explained the R&A's Head of Rules David Rickman. 'These measures give us the potential to accommodate up to five hours of delay and still complete the third round tomorrow evening. All the professional advice that we are receiving tells us that significant disruption is highly likely and it's only responsible of us to react appropriate to that.'

It meant that McIlroy would tee off at 11.01 a.m., alongside his closest rivals Johnson and Francesco Molinari. By quirk of fate, Woods began his round at exactly the same time. Woods, though, was banished to the inward nine holes for the first half of his round, along with the rest of the backmarkers. The R&A were using the 'U-shaped draw' employed by all the leading tours in such circumstances. Having the worst scorers starting at the same time as the leaders means there is a smaller gap in tee times for those in the middle of the field on similar scores. This is deemed the fairest way to proceed. Conspiracy theorists mistakenly thought that it was a ploy to allow Woods to share the same television airtime as the leaders.

This change of approach was not only unprecedented, it was also potentially controversial. To win the Open, you are meant to deal with everything that chance and the elements can throw at you. On this occasion, the players competed in damp yet benign conditions, that July Saturday. The round was over at 3.47 p.m. and McIlroy was in the interview room by the time the hostile weather struck. The rain pounded the canvas covering the media centre so hard he could barely be heard above the noise. 'This is the second-best decision the R&A has made this year. The first was taking the Open to Portrush,' said McIlroy, referring to the governing body's plan of taking a future championship back to Northern Ireland.

Had the R&A stuck with the original Hoylake timetable, the leaders would have been on the third or fourth hole as the storm broke. They would have needed to battle through the most difficult weather of the week, like Ernie Els did on the Saturday in 2002 when he won the Open at Muirfield. Play might have been suspended for a while, but the round would have been completed by Saturday night. McIlroy was spared this test and it was undoubtedly a fairer scenario for all concerned. But who said golf should be fair? That was a question posed by critics of the decision.

McIlroy took full advantage, especially when the clouds started to muster towards the end of his round, which he finished in breathtaking fashion.

Throughout the week he spoke of making the most of the par fives. This is exactly what Woods, as the longest driver in golf, did when he was at the top of his game. That mantle now belonged to McIlroy. He led the driving statistics at Hoylake by averaging 327.8 yards off the tee. The Royal Liverpool course is unique among Open venues in that it finishes with two par fives in its last three holes. This creates the prospect of rapid changes in leaderboards, as McIlroy was about to demonstrate.

He had completed the first 12 in a relatively lacklustre level par. Up ahead, Rickie Fowler was again demonstrating his taste for big-time golf, reeling off seven birdies to join McIlroy at the top of the leaderboard. It was time for the overnight leader to reassert his authority.

At the 14th, he was fortunate to get a read on a lengthy birdie putt from Johnson's even longer attempt. McIlroy saw that the ball initially moved right to left, then turned the opposite way at the end of its journey. He picked a spot that allowed for both breaks. His sole aim was to roll his ball over that point on the green. His ball duly dropped into the hole for only the third birdie of his round. It was the timing of a champion – again one of the hallmarks of Woods in his pomp.

Back in sole possession of the lead, McIlroy dispatched a mammoth drive down the centre of a generous fairway at the 16th. In the distance, he could see a packed grandstand ready to greet his approach. He belted a four iron 252 yards and the ball came to rest 20 feet from the flag. It was a moment to be seized and McIlroy was in the mood. He rolled in the putt, seemingly effortlessly, for the only eagle to be recorded on that hole all day. McIlroy then dropped a shot at the 17th while, up ahead, Fowler was holing out for a birdie and a round of 68. The young American trailed by four strokes. But the leader still had the last to play.

The closing hole at Royal Liverpool is a dangerous drive, with out of bounds creeping in from the right and bunkers down the left marking the point at which the par five doglegs right. McIlroy was fearless in firing his drive between both hazards. It was imperious golf, elevating him above the rest of his competitors. He had 239 yards to the pin – a five iron. The safe play was to aim to the right of the flag, but McIlroy was so pumped with confidence that he flew it straight at the hole. It rolled up to 11 feet. He strode onto the home green to tumultuous applause. Walking alongside, I commentated for BBC 5Live, unable to hear the words I was yelling to try to convey the moment.

McIlroy was certainly in no mood for an anticlimactic finish. He looked at his putt from every angle before coaxing it home. As the roars went up – it was the day's first eagle on the 18th as well – he greeted the moment with the gentlest of fist pumps. McIlroy appeared so loose and confident in producing two eagles in the last three holes, both born of golfing perfection. They had seemed so inevitable in their execution. The word 'Tigeresque' started to trend.

Earlier that afternoon, with six holes to play, McIlroy had been caught at the top of the leaderboard. Now he led by six shots, heading into the final day. 'This is the third night in a row that I'll sleep on the lead,' McIlroy commented. 'So I'm comfortable. It helps that I've been in this position before and I've been able to convert and I've been able to get the job done.

'I knew that Rickie was playing well in front. I didn't know how well. I saw on 12 that he got to within one of me, and then I bogeyed the hole and then it was tied,' McIlroy said. 'But I never panicked. I knew that I had some holes coming up that I could take advantage of and make some birdies on the way in. I just wanted to try and be as much ahead as I possibly could.

And that's why I was grinding over the putt at the last, just to try and finish the round off well. I felt like those two shots into 18 deserved an eagle.'

It was an audacious finish, leaving the 25-year-old on the threshold of his third major. He allowed himself to contemplate moving three-quarters of the way to a career grand slam, but this wasn't someone getting ahead of himself. This was someone who knew his elevated place in the game, who was undaunted by the magnitude of what he was about to achieve.

The next afternoon, McIlroy began with intent, birdieing the first to move seven strokes clear of Fowler. It looked like being a procession, with the record books providing the only opposition. Fowler and Sergio García, however, had other ideas and the leader was made to work for his title. His two previous majors – the 2011 US Open and the PGA in 2012 – had both been won by eight strokes. This time McIlroy needed to demonstrate resilience.

García went to the turn in three under par while a more hesitant McIlroy dropped shots at the fifth and sixth. His lead narrowed from seven to three shots and the pressure was on.

The pacesetter responded by holing from 15 feet for a birdie at the ninth, but up ahead the Spaniard knocked in an eight-footer for eagle. He was now within two strokes and this was turning into a vintage Open Sunday. As McIlroy climbed up to the par-five 10th green, García was departing the next tee. He threw a sideways glance to his right, to see how the man at the top of the standings was faring. The leader was in decent shape and coolly made a vital birdie.

García rode his luck when his wild approach to the 12th bounced off a grandstand to the edge of the green before McIlroy's poor tee shot at the 13th led to another bogey. There was a freshening breeze and plenty of tension in the air.

Crucially, though, García was too cute with his bunker shot at the par-three 15th and that dropped shot allowed McIlroy room to breathe on the home stretch. He sent out another monstrous drive down the 16th, before pointing out a heckler who had been trying to distract him all the way round. That drive set up the birdie that took him back to three strokes clear with two holes to play.

García went on to complete a brilliant 66 and shared second place with Fowler, who was round in 67 for a second consecutive major runner-up finish.

And so, after a tortuous, stressful and ultimately glorious afternoon, McIlroy was able to par in for a 71 to finish at 17 under and claim his first Open. It had been a performance of breathtaking brilliance that took full advantage of a favourable draw and the unprecedented rescheduling of the third round. He became the first European to win three of the four majors.

At 25, he had achieved something that had eluded the most revered figures of the continental game such as Sir Nick Faldo and Seve Ballesteros. Only Nicklaus and Woods had realised the feat at a younger age. McIlroy was again putting his name next to the greatest figures in the history of golf. His father, Gerry, was also £100,000 better off, thanks to a £20 bet he had put on his son to win the Open before he turned 26. The bet was struck a decade earlier, at odds of 500–1.

'I never dreamed of being at this point in my career so quickly,' McIlroy reflected. 'The Open Championship was the one you really wanted, growing up, and the one you holed so many putts on the putting green to win; to beat Tiger Woods, Sergio García, Ernie Els, whatever. I didn't quite need to hole a putt to do it, just a little tap-in, which was nice. The more I keep looking at this trophy and seeing my name on it, the more it will start to sink in.'

García's spirited charge was arguably the best major performance of his career. Still the Spaniard waits to win one of the biggest titles, but he showed a growing maturity in 2014 that suggested he would be one of the wisest heads in the European team room at Gleneagles.

Fowler had, once again, saved his best golf for the major stage. He came up two strokes short despite four rounds in the 60s and a 15-under-par total. There was, though, significant consolation.

'Going into the year, the goal was to be in contention at majors and play well and have chances to win,' he said. 'And with the good play, the long-distance goal was to be on the Ryder Cup team. With the way I've played in the majors this year, that's definitely what has given me the opportunity to represent the country and play in the Ryder Cup.' His major finishes now read: fifth, second and second.

Tom Watson was thrilled to have such an effervescent force in his team. 'I like Rickie. I like his attitude,' he said. 'He's playing well. He's about ready to run the table. Working with Butch Harmon, I think, has given him a good lift, taken some of the pressure off. Made life a little lighter. When you're playing well, life is good. Rickie is at that stage right now.'

Veteran Jim Furyk closed with a 65 for fourth place, which solidified the 44-year-old's Ryder Cup place, and ensured a continued unbroken run of representing his country in the event that stretches back to 1997. After the heartbreak of Medinah, where he let slip a late lead to García in a pivotal singles, Furyk was able to contemplate another crack at Europe.

But would the game's biggest name be there with him?

Woods completed an indifferent week with a closing 75 to finish six over par in a share of 69th place. He was beaten by 18 places by the 64-year-old American captain, Watson himself, who finished with a superb 68. To add perspective, Woods ended up 23 shots behind McIlroy. The game was moving on, and an increasingly desperate-sounding ex-champion was being left behind.

If Woods were Watson, would he pick himself for the Ryder Cup? 'I would say yes. But that's my position, my take on it,' Woods said after emerging from the Hoylake recorder's hut. 'Obviously it's his decision. He's going to field the best 12 players that he thinks will win the Cup back and I hope I'm on that team.'

With typical bravado, Woods deflected a question over whether he might consider playing outside the US to prove form and fitness ahead of the Ryder Cup if he failed to qualify for the FedEx Cup series. 'Well, I'd like to win the next two tournaments I'm in. That should take care of it,' he said. Only Woods could talk so positively of his chances at a WGC and then the PGA Championship after such a chastening week.

'I got picked by Corey (Pavin) when we played in Wales in 2010. I was coming off an injury as well there with my Achilles, and I'd sat out for most of the summer. And I felt like I was able to contribute to the team,' he added.

With one major to go, Watson was looking at a qualifying table that didn't include either Woods or Mickelson, the two greatest names of 21st century golf. 'If Phil and Tiger don't make it in the mix there, I've got some real thinking to do,' Watson admitted. 'Everybody is thinking that I'm going to pick them automatically. I can assure you that I'm not going to pick them automatically. I said about Tiger that I'll pick him if he's playing well and he's in good health. And Phil is the same.'

McGinley also had concerns, centered around stalwarts of past Ryder Cup glories. Ian Poulter missed the cut in a Championship where he had previously excelled and Lee Westwood also crashed out at the halfway stage. Luke Donald finished in a lowly tie for 64th and was showing little sign of the form the skipper would need at Gleneagles.

On the other hand, Europe's leader – who spent Open week grabbing a short family holiday in Portugal – knew that his team would contain the man who had now made himself the hottest property in golf. What was not yet apparent was just how blisteringly hot the phenomenon that is Rory McIlroy was about to become.

CHAPTER 13

The PGA

'He's a talisman; you know he's always going
to raise himself coming into a Ryder Cup . . .
he knows he's going to be the man with the "X"
on his back; the American players will relish
playing against him. But if anyone is ready
for that challenge it'll be Ian Poulter.'
Paul McGinley

For most players, landing a major is a crowning moment, especially an Open, the oldest and most revered prize in the game. It is an exclamation mark to be celebrated long and hard. In Rory McIlroy's case, it was no more than a semi-colon; a brief pause in the narrative of an astonishing season.

His head had long since cleared in the wake of his split from Caroline Wozniacki, his appetite for golf had never been higher and his game had never been better. There was no way he wanted the momentum generated by his thrilling, accomplished victory in the 143rd Open Championship to grind to a halt. He wanted to avoid the temptation of believing that the job had been completed. This hunger for more trophies was another indicator that he was reaching the levels of Tiger Woods at his best.

Victories are exhausting, especially the big ones that form an indelible mark on the history of the game. McIlroy knew he should celebrate his Hoylake triumph but also that he needed to move on quickly. This would enable him to tap into the driving perfection and putting prowess that was rapidly taking him to golf's summit. He had a couple of nights of raucous celebration with friends and family back home in Belfast but, as soon as he washed the dregs of Jägermeister from the famous Claret Jug, it was time to focus on achieving more glory. He wanted to live up to his claim that winning two major victories in one year was within his compass. And he fancied landing his first World Golf Championships title along the way.

Those goals were achieved in a tumultuous spell of 34 days during which McIlroy took control of the golfing globe. At the same time, both Ryder Cup captains applied the finishing touches to their teams. Between 31 July and 2 September, golf was rarely off the sports news agenda. The game generated banner headlines almost every day. There was intrigue, drama, controversy and some of the best and most thrilling play witnessed in years. The barren times earlier in the year, when golf struggled for relevance, when McIlroy bemoaned the lack of emerging champions and when the Woods injury saga provided the only consistently compelling storyline, faded fast from the memory.

Woods' attempts to recover from his back surgery and force his way into Ryder Cup reckoning was also building to a crescendo. But it was the struggles of another troubled American that captured most attention when the sport's entourage headed to Akron, Ohio, at the end of July.

The Firestone Country Club was the home of the WGC Bridgestone Invitational, a tournament where Woods was defending champion and had won on no fewer than eight occasions. Some players took the previous week off to recover from the exertions of trying to halt McIlroy at Hoylake. Others went to the Canadian Open, where the South African Tim Clark shot a final-round 65 to overtake Jim Furyk, who failed again to convert a third-round lead into victory.

Dustin Johnson, one of the stand-out performers for the US at the 2012 Ryder Cup, also played in Canada. The big hitter went there after a fine effort at the Open where he accompanied McIlroy in the third round before finishing in a share of 12th. His momentum came to an abrupt end at Royal Montreal, though. He shot 74–68 to miss the halfway cut and it soon became apparent his season was over.

Rumours spread across the range at Firestone the following week as players, caddies, coaches and journalists swapped gossip over the nature of Johnson's absence from the field. While the first round of the WGC event was being played, he issued a statement that posed as many questions as it answered. 'I am taking a leave of absence from professional golf, effective immediately,' Johnson said. 'I will use this time to seek professional help for personal challenges I have faced. By committing the time and resources necessary to improve my mental health, physical well-being and emotional foundation, I am confident that I will be better equipped to fulfil my potential and become a consistent champion. I respectfully ask my fans, well-wishers and the media for privacy as I embark upon this mission of self-improvement.'

It wasn't clear whether Johnson had been instructed by the PGA Tour to take his 'leave of absence' or whether it was voluntary. The Tour were in no mood to clarify the situation and issued a brief missive: 'We have nothing to add to Dustin's statement, but we wish him well and look forward to his return to the PGA Tour in the future.'

The player's agent, David Winkle of Hambric Sports Management, informed the PGA of America that Johnson would not appear at the following week's PGA Championship and would not take part in the Ryder Cup. Having won the WGC HSBC Champions tournament in Shanghai at the start of the year and with six other top-10s, the 30-year-old lay fifth in the qualifying table and had been regarded as a certainty for Gleneagles.

'We will certainly miss Dustin Johnson at Gleneagles,' Tom

Watson said. 'We wish him the best. As one of the longest hitters in the game with an undefeated record of 3-and-0 at Medinah in 2012, he has clearly been an asset for the United States team.' Watson later went further, with a nod to the battle against alcohol abuse that he had endured. 'I understand a little bit of what he is going through, frankly, and I want him to get well. I think that's the most important thing he needs to deal with right now.'

Within a day of the news breaking, allegations were published on an American website quoting an unnamed source. It reported that Johnson had been banned by the PGA Tour for failing a test for recreational drugs. The Tour refuses to publish details of punishments it imposes except where performance-enhancing substances are involved. It is a stance aimed at protecting the interests of players and covers all disciplinary matters, ranging from issues like slow play to audible obscenities picked up by microphones. The policy does nothing for the transparency of a sport that invests heavily in the concepts of integrity and fair play. In this case, few people other than those closest to the player knew the circumstances surrounding the absence of one of golf's biggest names.

The website publication of this story did yield a response from the Tour, who – as ever – chose their words very carefully. The statement said: 'With regard to media reports that Dustin Johnson has been suspended by the PGA Tour, this is to clarify that Mr. Johnson has taken a voluntary leave of absence and is not under a suspension from the PGA Tour.'

Aside from re-opening a long-running debate on the secrecy surrounding the Tour's disciplinary process, the only other certainty was that Johnson was out of golf for the foreseeable future. At a time when he should have been at the height of his powers, he sat out the PGA Championship, FedEx Cup play-off series and the Ryder Cup. Team USA was undoubtedly the poorer for his absence.

'You always want guys with that kind of power to play on any team,' Tiger Woods acknowledged. 'I've been his partner in the Presidents Cup in Australia and the firepower that he has, it's pretty cool to be around. It's not too often you see a guy carry the ball 320 yards without even trying, and then when he steps it up, he can hit it even further. When he gets it going it's awfully impressive.'

The controversy surrounding Johnson overshadowed the first couple of days of the WGC event in Ohio. Familiar names led the way, with McIlroy and one of the men he beat into second place at the Open, Sergio García, delighting European supporters with their good form. García, in particular, was breathtakingly impressive on the Friday afternoon when he finished with seven straight birdies, single-putting the last 11 greens for an astonishing 61. He held the halfway lead at 11 under par and McIlroy trailed by four strokes after a second-round 64.

This was scoring reminiscent of Woods' glory days. Hoping the familiar and fruitful surroundings might reignite his season, the 38-year-old began with a respectable 68. 'I hit a lot of good shots,' Woods said. 'I dropped strokes at three holes out there and got it right back on the very next hole. That was nice, to have three good bounce-backs. It was a good, solid day.

'This is only my seventh round back, so it's just going to take a little time. I'm starting to get in the flow of things. If you look at my iron shots, the majority were pin-high. I'm starting to get the feel back in my hands and get the ball and my trajectory under control.'

A day later he carded a one-over-par 71. Not only had he scored worse but his mood had swung the wrong way as well. 'I didn't hit the ball well,' he said. 'I didn't putt well. I didn't do anything well. The only thing I did well was I fought hard. The good news is I'm still getting stronger. I've still got a long way to go as far as my strength and explosiveness is concerned, but all that's coming round.'

Naturally, given the opportunity to talk himself up, Woods needed no second invitation. He was asked whether he could envisage shooting a pair of 65s over the weekend to get into contention. 'Absolutely, absolutely,' he said.

That proved beyond him as he slipped to an unconvincing 72 on Saturday. Woods went back to the driver he had used the previous year, with a lighter shaft, to try to find more reliability from the tee, but he still struggled. His putting was also erratic but he continued to insist he was getting more and more feel for competitive golf. There was, though, a hint that his physical condition was still some way from its best. By devoting so much time to playing golf, his usual gym regime of lifting weights to condition 'fast twitch' muscles was on hold.

'I can't burn the candle at both ends,' he said. 'I can't go out and play golf at full speed as well as do that, because I won't have the chance to recover for the next day. The whole deal, any time you lift, is being able to recover by the next day. Just not quite ready for that yet.'

By contrast, McIlroy was in peak condition and able to sustain a full gym regime as well as compete on the course. He added a third-round 66, coming back after a rain delay to birdie the last two holes and stay in touch with García at the top of the leaderboard. The Spaniard was round in 67 for a three-stroke advantage going into the final round.

More rain on Sunday morning led to a 90-minute delay to the closing 18 holes. No one wanted the action to spill over until Monday with the final major, the PGA Championship at Valhalla, looming. There were a few anxious glances skywards once play started but, thankfully, the skies cleared.

McIlroy was in the clubhouse before heading to the range for his warm-up and watched the television coverage of the early starters. He saw Woods produce glorious swings with his drive and nine iron down the par-four first. Then, at the long second, his ball came to rest at the top of a steep-faced fairway bunker. He had an awkward stance, with his left foot out of the hazard and his right lower down on the banking.

In the media centre, the large screen conveying the action was filled with the image of Woods addressing the ball. I turned to the *Daily Mail*'s Derek Lawrenson and said: 'We better watch this, his season could end here.' He smiled and raised an eyebrow. I was joking, but we'd both covered too many Tiger Woods injury stories in recent years.

Woods piled into his second shot. It was only a lay-up to the par five and he successfully advanced his ball. On the follow-through he wheeled round, gravity forcing him back into the bunker from which he skipped out, apparently unscathed. But then his game fell apart.

At the par-three fifth his tee shot inexplicably finished 64 yards short of the green. He showed no outward signs of discomfort, just anger at his poor swing. His caddie Joe La Cava later admitted: 'He did a great job of masking it.'

At the ninth, he hit a 318-yard drive but struggled to bend over to pick up his tee. Woods' back had gone into spasm and, in clear distress, he called for a buggy to take him back to the car park. It was only his 10th round since coming back from surgery and it ended before the halfway mark. It was a savage blow. Anyone witnessing his distress couldn't help but fear for his future. He appeared back to square one.

'I was watching and I said to myself before he withdrew that something is wrong with Tiger, I knew it when he hit that tee shot on the par three,' Tom Watson told PGA Tour Radio the next morning. 'It concerns me because that's an injury he had tried to correct. Tiger would be a great addition to the team, but this doesn't bode well. I just hope it's an isolated injury and he can tee it up at the PGA.'

In the car park, Woods had barely been able to change his shoes before being driven off to his private jet, which whisked him back to his home in Florida. He managed a few brief words with PGA Tour media official Chris Reimer. 'It happened on the second hole when I hit my second shot, I fell back into the bunker,' Woods said. 'I just jarred it, and it's been spasming ever since.'

Experts believed Woods' latest swing, under the tutelage of coach Sean Foley (with whom he later split), was the source of his back trouble. 'There is a lot of torque on his back with his swing at the moment,' Sir Nick Faldo noted. 'Adam Scott used to try to copy Tiger, but Tiger should now watch him. Adam "covers" the ball with his right shoulder and there is absolutely no stress on his spine. Tiger has a problem and has to make compensations with his swing.'

Faldo's colleague on the Golf Channel and long-time Woods critic Brandel Chamblee went further. 'Woods reminds me of an ageing Hollywood actor who has had too much plastic surgery,' said the former Tour player, who has become one of the most respected voices in the game. 'He is unrecognisable.'

McIlroy, who has a strong bond with Woods that runs deeper than merely being Nike stablemates, had been distressed watching the developments on television. He told me: 'I felt bad, I really did. Golf really needs Tiger and he's had a few withdrawals over the past few years. I think the first thing he needs to do is just get fit and 100 per cent healthy. Even take the year off, just to be able to do that. And come back next year ready to play again.'

Woods, though, had already issued the instruction to his caddie Joe La Cava to head the 300 miles south to Valhalla to scout the course for next week's PGA.

Woods didn't know it, but he was going through precisely the scenario that faced Graham DeLaet when he had rushed his return from a similar operation. In sporting terms, this colossus who bestrode the game with such majesty for almost two decades, departed Akron, Ohio, resembling a beaten, frail, old man.

McIlroy, meanwhile, headed into the final round at Firestone imbued with the confidence that had come with his Open triumph. García's advantage quickly disappeared, and on the third hole he hit his drive into the crowd. It struck a recently engaged spectator on the hand, knocking the diamond from her ring. The Spaniard offered to pay for a replacement but the jewel was found in the rough soon afterwards.

Of more concern to García was trying to keep pace with a rampant McIlroy and, just as at the Open, it proved beyond him. A second successive 66 brought McIlroy back-to-back titles and returned him to the top of the world rankings. García shot a tame 71 to finish two strokes behind at 13 under par.

It seemed natural that McIlroy should be clutching another trophy. Standing on the 18th green, with flash bulbs illuminating the gloaming, he smiled broadly. I stood next to his father, Gerry, as the prize was handed over.

'Yes, he's playing some golf at the moment,' was his understated yet proud summation. After the speeches and yet more television interviews, the champion climbed aboard a buggy to ferry him to the media centre. I sat with him and we discussed the magnitude of this latest victory, one that emphatically backed up his triumph in the Open Championship a fortnight earlier.

'I kept saying at the start of the week, this is what I wanted to do,' he said. 'I didn't want to dwell too much on the Open. It was a huge achievement and probably the biggest title of my career, but to back it up with a World Golf Championship win here at Akron, you know, one of my favourite events of the year, is great. I love this golf course, I feel like I'd always do well here and just to keep the mindset, that's what I'm most proud of, just not letting myself fall into any sort of complacency.

'It feels great to get that number one spot again. It's very special. It's a nice title to hold and hopefully I can hold on to it for a little while longer. I did say it at the start of the year, that golf was looking for a guy to try to become one of the dominant players and I've put my hand up there and won a couple of big tournaments the last few weeks and hopefully I can just keep that going.'

McIlroy's triumph and Woods' setback dominated the head-lines but this was also an important week in terms of Ryder Cup qualification. Like McIlroy, Graeme McDowell fired closing rounds of 66 over the weekend to claim a share of eighth place on a course where he had struggled in the past. The man from Portrush moved into the automatic qualification places for the European team for the first time.

Lee Westwood, a veteran of the eight previous Ryder Cups, was nowhere near qualifying. He had cut a thoroughly dispir-ited figure when he missed his fourth cut in a row at the Open and Paul McGinley made it known that he would need to show some form to put himself in the picture for Gleneagles. On that rain-softened final day the 41-year-old from Nottinghamshire produced a brilliant 63.

'I felt like I needed it and I felt like it was coming,' Westwood told me. 'The first three rounds were frustrating but I was gradually getting better, dropping too many silly shots but making a lot of birdies. Today I knuckled down and concentrated on those first few holes and I just kept it going. It's just a case for me of getting feelings in my golf swing that I can take on to the golf course.'

He was reluctant to be drawn into talk of the Ryder Cup. 'The bigger picture is next week, the PGA Championship, the final major of the year,' he said. But when pushed, Westwood provided words that were music to McGinley's ears. 'I think the captain knows what I can do, my record speaks for itself, but he wants to see some form from me and I think 63 is form.'

McGinley spent the summer trawling through transcripts of interviews given by players on his Ryder Cup radar. When he read Westwood's response, he was delighted. 'Thank you for asking him, that's just the sort of thing I want. I like the fact that the Ryder Cup is in their heads – keep asking those questions,' McGinley later said to me.

The Akron week had been even more significant for the Americans. This was the penultimate qualifying tournament, with only the PGA Championship to go. Johnson was out of the picture, and it also looked as if Woods would not be ready in time, although he would give it one last try to prove form and fitness the following week.

At Firestone, Patrick Reed had found a new driver to his liking. In the wake of his early-season success, the 24-year-old had accidentally broken the previous club he had used and his results suffered. In the final round of the WGC, the abrasive American fired a 65 to share fourth place with Justin Rose. Keegan Bradley, so desperate to retain his place in the US team, also shot four rounds in the 60s to finish tied third with Australia's Marc Leishman. And of even more encouragement to Watson, an out-of-sorts Phil Mickelson closed with a brilliant eight-under-par round. 'That 62 was good to see,' Watson said. 'Mickelson is one of those players who can just turn it on. I'd certainly like to have him on my team.'

Watson needed all the good news he could get because it had been an otherwise calamitous week. As one leading American writer sarcastically quipped: 'What a great week. We lose Johnson and Woods and gain Patrick Reed. Just what we needed.'

Heading into the last qualifying event with double points on offer as well as $1.8 million, the biggest first prize in the game, this is how the American qualifying table looked, with the leading nine players claiming automatic places in the team:

1. Bubba Watson   6,828.138
2. Jim Furyk   5,875.194
3. Jimmy Walker   5,510.205

4. Rickie Fowler	5,403.253
5. Matt Kuchar	4,999.665
6. Jordan Spieth	4,781.828
7. Jason Dufner	3,516.345
8. Zach Johnson	3,450.894
9. Patrick Reed	3,301.393

Mickelson was around $105,000 outside the standings, while Dufner, the defending champion at the PGA Championship, was increasingly hampered by a neck injury.

The Valhalla course that was staging the PGA is located just outside Louisville in Kentucky. It hosted the 2008 Ryder Cup, the last one that had ended in US victory. For those looking to shore up their places in Watson's team, it was the perfect setting. 'It really is a fun place for us to play because of the memories that we have,' Mickelson said. 'Winning the Ryder Cup here, it's a very emotional experience, and the people here in Louisville, we kept calling them our 13th man because they were such an asset in keeping us motivated, excited and giving us momentum. It's a great golf town.'

Mickelson had qualified for every Ryder Cup team since his 1995 debut and was determined to feed off the previous Sunday's 62 to keep his run intact. 'I think I'll continue that play into this week and I'm confident that I'll get on the team on my own and won't require that pick,' he said.

The PGA of America decided to introduce a long-driving contest for the Tuesday practice day. Drives were measured off the par-five 10th and most players embraced it as a bit of fun for the fans. The big-hitting Bubba Watson was expected to be one of the main contenders but, in an increasingly tetchy week, he undermined the idea by taking an iron off the tee. A far cry from the bubbly, engaging character who had set in motion a stunning year of major golf with his Masters win back in April, he came over as precious and out of touch.

'I don't see that we should have a competition like that while we're playing a practice round and learning the golf course, trying to win a great championship,' he complained. 'There's no reason to make something up in the middle of the practice round like that. That's just me. Like it or not, that's just who I am.'

This seemed a surprising reaction from a man who had spoken so glowingly about his desire to grow the game in the wake of his Augusta triumph. At Valhalla, Watson shot 70–72–73–72 and was irritable throughout, berating himself and caddie Ted Scott with such venom that he ultimately felt obliged to apologise. He tweeted: 'Sorry for my actions today! Trying to get better as person. Thanks to all who support me. #YallDontGiveUpOnMe' and later: 'Thanks to everyone for holding me accountable for my actions, it's helping me to get better!! #Thanks #Blessed'.

As the *Guardian*'s Ewan Murray put it: 'Bubba the Man Child was back, which is never a pretty sight.' The episode revealed him to be a complex and potentially difficult character who would need to be handled carefully with regard to potential partners in the Ryder Cup team.

Twitter was also awash with pictures of Woods' empty parking space in the days leading up to the championship. He was in Florida, receiving intensive treatment to try to ready him for the final major of the year. He eventually arrived at around 2 p.m. on the eve of the tournament. The timing was not helpful to Tom Watson, who was giving a news conference in the media centre at the time. Just when the US captain wanted to be at his most assured, he found himself bombarded with questions about Woods. They were questions he simply could not answer.

'I can't tell you what's going to happen with Tiger,' Watson admitted. 'I don't know his physical condition right now. And I said right from the beginning, if he's playing well and he's in good health, I'll pick him. Obviously he's not in great health right now and he hasn't played very well. So the question is: "Will I pick him?" Well, I can't tell until things happen in the next three or four weeks. Honestly – I can't answer this.'

At the same news conference Watson announced the experienced but semi-retired Steve Stricker as his third vice captain to supplement Ray Floyd and Andy North. Stricker was playing in the PGA and had an outside chance of grabbing a qualifying place. He had also acted as a putting coach with Woods in the past, and later that afternoon played nine holes with him. It was probably the most scrutinised warm-up round in the history of the game and – given how badly injured he had looked the previous Sunday – it was a remarkable turnaround to see Woods apparently ready to compete.

Woods, though, went on to card disappointing rounds of 74–74 and missed the cut by four strokes. He could easily have walked off after nine holes of his second round because, again, it was clear he was in great discomfort. It is testament to his fighting qualities that he continued, but it was a vain attempt to prove his fitness and he never looked like achieving the high finish he needed to make it into the PGA Tour play-off series. His season was effectively over.

'I couldn't make a back swing. I can't get the club back,' he said. 'I felt like I wasn't that far away when I came back at Quicken Loans, but obviously you can't develop strength the same time as you are playing a lot. I need to get back in that gym and get stronger.'

While Woods' pain showed no sign of ending, nor did McIlroy's ride upon the crest of a wave of confidence. Golf had not seen the like since Woods was in his prime. Before teeing off in his quest for back-to-back majors and three wins in a row, observers acknowledged a new man was now in charge.

'Really, without the Tiger Woods dominance, when Rory plays well he is the best player in the world,' McIlroy's former

Ryder Cup captain Colin Montgomerie told me. 'We have a rightful number one in the world, with all respect to everyone else. When he plays his best, he wins. I could have said the same about Woods in the year 2000. And this course suits Rory down to the ground. If he's not too tired from last week and his exploits at the Open, he should win.

'He's taken a few years to learn how to cope with stardom, and it's not easy living one's life in the public eye. He's managed it very well, especially over the last month, and I expect him to go on and win his fourth major. He's on his way to greatness.'

McIlroy had arrived at Valhalla on the lunchtime after his Akron victory. He abandoned his plan for nine holes of practice that Monday and chose to sign in and get settled. I saw him briefly that day and he said it had been a quiet night after his win because he didn't want to disturb his momentum. It was as though all he was doing was satisfying his own expectations, that these wins were nothing out of the ordinary. He would maintain that mindset for the final week of major championship golf in 2014.

The new world number one began in a manner befitting such an elevated status. The course was relatively soft and he took full advantage with an opening 66. Americans Ryan Palmer and Kevin Chappell, along with Westwood, were the only players to outscore him on the first day, by a single shot. McIlroy then added a 67 to move to nine under par.

'Mentally, I'm in a really solid place in terms of not getting ahead of myself on the golf course,' McIlroy revealed. 'I've got little trigger words that I'm still using and that seems to be getting me through. I can't really explain it any better than that. Obviously my swing is technically in a good place at the minute, I'm able to shape the ball both ways. I'm confident and I'm just on a good run.'

From the American point of view, Mickelson was showing

up well, trailing by only three strokes, and Fowler was just two back at halfway. McIlroy didn't let up, with a third-round 67 matched by the two Americans, while Henrik Stenson was also within three.

Torrential rain then pounded the area, more than an inch falling in 45 minutes around lunchtime, and play was suspended. Players complained at having to perform on a waterlogged course but, as Montgomerie pointed out: 'They wouldn't be playing if they were not desperate to finish today.' Paul McGinley was watching from the Sky Sports commentary box and quipped: 'I hope nobody will be giving us a hard time at Gleneagles next month if we get some rain.'

The saturated conditions, and the probability of mud influencing the flight of the balls, didn't spoil one of the most dramatic days of golf witnessed in recent years. McIlroy led by one stroke from Bernd Wiesberger heading into the delayed final round. A bogey at the first drew him back into a five-way share of the lead with his Austrian playing partner as well as Stenson, Mickelson and Fowler.

Fowler then chipped in at the fifth to steal the lead, Mickelson briefly joined him on the seventh only for Fowler to nudge ahead again moments later. There was an extraordinary spirit between the two players as they regularly fist-bumped each other. Mickelson was playing an avuncular role but relishing the battle. Stenson made his move as well while, despite a birdie at the par-five seventh, McIlroy struggled on the front nine. By the turn, he was trailing by three.

Throughout this glorious summer, though, McIlroy had been able to conjure magic when he needed it most. It came on the par-five 10th, a hole where he had run up a seven in the first round after hoiking his second stroke out of bounds. This time his 281-yard three wood was more fortunate. He didn't hit it well, it squirted out of the neck of the club, but its lower than intended trajectory enabled the ball to bound towards the green and run up to eight feet from the hole. 'I didn't hit a very good shot there but it worked out well,' he admitted. Typically, McIlroy rolled in the putt for an eagle three to move back within a stroke of the lead.

His name is now feared on leaderboards and that ability to influence others should not be underestimated. The pace-setting trio of Stenson, Mickelson and Fowler all faltered on the inward half.

By contrast, McIlroy grew more composed. From a fairway bunker on the 17th he powered a nine-iron approach to set up the decisive birdie. Darkness was descending and, sportingly, Mickelson and Fowler in the group ahead allowed McIlroy and Wiesberger to drive before the American duo played their second shots. Officials then encouraged the same process for the approach shots from the final pair. This didn't sit quite so well with Mickelson and Fowler, who were understandably keen to set a target that might force McIlroy into doing something injudicious. As it was, the leader only just missed the water down the right with his tee shot.

'It didn't affect the outcome, I think,' said Mickelson. 'It's not what we normally do but it's not a big deal. It's a courteous thing to let the guys tee off in case they blow the horn. It gave everyone a chance to finish just in the nick of time.'

Mickelson, trailing by two, came desperately close to a sensational pitch-in for eagle while Fowler, one behind, lipped out for a birdie. It all fell into place for McIlroy, who could now par in for victory. Despite the darkness, he duly obliged.

This was a man who seemingly could do nothing wrong – he even swooped to make a timely catch when PGA President Ted Bishop dropped the lid of the enormous Wannamaker Trophy while handing it over at the presentation ceremony.

'This has been incredible, never in my wildest dreams did I believe I would have a summer like this,' said McIlroy. 'I think I showed a lot of guts out there and I'd like to thank Rickie and Phil for letting us play up. They showed a lot of class and sportsmanship.'

It was Fowler's third major runner-up finish in a row, to follow his fifth place at the Masters.

'This is the first one that hurts,' he admitted. 'The performance in the majors is something I can be proud of but Rory has been a deserving champion every time. We will see if we can get one away from him at some point.'

McIlroy now had four majors to his name. The first two had been won with ease, by eight strokes. At the Open, he was forced to hold at bay a chasing pack. This time he had come from behind to secure the spoils.

People could not get enough of him. After the presentations and photographs he sat for half an hour answering questions from the world's media. From the main interview room he was whisked up to the clubhouse, which had been turned into a television studio, and he completed a string of one-on-ones with broadcasters from across the globe.

Finally he sat down with a group of British and Irish journalists. Greg Allen from the Irish broadcaster RTÉ and I, with my BBC microphone, were also there, flanking the champion as he sat signing souvenir flags.

Inevitably the conversation turned to the Ryder Cup. McGinley had already identified that the world number one would carry a target on his back all week at Gleneagles. The Americans would be desperate to rattle him and deny him points.

'It's not just how the Americans view me but how I'm viewed by my own team,' McIlroy said. 'It's going to be my third Ryder Cup. I'm not one of the most experienced guys but I'm going to have to be some sort of leader, be a talisman and drive us forward. I'm realising that I have to accept that responsibility. I'm comfortable with that. The first couple of Ryder Cups I maybe felt a little out of place, not able to put my hand up and offer my opinion. "Who am I? I'm only a rookie." Now I've experienced a couple, and I'm in a place in the game that warrants me leading the team.'

The US also knew they would have a leader in place. Despite not winning, Mickelson was true to his word that he would play his way onto the team. Dufner withdrew injured during the first round of his title defence and, at the end of the qualifying process, there were nine men who had earned their way into the 2014 Ryder Cup: Watson, Fowler, Furyk, Walker, Mickelson, Kuchar, Spieth, Reed and Zach Johnson.

Tom Watson had until 2 September to finalise his three wildcard picks. He said: 'I'm looking for players who, in the words of a football coach, demand the ball with 10 seconds to play and show me they can get the job done.' Watson's opposite number would also name his wildcards on that day, but the Europeans had until the end of August to force their way into the automatic places.

Within a week, Woods bowed to the inevitable. He announced on his website that his valiant bid to play at Gleneagles had come up short. 'I've been told by my doctors and trainer that my back muscles need to be rehabilitated and healed. They've advised me not to play or practise now.

'I was fortunate that my recent back injury was not related to my surgery and was muscular only. I have already spoken to Tom [Watson] about the Ryder Cup and, while I greatly appreciate his thinking about me for a possible captain's pick, I took myself out of consideration. The US team and the Ryder Cup mean too much to me not to be able to give it my best. I'll be cheering for the US team. I think we have an outstanding squad going into the matches. I plan to return to competition at my World Challenge tournament at Isleworth in Orlando, Florida, Dec. 1–7.'

Clarity at last, although Woods gave the impression that he had made the call to the American captain. Watson later said this was not the case: 'Tiger told me when I called Tiger. He didn't call me. I called him.'

For two of the most seasoned professionals on the European Tour, the final two weeks of qualifying were a vital period in securing their Ryder Cup debuts. Welshman Jamie Donaldson had seemed certain of his Gleneagles spot with sustained early-season consistency. He backed up his runner-up finish to Reed at Doral in early spring with top-five finishes at the lucrative French Open and the BMW International in Germany. His aim was to try to keep the Ryder Cup in perspective, knowing that consistently good results would see him fulfil his ambition of making it into the team.

It was the right approach, but he admitted: 'There's always that little fella on my shoulder, getting into my head and nagging away at me.' To boost his chances, he added the Scottish Open to his schedule and promptly missed the cut. Confidence dented, he then failed to make it beyond the halfway stage at the Open. Suddenly the pressure was on and a top-40 in Akron and a top-25 at Valhalla were not enough to complete the job.

McGinley told him that he still needed to do more. 'Wildcards tend to go to experienced players,' the captain said. The implication was clear – Donaldson had to keep on playing to earn enough to claim an automatic place.

Turning up at the D+D Real Czech Masters was a step down in the class of tournaments he had been playing but he knew that a strong showing would give him a place in McGinley's side. Donaldson produced a stellar display. Rounds of 66–69–71–68 gave him a two-stroke victory over compatriot Bradley Dredge. He took home £128,000 from Prague, having needed a mere £24,000 to qualify.

'This is big. It's been an amazing week,' the 38-year-old from Pontypridd said. 'I needed to play well either this week or next week to guarantee my place in the Ryder Cup team, so there was a lot on the line and I played really well.'

It was his third European Tour win and, given the Ryder Cup implications, it was the sweetest. 'It's so difficult to get into the team,' Donaldson added. 'The lads are playing so well. You know that you have to play well to secure your place and it did come down to the wire. But that's how it is to get into the team. I played as well as I can play for 18 months, and then a couple of slow events and you rocket down the list, so it's great to come here and play so well and do enough to get into the team.'

Trailing in Donaldson's wake was Stephen Gallacher, who shot rounds of 71 and 73 over the weekend to finish in a share of seventh. It was a much-needed top-10 for the Scot, who was bidding to emulate his illustrious uncle, Bernard Gallacher, in becoming a Ryder Cup player.

One of the most popular players on tour, Gallacher had successfully defended his Dubai Desert Classic title in January and his Czech finish was a fifth top-10 since that victory. He was very close to becoming a Scottish Ryder Cup player at a Scottish Ryder Cup, but needed one more good result to be sure.

There was a strong feeling that he would have to play his way into the nine automatic qualifiers because stalwarts Ian Poulter, Luke Donald and Lee Westwood required wildcard picks. Given their past heroics, the three Englishmen were favourites to receive the captain's vote.

There was one week to go before the 31 August deadline and only one more tournament of influence. The Deutsche Bank event in Boston couldn't count because it finished on 1 September, America's Labor Day holiday. It all came down to the Italian Open in Turin. A top-two finish for Gallacher would edge out McDowell as an automatic qualifier. McIlroy, García, Kaymer, Rose, Stenson, Dubuisson, Bjørn and Donaldson were in the team. Could McDowell be overtaken by the Scot?

As Gallacher set about his task, McDowell was at home in Orlando welcoming his first daughter into the world. As he told his BBC blog, 99 per cent of his attention was on his newborn. The other one per cent was focused on the European Tour App, and the leaderboard in Italy. But it wasn't until the Friday afternoon that Gallacher's name hoved into view on the McDowell iPhone. An inward half of 30 for a fine 65 made significant inroads into what had been, at one stage, a 14-stroke deficit. In the third round the Scot maintained the momentum with a 69 and second place was now within striking distance. Bit by bit he appeared to be getting into range.

The final day of European qualifying was a thriller. Over the opening holes Gallacher's approach play suggested his ball was on the end of a piece of string. He carved out seven birdies in 12 holes to surge into second place. Up ahead, though, David Howell was sinking putts for fun. The Englishman went on to card a 63 and finish at 18 under par, two behind eventual winner Hennie Otto of South Africa.

For Gallacher, it came down to the final hole. He had drilled home a 10-foot par save on the 17th to keep alive his hopes. He needed a birdie at the last to tie with Howell and give him enough prize money to oust McDowell, who by this time had camped down in front of his television. Gallacher's tee shot flew right of the fairway. In frustration, he shaped to demolish an advertising hoarding on the side of the tee and only thought better of it at the very last second. Confronted by a difficult approach, the 39-year-old did well to force his second shot into a greenside bunker. Hole from there and he was in the team. He did not. He came up 10 feet short. One putt later and he had missed out by a single stroke.

It had been a magnificent effort, a final-round 65 to finish at 17 under. 'My emotions were a bit mixed,' Gallacher recalled. 'I was delighted with the way I had played, and I was disappointed I didn't qualify automatically. I had it in the back of my head that I was up against a lot of really good players for picks. I didn't really have a clue what was going to happen.'

There was a strong feeling that, although he had come up

just short, Gallacher had done enough to warrant a wildcard. If just one of Howell's birdie putts had lipped out rather than disappeared, the Scot would have been in the team. It was that close.

'I really hope Stephen gets a pick,' said Howell, who played in the 2004 and 2006 matches. 'He'd make a fantastic Ryder Cup player. If a captain needs any nudge to realise that someone is in form and can play well under pressure, then Stephen has done it over this weekend.'

There was much for McGinley to ponder as he left Turin. The following day he would make his decision ahead of the 2 September wildcard announcements. He texted the players under consideration – Gallacher, Poulter, Westwood, Donald and Francesco Molinari – to tell them not to expect any calls until early Monday evening. 'It was a long day,' Gallacher said later.

McGinley spent it in the company of his vice captains, Sam Torrance and Des Smyth, two of the wisest old heads in European golf. They met at the exclusive Queenwood Golf Club in Surrey and shared a morning round while discussing their options. Then they retired to a private room where they had a presentation from two statisticians, Chris Sells and John Franks from strokeaverage.com, who had been monitoring the players' performances during the season.

'It was very short and concise,' McGinley said. 'We reconvened and we had a bit of a chat regarding it. We were all very much on the same lines. We went away, had a shower, came back, had dinner around 7 p.m. and firmed up our ideas.'

The decision was made and at around 8.30 p.m. McGinley decided to get the hardest phone call out of the way first. He rang Donald, back home in America at the end of a disappointing summer in which a share of 16th place at the Scottish Open in early July had been his best showing. McGinley called it 'the toughest call of my career' and confirmed that Donald had not expected to be left out.

'It wasn't nasty but I wanted to do it in the right way. Let's not get things out of perspective, there are bigger things in life than having to make a call about sport. But it was a very, very difficult thing for me to do because of my personal relationship with Luke.'

McGinley had partnered Donald, who had never been on a losing team in four appearances, in his first Ryder Cup match in 2004. 'I have a very strong bond with Luke and when I see him the next time it is going to be tough.' McGinley said. He admitted the Englishman was very disappointed but added: 'Luke was incredibly accepting of my decision and the last thing he said to me was: "Go Europe." '

It was a much more pleasurable experience to call Gallacher. 'Steve's performance last week was one of the best I've seen with Ryder Cup qualification on the line. It was spectacular,' McGinley said. The Scot had earned the right to play at a course that lies a mere 35 miles from his Linlithgow home. 'That's brilliant, wee man!' Gallacher responded when McGinley imparted the good news.

McGinley's other two picks were bigger gambles. Neither Poulter nor Westwood had shown much form throughout the season. Poulter was always likely to get a pick because he always reserves his best golf for Ryder Cups. He inspired the comeback from 10–4 down at Medinah with his five birdies in a row late on the Saturday and had an 80 per cent winning record from his four previous appearances. 'To accept the call from Paul was amazing,' Poulter said. 'Ryder Cup means a lot to me and I guarantee I'll be ready to perform to my best.'

Poulter failed to qualify for the third leg of the PGA Tour play-offs but turned down McGinley's suggestion to play the Wales Open the week before the Ryder Cup. It meant that he went to Gleneagles without having played competitively for three weeks.

'Paul did ask, but I've played a lot recently and I feel I can get more done at home,' he said. 'I know how to prepare for a Ryder Cup and get it right. My record, in terms of turning up ready to play my best golf and go out there as often as the captain wants me to, stacks up pretty well. I told Paul that, and he said he's got faith in me to turn up on the first tee ready to play my heart out.'

Speaking to me in a BBC interview, McGinley explained: 'He's a talisman; you know he's always going to raise himself coming into a Ryder Cup. He very rarely has a lot of form going into a Ryder Cup, but somehow manages to produce on it.

'He knows he's up against it in this Ryder Cup, he knows he's going to be the man with the 'X' on his back; the American players will relish playing against him. But if anyone is ready for that challenge it'll be Ian Poulter.'

Westwood entered the Wales Open as soon as he received the call. The 41-year-old, set for a ninth Ryder Cup appearance, didn't make it past the first week of the play-offs and was in desperate need of a competitive outing. The closing 63 at Bridgestone was the sort of form to impress the captain, as was his opening 65 the following week at the PGA Championship. Donald did not hit such heights and that's why the decision went the way of Westwood. 'He showed a flourish at Firestone and Valhalla that Luke wasn't able to do,' said McGinley. 'I'd asked Lee through the media to show some form, he wasn't going to get in on reputation alone. Lee did that. He beat Luke by a short head.'

Westwood thought that he also brought another dimension to the team. 'Paul obviously felt that he needed experience,' he said. 'I have played in eight teams and I have a lot more experience than a lot of captains. He picked me to do a vice captain's job in the team room as well.'

McGinley's line-up was complete.

Throughout the qualifying period he had been in constant touch with all the candidates. His message was that they shouldn't be carried away by their favourites' tag and he encouraged them to talk up the status of the legendary figure leading the American team.

But, given the way Europeans had dominated the last three majors, McGinley had to concede that his team were worthy of their short odds going into their defence of the trophy.

'To be in a situation where we are favourites is something to embrace, something to be proud of,' McGinley told me. 'With the number one player in the world in Rory McIlroy, with Martin Kaymer winning the US Open and Justin Rose winning the US Open last year and on and on. But we are under no illusions whatsoever how difficult this is going to be.

'Anyone who follows Gaelic football will know Dublin were 1 to 7 favourites to beat Donegal and lost by four points. So the favourites' tag is great but it's also something that we're very wary of. We are up against some opponents who will rally and galvanise themselves as underdogs.'

Precisely 12 hours after the announcement of the European wildcards, Watson did the same for the Americans. It was a remarkably lavish, drawn-out affair in New York that saw the American skipper take half an hour to reveal the names of Keegan Bradley, Hunter Mahan and Webb Simpson. The captain had gone through a late change of heart when Simpson texted him late at night on the eve of the announcement. In the phone conversation that followed the 2012 US Open champion convinced the skipper that he should receive the last pick.

Mahan was a certainty for his third Ryder Cup after winning the Barclays tournament in the play-offs. He shared the 'redemption' DNA that coursed through the American Ryder Cup effort. It was his duffed chip at Celtic Manor that helped deliver the winning point to Europe when he lost to McDowell in the final match. Having missed Medinah, Gleneagles would provide Mahan with his first opportunity to atone for an error that had left him in tears.

Simpson was the curious choice, bearing in mind Watson's football analogy that he was looking for someone to grab the ball and score in the last ten seconds. Chris Kirk had seized the moment in exactly that fashion at the Deutsche Bank tournament, the final event of any influence. The 29-year-old from Knoxville, Tennessee, played with and beat McIlroy over the last 36 holes to claim his second title of the year on the eve of the captain's announcement.

But Watson's team already had three rookies in Spieth, Reed and Walker. The skipper clearly didn't want a fourth. Watson's preference was experience, and so Simpson received the call despite finishing eight places behind Kirk in Boston.

The captain also had in mind that Simpson had forged a strong partnership with Bubba Watson at Medinah, where they collected two wins out of three and both by thumping 5–4 margins.

The first wildcard to be named was Bradley. No one epitomised the spirit that Watson wanted to take to Gleneagles more than the Vermont-born 28-year-old. Bradley famously refused to open his holdall containing his Ryder Cup clothes when he returned home from Medinah. The bag sat unopened in his Florida home for two years as a symbol of his own desire for redemption.

'It was pretty emotional when the captain phoned me,' Bradley, who finished 13th in the qualifying table, admitted. 'I had been down and thinking there was a good chance I wouldn't be on the team.' He impressed Watson, though, with his desire to right the wrongs of Medinah. Bradley also gained favour by joining Watson on a scouting trip of Gleneagles during the weekend before the Open.

'There's a lot of great plusses about Keegan,' Watson said. 'But the most important thing is his unbridled passion to play in the Ryder Cup.'

Furthermore, the player promised to impose his personality

on Gleneagles. 'I'm not going to suppress any emotion. I think the Ryder Cup is the time to let the emotion come out of you. Sometimes it can make you play great golf.'

But no one knew better how to play his best golf than McIlroy in that glorious summer of 2014. He was aware of Bradley's threat. 'Keegan is the guy on the US team who could get close to the passion that Poulter shows,' McIlroy said.

With Bradley and Poulter, the Gleneagles cast list had been completed by two characters who could define the event. At the end of a tumultuous season of golf, Europe and America had produced two well-balanced teams. The home side had the superstars and the stalwarts trading on past glories, while the US could boast a solid rump of consistent performers, fuelled by a deep-seated desire for revenge.

The stage was well and truly set.

CHAPTER 14

The final build-up

'Well, not only are we able to play together, we
also don't litigate against each other and that's
a real plus, I feel, heading into this week.'

Phil Mickelson

One week before packing his equipment to travel to his ninth successive Ryder Cup, Jim Furyk was branded 'golf's biggest choker'. The 44-year-old from West Chester, Pennsylvania, had qualified third for the US team despite not winning a tournament for four years. During the 2014 season he was a model of consistency, with four runner-up finishes and seven more top-10s. But no victories. Britain's *Sun* newspaper therefore felt justified in referring to the man who had played every Ryder Cup since 1997 as someone lacking the nerve to win.

Still fresh in the memory was his pivotal defeat on the final day at Medinah where, leading one up with two holes to play, he made two bogeys to lose to Sergio García. If he had preserved his advantage. America would have won the Cup.

'I feel like every time I go to the press room, I understand the questions that are coming and I feel like we're in a morgue,' Furyk said. 'Everyone is looking at me with this blank stare and they ask me depressing questions. And they bring up the Ryder Cup and the loss to Sergio García, and we go through Akron (in 2013) and my double bogey on the 18th hole to lose there. I get asked if there is a common denominator for these things, where I just can't punch it in on Sundays with that really low round, and — I'll be honest with you — I think it's kind of a crappy thing to say. And the reason I say that is I had three seconds this year with a 65 and a 66 on two of those Sundays. I've played great this year – no, I've played very good this year, I won't say great because I haven't won. And I'm not going to hang my head and I'm not going to just walk away.

'But I chuckle every time I leave the media room, because it's almost as if everyone expects me to be depressed. I mean, there's a lot worse stuff going on in the world than me shooting 70 on a Sunday. Every time I lose I'm disappointed. I will learn from it, and I feel like I'm getting closer. I understand why y'all ask the questions. But I guess I want everyone to know that I'm thinking like: "God, this is kind of a sad conversation." I want to walk in there happy. I guess I've got to win to do that. So if and when it happens, I'll have a big smile on my face.'

And nothing would surely give him a bigger smile than playing a part in a US victory at Gleneagles. In his eight prior appearances, Furyk was on the losing team six times. 'I'm very proud to represent my country and when I look back on my career and the things I've done, making nine teams means an awful lot,' said the man whose idiosyncratic, loopy swing had netted in excess of $65 million in prize money. 'You have to be consistent and to be able to qualify by right for eight of them, to be in the mix that often, I'm proud of that.'

But Medinah hurt most of all, especially since he had been one of Davis Love's wildcard picks. 'I think if you ask Sergio he would agree I outplayed him,' Furyk added. 'But it doesn't matter if you don't win the point. I think I was the most disappointed of our team because I felt bad for Davis. He got everything right as captain but, quite honestly, we laid an egg on Sunday and the Europeans got the momentum.'

It would have been fair to assume that Furyk, harbouring such heartache, would head the queue of those buying into Gleneagles as a mission of American redemption. But he bristled at this thought, in the same way he rejected any suggestion that US teams had lacked motivation and spirit during Europe's recent period of domination.

With Tom Watson stating that Medinah should 'stick in the craw' of all the Americans on duty in 2014, and with his players overtly embracing the effort to regain the trophy, it seemed fair to suggest that this must be the most driven US team in the history of the Ryder Cup. But, when I made this point to Furyk at the Tour Championship, his last outing before Gleneagles, he was having none of it.

Our interview came at the end of a lengthy media session, during which the tour veteran had been affable and patient throughout. He was happy to talk to all and sundry and remained in his chair long after the formal press conference had ended. But suddenly, in this BBC interview, his eyes narrowed, and he adopted a stern, reproachful expression. Furyk's bald head edged towards my microphone to ensure his message would be heard loud and clear, and he paused before saying: 'I would go with probably not. I would also say, you'd be next to say that we look like a bunch of individuals and they (the Europeans) look like a team. And let's go through the other clichés – there's probably one more in there that I'm missing.'

While we were speaking Jimmy Walker, Rickie Fowler, Jordan Spieth and Zach Johnson were playing nine holes of fourball matchplay. It was their last golf before competing for a potential $10 million payout from the FedEx Cup play-offs, but already it was clear their mind had turned to the format and style of play required at Gleneagles.

'No, I was deliberately trying to get away from those clichés,' I replied. 'What I'm saying is you've got guys who are out on the course here now, playing matches against each other, obviously with Gleneagles in mind on the eve of the Tour Championship. The fact that you had a team dinner in Denver last week (at the BMW Championship play-off event) and the kind of things that Tom Watson has been saying about redemption?'

'I think we have always done that,' he replied tartly. 'You're just noticing it. Do you spend a lot of time here in the States watching golf tournaments?'

'Yeah, yeah, absolutely.'

'How many events to do you attend?'

It made a change to be the one answering rather than asking the questions.

'I'd be here for the majors, WGCs, the Players' and Tour Championship,' I replied. To be honest, it wasn't a comprehensive list.

'So the standard game is Mickelson, Keegan and Dustin Johnson [none of whom were at the Tour Championship] and maybe Rickie Fowler – all Ryder Cup guys who have a standard Tuesday game that they always play together. I think the fact that you see the guys out there playing isn't really much different than usual. And as far as the dinner thing, that's something we've always done; it probably just caught wind in the media this year.

'I think the Ryder Cup's an event we've always been excited about and, if we look more excited this year, I think that's great. Hopefully we are, but I feel like, for myself personally and from most of the guys I speak to, I don't think I've ever not been at basically the highest excitement level I can get to – which maybe isn't that high for everyone else – but I'm at my high, put it that way. I enjoy it and I love it. When the start of the season came around, I wasn't sure if Medinah was going to be my last or not and I couldn't be happier that I get another crack at it.'

Furyk's commitment to the Ryder Cup cause was evident earlier in the summer when he interrupted his preparations for the Open to join Watson on a scouting mission to Gleneagles. The US skipper had been hoping to attract several of his likely team members to check out the Centenary Course during the weekend before the Championship at Hoylake. The inland course overlooking the spectacular Ochil Hills, however, bears no resemblance in style to the seaside links they faced for the third major of the year, so Mickelson, Walker and Fowler chose to compete in the Scottish Open at Royal Aberdeen instead. But Furyk preferred to accompany his skipper to acquaint himself with the course, safe in the knowledge he was well on the way to qualifying for the Ryder Cup.

Keegan Bradley, on the other hand, still had much to do to make the team and would ultimately need a wildcard selection to retain his place. He joined Watson the day before Furyk arrived and played a fourball with the captain on the Ryder Cup course. PGA President Ted Bishop and *Golf Week* senior writer Alex Miceli made up the numbers.

Miceli was there to write about the reconnaissance trip, having provided statistical analysis for every American skipper since the victorious Paul Azinger in 2008. As Miceli made his way through the Gleneagles car park he saw Watson driving through in a buggy and the captain beckoned him over. 'Do you want to make up a fourball?' asked the five-times Open Champion to the eight-handicap journalist.

Miceli needed no second invitation and was able to observe the scouting process first hand. The PGA's Chief Championships Officer, Kerry Haigh, was also present. 'On every green Kerry would place a little disc where the hole locations had been at the Johnnie Walker Championship,' Miceli told me. Clearly the Americans thought it likely that the pin positions used in the regular European Tour event would provide the blueprint for the Ryder Cup. 'Tom and Keegan could see where the hole locations were and that was, I'm assuming, helpful for them. I think the whole thing was helpful in the fact that Tom could see how a modern-day player would play Gleneagles.

'Tom was grateful that Keegan went there,' Miceli added. 'At the time Keegan paid for the trip. He flew up on his own and paid for the private jet to go back down to Hoylake, but I think there was a discussion afterwards that said he shouldn't be paying for this and the PGA of America should pick up the tab. They talked a lot, especially around the greens, looking at different pins, looking at when you hit shots on the fairways, seeing where you could go.

'Obviously Tom's seen the golf course before but when we were there a year out it was raining. This time it was dry, it was pretty good. I told Keegan when we were playing that I thought he'd done himself the world of good by making that trip. I think because of that trip he was always going to be on the very, very short list for a wildcard pick.'

Once the practice round was completed (Miceli took the money from Bishop), the group retired to a small room at the side of the Gleneagles clubhouse. Watson's mind was at its most enquiring.

'We sat there for three hours,' Miceli said. 'Keegan had to leave after an hour or so.' Watson spent his time pumping Miceli for information about the likely figures in his team, come the end of September. 'It's interesting, I got the chance to play with McGinley in the pro-am at the Scottish Open last year and I hardly asked him anything, he asked me everything. He wanted to know everything about our players. Tom was the same way. He would throw a name out. "What do you think?" We talked about everything and anything . . . At the time, we didn't know about Dustin Johnson – Dustin Johnson was a conversation. Nobody knows Patrick Reed, so Patrick Reed was a conversation . . . we talked about Bubba [Watson] . . . I like Bubba's game, I think his game is perfect and at the time Webb Simpson wasn't even on the radar screen.

'I said: "Look, you're going to have to figure him out, you really have to understand him." I said I would go to Angie [Bubba's wife] and to Teddy [Scott, his caddie] and talk to them to see what it's going to take to get him engaged and motivated. Those were the kind of conversations we were having.

'I know a hell of a lot more about these guys than he does because I'm out there on tour the whole time and he knows that too. He would always say to me: "Look, I'm relying on you, you know these guys." And at the end of our conversation I said to him: "You know, you have one job, that's all you have, one job – win back the Ryder Cup. I don't really care how you do it, as long as you do it." And he knows. At the end of the day, he understands that more than anything else,' Miceli added.

That task was made no easier in the weeks following Watson's wildcard selections of Bradley, Hunter Mahan and Simpson. As the play-offs built to their climax at the Tour Championship in Atlanta, the captain's decision to overlook Chris Kirk began to look more and more flawed. The 29-year-old from Knoxville, Tennessee, had gone 64–66 to outlast Rory McIlroy and win the second of the play-offs in magnificent style. But that victory at the Deutsche Bank wasn't enough to convince Watson when he made his announcement a day later. Instead, he went for Simpson, who finished ninth in that Boston tournament and, at 32, was the lowest-ranked player in the American team. Kirk, meanwhile, maintained his impressive form and finished in a share of fourth place at the Tour Championship to claim second spot in the FedEx Cup play-offs.

It meant that Simpson went to Gleneagles with huge pressure on his shoulders. It was made even greater by the exploits of another overlooked American, Billy Horschel. Before finishing second to Kirk in Boston, the 27-year-old had posted just three top-10s all year. He had hardly shown the form that might make him a Ryder Cup player and threw away his chance of beating Kirk with a poor final hole at the Deutsche Bank.

The 69 he posted that day, however, was the fourth of 12 consecutive sub-70 rounds to complete his season. Horschel finished 14 under par at Cherry Hills in Denver to win the BMW Championship and promptly followed it with victory in the Tour Championship. He brilliantly saw off a fatigued Rory McIlroy, who shared second place with 'Mr Nearly Man' Furyk (who bogeyed the last two holes to lose by three strokes).

Despite his early season inconsistency, Horschel is the sort of combative character who would thrive in the Ryder Cup environment. The form he and Kirk showed during the play-offs meant the US were now heading to Gleneagles without the country's two most in-form players. That was something they could ill-afford, bearing in mind that injury and circumstance had already robbed them of three of their most valuable assets; Tiger Woods, Dustin Johnson and Jason Dufner.

Nevertheless, Watson remained defiant over his selections and the fact that they had to be made before the lucrative play-off series was completed. 'In 1993 I made my two picks after the PGA (Championship), six weeks before the Ryder Cup,' he said. 'Three weeks out is a logical place to make your final picks because, logistically, there are so many different things that go into getting the players over there; get their clothing, get their families involved. It would be awfully difficult to make a decision the week before. From a time standpoint, it would not make any sense.'

Horschel won $13 million in the final three weeks of the American season. Watson added: 'I texted Billy last week and said: "You're a day late but not a dollar short." He was on my radar earlier in the year and I like his swing, his fundamentals and his attitude, but he just did not perform well enough to get on the team.'

The captain knew, though, that the way the PGA Tour campaign had ended was heaping pressure on his wildcard picks as well as his captaincy. If America were going to lose, he would be the man in the firing line. 'I'm prepared for that. I have some thick skin,' he said. 'I'm trying to make the best decisions I can at the time. If the players lose rather than win, I don't care, I will take the blame. If and when we win the Ryder Cup, I will stand aside and give all the credit to the players and caddies. That's where it's due.'

For Paul McGinley, a different kind of pressure was

building. No one had questioned the wisdom of his picks, although there were a few voices wondering whether Luke Donald's putting prowess might have proved more valuable than Lee Westwood's consistency from tee to green. At a corporate event in central London, vice captain Sam Torrance revealed that it had been another assistant, Padraig Harrington, who made the telling contribution in the European wildcard debate. The Irishman pointed out that Donald was struggling for consistency with his newly re-modelled swing and if, as anticipated, the weather was bad at Gleneagles he would find it even harder to find a dependable action. 'That's what swung it and made up our minds,' Torrance told an audience of bankers and fund managers.

And Europe's stock was continuing to rise as Watson's captaincy came under scrutiny. The one area of worry for McGinley, however, was that only four of his team turned up to play the Wales Open the week before the Ryder Cup. The skipper had hoped six or seven would use the chance to warm up on a course which had been set up specifically with Gleneagles in mind. Ian Poulter preferred to practise at home while Graeme McDowell reversed a late decision to enter the Welsh event. The lure of spending time with his newborn daughter was too great and, instead, he, Poulter and Henrik Stenson chose to establish their own Ryder Cup training camp on the range at Lake Nona, the Florida gated community where they live.

Victor Dubuisson's absence was harder to explain. The mysterious Frenchman played only once after the PGA Championship in early August. He finished 29th at the Omega European Masters in Switzerland. It was around this time that stories began to surface of an airport incident involving Dubuisson ahead of the PGA, where he had argued with an immigration official over the state of his passport and was sent to the back of the queue. The enigmatic 24-year-old threatened to leave even before he had officially entered the US. He was prepared to forego his place in the final major of the year. It was only after he had calmed down that he cleared immigration and took his place in the Valhalla field where he proceeded to claim a share of seventh place.

'Victor is Victor, as we all know,' McGinley acknowledged on the eve of the Wales Open. 'He decided at a very late stage to say, you know what, I'm going to prepare better I think down in France. I know he's down there with the French Federation, doing some work for them. The one thing that makes me feel happy and secure in terms of Victor's preparations is the fact that he's a guy who disappears and then all of a sudden comes out of nowhere and plays well in a tournament.'

Dubuisson was out of action for almost the whole of May before bursting back onto the scene to lose a play-off in the Nordea Masters. 'The whole world is like: "Where's Victor?" And then he comes out and nearly wins,' McGinley added.

The skipper made a point of getting to know the Frenchman as soon as it was clear he was destined for his Ryder Cup debut. He ensured they spent plenty of time together when Europe took on Asia in the EurAsia Cup in Kuala Lumpur in March. 'I had dinner with him most nights. We conversed, had a bit of fun, a bit of craic, I got to know him and got to understand him. I know who he is, and I think Victor is very much his own man and I'll certainly be letting him be his own man and letting him make his own kind of way. I think it's important that Victor has that freedom to make his own decisions.'

The process of getting more acquainted with Dubuisson wasn't restricted to the trip to Malaysia. McGinley is close friends with Eddie Jordan, the former owner of the Jordan Formula One team who acted as a sounding board throughout his fellow Irishman's captaincy. McGinley also knew that Dubuisson has a passion for motor racing and capitalised on it.

'Paul came down to Monaco. He asked me to set up a dinner,' Jordan told Kevin Garside of the *Independent*. 'It was an opportunity to get to know Victor better. Victor came with a mate, Paul came with Ally (his wife), there was myself and Marie and a few others. I had not met Victor before but there wasn't anything he could not tell me about Jordan. He is a motor racing fanatic. He has real style. He brought with him one of the most expensive Bordeaux wines money can buy, a Rothschild. Let me tell you he will be a big thing in this Ryder Cup, maybe a surprise for a lot of people. He is very much his own man, a fantastic character, and he won't be overawed.'

Westwood was the most experienced man in the European team. Part of his brief when he was selected was to take on an avuncular role towards the rookies. 'It's very difficult to know what to make of Victor,' said the veteran of nine Ryder Cups. 'He's quite shy. He's quite unpredictable. He's got a lot of flair. He's got tons of game. He's obviously good at matchplay, as he proved in Arizona at the start of the year.'

Back in Wales, with the Ryder Cup just nine days away, McGinley sat down in the press conference room with the brown leather folder that had been at his side throughout his captaincy. It was crammed full of notes, some of them detailing how to deal with the trickier questions that might come his way in his last public appearance before the event. Scotland's Paul Lawrie, one of the Medinah veterans, had expressed disappointment at being overlooked for a vice captain's role. McGinley thought he would be challenged on this by Scottish reporters and so had his answer noted down. The question never came up, but he had been prepared for every eventuality.

It was another accomplished media performance from a man who seemed much more at ease in the spotlight than his opposite number. He prepared booklets filled with inspiring photographs and essential information on how Ryder Cup week would work. He handed them to Thomas Bjørn, Jamie Donaldson, Stephen Gallacher and Westwood when they had dinner on the eve of the Wales Open. The captain gave a positive impression with his every utterance, his puffed out chest and ready smile suggesting this was a man relishing his role.

When he was reminded of Watson's difficulties regarding his wildcard picks, McGinley immediately downplayed their significance. 'It's not a case of turning up and thinking the Americans will roll over,' he stated. 'We know it's going to be a very strong American team. We know it is going to be a very strongly motivated team and a very strongly led American team as well. This is going to be very, very difficult to win the Ryder Cup. I think we've got a slightly different threat from America than we've had in the past, in as far as they feel like they are underdogs and they are up against it.'

McGinley also pointed out that questions over whether Watson had picked the correct side could be used to galvanise their effort at Gleneagles. 'We've seen that in the past, certainly from a European perspective. We are not underestimating America, I can assure you of that. We will be absolutely ready for this.'

The build-up to the first ball being struck early on Friday morning is the longest week in golf. Players, fans and media arrive early and enter into a week of seemingly endless preparation and deliberation.

McIlroy had needed time away from his clubs after finishing tied second at the Tour Championship. He flew to the UK and embarked on a round of sponsor appearances. On the Saturday evening he took in the European super-middleweight fight between Britain's George Groves and Frenchman Christopher Rebrasse at London's Wembley Arena. On Sunday, he appeared on a Sky Sports football show to review the weekend's goals before flying north to Gleneagles. The world number one was the first man from either team to arrive. The main mission was to re-acquaint himself with his clubs, which had lain dormant for six days.

McIlroy was joined on the range on Monday morning by Bjørn, who the day before had finished disappointingly at the

Wales Open. Just as these two Europeans were warming up, the American team touched down at Edinburgh airport. Eleven of the players had travelled together while Mickelson made his own way in his private Gulfstream Jet. When the team plane landed at Edinburgh airport, Mickelson, who was already there, was spirited onto the aircraft so that he could disembark with the rest of the line-up before a throng of media photographers.

The American team seemed in buoyant mood, as reflected by the exuberant Fowler. The 24-year-old's last act before boarding for his second Ryder Cup was to have the letters 'USA' shaved into the side of his cropped hair. 'I thought it was terrific,' said Watson. The skipper confessed that, in many respects, he was a father figure to his team, but he was an approving parent as far as this fashion statement was concerned. 'It brings a spirit, a light spirit to the team and I wouldn't be surprised if, heck, even Ted Bishop puts USA on the side of his head if it means we're going to win.' Bishop duly obliged, using the Gleneagles Hotel hairdressing staff to adorn his grey hair with a red, white and blue USA of his own.

Watson's comments came at a joint news conference with McGinley in the vast media centre. For some, the build-up was already proving too slow and too long. The sardonic *Golf World* journalist John Huggan tweeted: 'Welcome to the Ryder Cup where one member of the visiting team has apparently had a haircut #breakingnews.'

Of more significance was the first indication that McGinley was considering ditching McIlroy's partnership with McDowell. The Ulstermen had teamed up in the last two Ryder Cups but their relationship was under the microscope because of McIlroy's ongoing dispute with his former management company. McDowell, represented by the same Horizon agency, had been drawn into the legal proceedings. Both players had been at pains to stress that the dispute wasn't going to have any influence in the team room.

In his blog for the BBC Sport website, McDowell wrote: 'Myself and the other 10 guys would all love to be paired with the world's number one player. There will be a queue out of the door, of players wanting to partner Rory and, absolutely, I will be among them. Who wouldn't want to team up with the guy who has played the best golf all summer? Yes, it has been a rough time over the last couple of years on the business side of things for both me and Rory because he's been involved in a lawsuit with my management company. And it certainly has stressed our relationship, but we have put those things behind us this year. If anything our friendship has been strengthened by what we've experienced. We have talked about it and we would certainly love to renew our partnership again. As Paul McGinley and Rory have said, there are no problems in the team room between myself and Rory.'

The only problem was their record together. Of a possible six points, the partnership had yielded only two-and-a-half at Celtic Manor and Medinah. 'If I want to put them together, I will totally put them together,' McGinley stated. 'But I'm looking at different ideas as well.' Their past performances were the key factor, he explained, before adding: 'I don't understand why there should be such an interest in whether they will play together. I don't see what the big fuss is about this. Having said that, two or three months ago I would have had a view that they certainly would have played together. Now, I'm looking at different options too.'

Watson, meanwhile, wasted no time in beginning to direct a charm offensive at the Scottish crowds. His remarkable record of winning four Opens in the country that gave the game to the world was one of the prime reasons behind his appointment. His hero status in Scotland, which had just rejected independence in a national referendum, was clearly seen as a key asset to the American cause. 'This is a special place,' he told the assembled press. 'Scotland is where the game of golf was invented and the history of the game here is rich. There's a certain element in me that feels like I'm part Scottish. I love the game so much and I think the reason is reading of the history when I was a young boy.'

Sitting alongside, McGinley quickly got in on the act. 'He's got a particular affinity with his successes around here that I certainly watched as a boy,' the Irishman said.

'Hey, wait a minute, you're older than that!' Watson replied. 'You've got grey hair to prove it.'

'I was a teenager,' McGinley laughed. 'I have memories growing up of Tom winning Open Championships. I was rooting for him. It's a great thrill for him to come back to Scotland; it is the home of golf. I go to St Andrews, and I can feel the spirituality. You know you are somewhere special. But I think Gleneagles is again a very historic venue in world golf and I think it will do the Ryder Cup a lot of justice this week.'

This was Monday. A day of welcomes and of charm. There was a strong bond of respect between the two captains, but both were desperate for victory.

Watson stated yet again: 'This trip is a redemption trip.'

McGinley reiterated that Europe were only slight favourites and that the Americans should not be underestimated. He also made it clear that he was determined to avoid mistakes with his pairings, identifying the fact that in the last two Ryder Cups Europe had suffered more than their share of losing sequences. 'It is a real concern,' he told me. 'We've won two out of nine sessions in the last two Ryder Cups and yet we've won both matches.

'We've been very fortunate because the two sessions we did win, we won by huge numbers. I'm really aware of that and so are the players and, again, it's another warning signal that this is not going to be a case of [just] turning up and all this talk about us being really big favourites, far from it. This is a really strong American team and if we are going to win this Ryder Cup we are going to have to play incredibly well.'

This was the last occasion the two captains were seen sitting side by side in the interview room. McGinley was the more accomplished speaker in this environment. He appeared confident, thoughtful and prepared. Watson was more hesitant. In his first answer he stated: 'The real thing that's on everybody's mind is Friday morning at 7:35, is it? Or 7:36?' The discrepancy over the first tee time was only one minute, but it was the kind of question mark over detail that never occurred with his Irish opponent. When moderator Scott Crockett said '7:35, Tom' the American captain smiled: '7:35. I better get that right, no late to the tee.' It was a light-hearted moment, but still a mini own goal.

European players were still arriving from a wide variety of places. McGinley had told them to be on site by Monday evening, free of jet-lag. McDowell was the last to make it to the Perthshire venue, having flown from Florida the previous Friday. He spent the weekend practising at the exclusive Queenwood course in Surrey, under the watchful eye of his coach Pete Cowen. McDowell then made a quick visit to his family in Portrush in Northern Ireland before hopping over to Scotland.

When he arrived, his hotel room, like those of all the European players, was filled with presents and the clothing they would wear for the next seven days. 'It's a bit like Christmas when you go in there and see what's waiting for you,' McDowell told readers of his BBC blog. 'We will have our suits and clothes laid out per event and per session. There will be the Gala Dinner suit, the opening ceremony suit and our clothing for the golf. We'll get the answer of how we will look on each of the days and, as someone who likes his fashion, I'm always impatient to know what we'll be wearing when we go into battle.' McDowell also revealed that there would be tailors on site to make last-minute adjustments.

In the Monday evening gloaming, McDowell was a solitary figure on the range, hitting a few wedges before heading off to the first team meeting at 6 p.m. Some of the American players ventured onto the course that Monday afternoon and played a fun six-ball for a few holes. A small knot of spectators accompanied them and the players were happy to take 'selfies' with the fans afterwards. It was all so relaxed that they even noted the fans' email addresses in order to send them the pictures as mementos.

The following day, both teams went out for their first full practice rounds. It was a chance to acquaint themselves with a Centenary Course that had longer and thicker rough than anticipated because of the excellent September growing conditions. It was a bright, chilly day. The Europeans played in four groups of three because McGinley didn't want the rounds to drag out. The golfers stopped for autographs and pictures, keen to embrace their support. In the first group McIlroy, Martin Kaymer and García played together. Then came Poulter, Justin Rose and Gallacher. The third trio was Bjørn, Westwood and Donaldson, with Stenson, Dubuisson and McDowell bringing up the rear.

The Americans played in three groups of four and Watson kept the same quartets for all three practice days. They were made up of Matt Kuchar, Spieth, Simpson and Bubba Watson. Then came Furyk with Johnson, Mahan and Reed, followed in the final foursome by Bradley, Fowler, Mickelson and Walker. The idea of keeping the same groupings echoed Paul Azinger's 'pod system' which was at the heart of the US victory at Valhalla in 2008. Revealingly, Ted Bishop said: 'I don't want to say Tom Watson is stubborn or inflexible but a year ago he wasn't interested in the pod system. That has been Steve Stricker's influence. When he was appointed a vice captain he told Tom how effective it was at Valhalla and Tom became convinced that was the way to go.'

As the players set about their work, former Manchester United football manager Sir Alex Ferguson was spotted on the grounds at Gleneagles. McGinley had indicated he would have a guest speaker for his team on the Tuesday evening and it became obvious his choice was British football's most successful coach. 'We'd heard about it the previous Thursday at the Wales Open,' said the *Daily Telegraph*'s golf correspondent James Corrigan. 'But the European Tour denied it. They obviously didn't want it to get out. It had obviously been planned for months and months and this showed how determined McGinley was to keep it secret. There was then a rumour on the Monday that David Beckham had turned up. We knew there was going to be an inspirational speaker and we were running around looking for Beckham. We had been put off the scent of Fergie. Then we were all sitting in the media room on the Tuesday and there he was, Alex Ferguson, on the screen and then we knew.'

The captain's thinking was to make a virtue of Europe's favourite's tag. He didn't want any complacency and he knew that Ferguson had led Manchester United into countless matches where they were heavily backed to win. How did he repeatedly ensure that his team didn't fall victim to complacency and shock results? McGinley had first met Ferguson 15 years earlier at a pro-am organised by Irish racehorse owner J. P. McManus and they had subsequently become firm friends. When McGinley became skipper he asked Ferguson to come and speak to his team. He wanted it to be a surprise for the European players, but the cat was now out of the bag.

'I've loved the way his teams played,' McGinley said. 'The more I've met him, the more I've known he will be a natural fit. It's not about him being a headmaster and coming in and preaching to them. This is about fun.' But it was also about ramming home key sporting thoughts to help put the European players in the correct frame of mind.

For McIlroy, it was a huge highlight. An ardent Manchester United fan, he revealed how excited he was, listening to Ferguson: 'Whenever he was managing, they made Old

Trafford a bit of a fortress. When teams went there, it was very hard to compete against United. He was just talking a bit about that. We're slight favourites for a reason. We deserve to be. We've played well this year. It's not something that we should shy away from. It's something that we should embrace.

'I was just sitting there and looking up at him, and I didn't take my eyes off him. I was sort of in this trance, just listening to everything that he was saying and I'm sort of thinking: "This is all the stuff that he's probably said to Manchester United teams over the years." He told us a couple stories, just of past experiences in some big games and big matches, and some of the players that he managed, and it was a great evening. It was a really cool thing to be a part of.

'It was very useful, because we got to ask some questions, just about different things and what he thought was the key element to being successful, and successful as a team. He's a very inspirational sort of man when he talks. He's got a lot of authority and the room just goes quiet and everyone listens. So, as I said, it was a great experience for everyone, obviously, but especially for me, being a big Manchester United fan.'

In between practice rounds, players carried on with their media duties. They were split into groups of three and the process lasted an hour. They moved in rotation. One player spent 20 minutes in the media centre being grilled by newspaper and agency reporters, while another was being interviewed by the home television network, Sky Sports, and the next was in the American NBC studio. Then they would swap positions. It was a slick operation, with most of the golfers trying to dodge any potential controversy and remain 'on message'.

There was one exception: Phil Mickelson. He was the saviour for a reporting pack desperate to find an edge, a rivalry and a source of debate. Mickelson is a skilled operator in media conferences. He is eloquent, intelligent, charming and invariably a strong ambassador for the game. But, like his veteran teammate

Furyk, he bridles at suggestions that the US are not as cohesive a team as their European counterparts. His press conference was progressing in predictable fashion until he was asked: 'One of the theories put out there is that the Americans are not as close, they don't get along, and yet you were leading in the team competition two years ago and lost in the singles. So does that knock down the theory that you can't play together?'

Mickelson produced a bombshell reply. It was a cocktail of Furyk-like indignation and mischief and it guaranteed newspaper headlines.

'Well, not only are we able to play together, we also don't litigate against each other and that's a real plus, I feel, heading into this week,' he said.

The biggest star in the American team had made a calculated jibe at McIlroy and McDowell over their management company differences. Amid shocked laughter in the vast interview room, European Tour moderator Michael Gibbons said 'Ouch' and Mickelson smiled: 'I couldn't resist, sorry.'

'We just thought: "Oh my God, did he just say that?"' recalled James Corrigan of the *Daily Telegraph*. 'Then came the general sense that, with it being such an interminably long build-up, this would get us through the next few days. It had all been a bit of a phoney war. His comments were obviously planted. He meant to say it and spice it up a bit.'

The headlines duly followed. The affair quickly became known as 'Liti-gate' and set the agenda. There was even a suggestion that McIlroy responded during the official pre-Ryder Cup gala event in Glasgow, attended by both teams. According to the *Sun* newspaper, McIlroy is said to have quipped, 'At least none of us are being investigated by the FBI', referring to the enquiry into insider trading, to which Mickelson had briefly been linked before the investigation was dropped.

While this was all being played out in newspapers, radio and television, the players battled to get to grips with the

Centenary Course. Nine holes were played on Wednesday and Thursday, with hoards of spectators following behind. The moment for hostilities to begin in earnest had almost arrived and the eagerly anticipated pairings for the Friday morning fourballs were announced at a glitzy opening ceremony staged on the Gleneagles Hotel's par-three course.

The home captain chooses the order in which the matches are played. At Medinah, Davis Love opted to start with the alternate-shot foursomes but Europe's preference this time was for the better-ball format.

McGinley explained to me: 'I don't want to change an order that's been so successful for us. If I changed it and we lost I would get heavily criticised.' Going first with fourballs poses difficulties, though. It is the more forgiving format and makes it easier to blood newcomers. On the other hand, there is the risk of sending them out in the highly charged atmosphere of the first morning.

When the pairings were unveiled it became clear McGinley was the more cautious of the captains on this issue. Of his rookies, only Gallacher was blooded while Watson fielded all three of his debutants: Spieth, Reed and Walker. Indeed, Watson made the audacious move of teaming up his Texan youngsters, Reed and Spieth, rather than pairing each of them with a more experienced player.

This is how they lined up:

07:35	Stenson and Rose v. Watson and Simpson
07:50	Bjørn and Kaymer v. Fowler and Walker
08:05	Gallacher and Poulter v. Spieth and Reed
08:20	García and McIlroy v. Bradley and Mickelson

There was a collective intake of breath among the thousands of fans who attended the ceremony when that final match was announced. Pitting McIlroy against Mickelson was just what they all wanted, after the US left-hander had spiced up the preceding days.

McGinley explained his choice of putting the world number one with García, who had been beaten by McIlroy at the Open and the Bridgestone event earlier in the summer.

'It was quite clear not just on the golf course but off the golf course, there's a real bonding going on,' he said. '[Their] statistics are very strong, they enjoy each other's company, and in a lot of ways it was a natural fit. They kind of raised it with me in May at Wentworth, and I said: "Okay, let me think about that." To be honest, I didn't really pay a lot of attention to it, and it was only at the US PGA, as they started talking to me more and more around that time, that my position became a little bit clearer. I thought: "You know what, yeah."'

It is a blind draw. The captains deliver their pairings in the order they want them to play and then they are matched up. It was little surprise that Watson had gone with America's two most successful pairings at Medinah in the strategically important first and last matches. McGinley had done the same, fighting fire with fire.

Watson was asked whether he was happy that Mickelson and Bradley would be facing the strongest-looking European pairing. 'Of course I am, sure,' he said. 'You always look and guess what Paul might do, but honestly, it was really where the players wanted to play rather than where we thought Paul was going to put his teams.

'It just fell like this, so we got a match! That's the striking contest. That's the main event in the first round, you'd have to say. You all know that. I mean, it's not rocket science here. We're going to be looking at the first three matches; oh, yeah, there's Sergio and Rory playing Phil and Keegan. I'm looking forward to that. But again, every match is really important. Every point is important.'

And, at long last, the contest for those points was about to begin.

CHAPTER 15

Gleneagles Day One

26 September 2014

*'If we don't hit them with the first wave, we
hit them with the second. And, if you see red
on the board, you are not to panic or worry,
there's another wave coming behind.'*

Paul McGinley

E urope headed into action having been bombarded by
messages of inspiration. Sir Alex Ferguson had told the
players to feel like a rock in a storm. They needed to
remain strong to withstand everything the Americans threw
at them. Paul McGinley spoke passionately about how the continental golfers needed to stick together and perform as a unit.
All those Gaelic football memories, from the dressing rooms
of his youth, resurfaced as he sought to maintain and enhance
Europe's renowned Ryder Cup spirit.

While the Americans were being told repeatedly by Tom
Watson that this was a mission of redemption, McGinley's
methods were more sophisticated. He enlisted a US-based
British coach, Nick Bradley, who specialises in areas of self-
motivation. Bradley was given the role of providing pictures
with messages to bolster confidence and cohesion. The images
hung in the team and locker rooms.

'Paul asked me to produce six or seven movie-like posters
with different messages on,' Bradley revealed. 'It felt a complete honour for me to do that. Each one needed to have a

different message. For example, we had the rock of Europe, which was the first thing they saw when they walked out of the team room after a meeting with Paul. The rock of Europe is basically a big peninsula with these waves crashing against it, and embedded into the rock are the stars of the European flag,' said Bradley.

'The caption said: "We will be the rock when the storm comes." It is very metaphoric, you know, we are going to stand still and not going to be moved. It signified resilience, the old Chinese proverb "fall down three times, stand up four". It looks at our heritage, our history together and the bonding of all of our cultures.

'Another popular one was an Ian Poulter one. Ian is pulling his heart out of his chest. The heart is blue, once again with the stars of the flag embedded in there. Poulter is in typical shouting fashion. Underneath, it says: "Europe, I give you my heart." The message is that this week isn't about money, not about a sponsorship deal, but about the glue between us and what this really means. The players loved it. Rory McIlroy said the images were fantastic and all Justin Rose kept saying all week was: "I am the rock." '

By the first morning, these images were etched into the psyche of the players as they made their way from the team room to the locker room close to the driving range. The message then became even more powerful. 'Just before they went out on the practice area, I did a massive picture of Seve Ballesteros which stood right next to the door. It looked like a shrine. It was Seve when he was 17 years old. He's staring into the camera and the caption read: "Look into his eyes, his mission is clear." If you didn't get goose bumps looking at that, you would never get them.'

This all played to McGinley's central message of resilience and inspiration. It was not all tub-thumping stuff, though. Another prominent message came from Bob Torrance, the legendary coach who had schooled McGinley through his career and had helped several of his team at various times. Torrance, Sam's father, had been a fixture on European Tour ranges for decades until he died in July 2014. 'Happiest days of your lives,' was his standard phrase to his players, the moment before they went out to compete. That saying was also prominent in the team room.

The Americans also had motivational signage in their locker room. The entrance was set in a giant flag of the Stars and Stripes with 'Team USA' emblazoned across the top. In simple white lettering on the secondary door read the message '12 STRONG'. A giant poster of the Ryder Cup stood in the middle of the changing area, leaving no one in any doubt over what the week was all about. Each of the lockers had a large action photograph of the player using it that week. And, on their departure to the range, the last thing they saw on the exit door was: 'UNITED WE STAND'.

The motivational imagery did not end there. Heading onto the range, the players walked down past the media centre and into a tunnel under the road which separated the Centenary Course from Gleneagles's famous Kings layout. The tunnel was illuminated and decorated with past Ryder Cup captains celebrating moments of glory. To the left were the Americans − Watson, Jack Nicklaus and Paul Azinger among others − all decked in red, white and blue. To the right were Europe's heroes: Colin Montgomerie, Ian Woosnam, Bernard Gallacher, José Mariá Olazábal and, inevitably, Seve. He was the last face on the European side. Sergio García would blow his mentor a kiss every time he made the climb to the first tee.

It could not have been a more emotive scene for the players as they headed towards what is regarded as the most nerve-wracking shot in golf − the first drive at a Ryder Cup.

A keen, chill breeze on a beautifully clear morning provided the perfect autumnal scene on that first morning. The

Ochil Hills, with the glorious valley of Glendevon carving through them, never looked more spectacular. The atmosphere around the tee, meanwhile, was boisterous but not to the extent witnessed two years earlier at Medinah, or at Celtic Manor in 2010. Large stands formed an intimidating, horseshoe amphitheatre around the teeing area. Although the spectators had been there for hours, it was only when vice captains and players started to emerge that the decibel levels started to rise. The European anthem of 'Olé, Olé, Olé!' rang out as first Padraig Harrington and then McGinley came into view. The American captain, Tom Watson, was there as well to see off his first pair.

As the visiting team, the US teed off first. Bubba Watson and Webb Simpson arrived, clad in white woolly hats, as did Rose and Henrik Stenson. The Europeans, though, seemed more elegant. They wore royal-blue sweaters with the cross of St Andrew emblazoned down the right front. It was a smart move, using the saltire to play to the Scottish crowds, and particularly so in the wake of the recent referendum on independence. The US players wore navy blue with a large emblem of the Ryder Cup. It seemed like a throwback to the sort of jumper you might receive as a 1980s Christmas present – one that would not emerge from the bottom of a drawer beyond New Year.

As the American pair wandered onto the tee, the atmosphere grew to fever pitch. A glance down the hole revealed thousands of people on the banks bordering this 461-yard par four. The entire hole was surrounded with people standing at least 10 deep. Behind the green, on a large hill, they stood 30 or 40 deep, tightly packed. It was an extraordinary sight. It was as though this golf hole had become an impromptu sell-out stadium, and all this at 7.30 in the morning. Commentating, I said I had never seen anything like it on a golf course before.

Bubba Watson looked jaunty and confident, his partner pale and nervous. Rose and Stenson appeared calm and composed.

The crowds synchronised their cheers with the players' lazy practice swings as they burnt up the time until the 7.35 start. Watson nodded to starter Ivor Robson, a silver-haired veteran with a distinctive, high-pitched Scottish accent, indicating that he would hit first. Robson nodded in acknowledgement. But it was Simpson who was on the teeing ground, while Watson stood at the side, arms folded across the top of his bright pink driver. Simpson kept practising his swing as Robson went through the preliminary announcements. He then said: 'On the tee, Bubba Watson!' But it was abundantly clear that Simpson was hitting first. The Masters champion had duped the most experienced starter in the game, and gave a broad grin. Robson rarely, if ever, makes public comment beyond who is next to tee off, but could hardly have been impressed by the prank. He was forced into a correction. 'Thank you, ladies and gentlemen . . . on the tee, Webb Simpson!' This was the cue for ironic cheers from the crowd.

The embarrassment switched immediately from starter to golfer. Simpson produced an unconvincing swing and skied the ball into the air. It was the kind of shot associated with a high-handicap amateur and only just made the fairway.

Watson then stirred up the crowd, inviting them to cheer at their loudest as he took his turn. This was the same trick he had played at Medinah, although he had stated he would not do anything similar at an away match. In a change of heart, he lifted his arms repeatedly to encourage the spectators. As had happened two years earlier, however, the party atmosphere did not help him find the fairway and his ball flew into the left rough. Rose and Stenson took a more conventional approach, launching imperious drives down the fairway to give Europe the confident start they craved. The 40th Ryder Cup was under-way. A day of extraordinary ebbs and flows was about to unfold.

The top match proceeded down the first and Rose and Watson traded pars. At the second, the big-hitting Watson was the only player to find the green of the par five in two. Stenson had to lay up from the rough, but pitched to eight feet. Watson charged his eagle putt long before the Swede carded the first birdie. The Masters champion then missed his return and Europe went one up. From then on, the home pair were in charge. Simpson was hopeless, and Watson not much better. The American pair, who had won both of their fourball matches two years earlier by commanding 5 and 4 margins, failed to register a birdie between them.

The only discomfort for the European partnership came at the par-five ninth. There, Rose hit into the water down the right and, while looking for his ball, was stung on his right thumb by a wasp. On the following green the Englishman was given a pain-killing spray and some antihistamine pills. Moments later, he drained a 30-foot birdie putt to take the home pair four up. The match ended when Rose holed a 10-footer on the 14th for his third birdie, and the fifth in total for an impressive combination that had been forged on the Lake Nona range where the players live.

'They know each other's games,' said Pete Cowen, who coaches Stenson. 'They don't play a lot together but they hit balls all the time. When I'm at Lake Nona there's always Poulter, Justin and Henrik on the range with GMac [Graeme McDowell] down at the other end. It's like a European Tour event when we are on the range.

'Henrik loved going out first on the Friday. He wanted to be there. The week before, I went out to Florida to work with Henrik and Graeme and at that point I honestly had never seen Henrik hit the ball better. For two days he never missed a shot. So expectations went up a bit. He didn't hit the ball quite as well at the Ryder Cup, which was a little bit difficult,' Cowen told me.

The 5 and 4 margin held a certain resonance, given that Tom Watson had said 'I kept seeing these numbers 5 and 4, 5 and 4' as his justification for handing a wildcard to Simpson. The selection had been a last-minute decision and he must have been wondering whether his original choice of Bill Haas would have been a better bet. The US captain certainly did not envisage those figures being posted in reverse. Europe emphatically secured the first of the 14 points needed to retain the Ryder Cup.

Elsewhere, the visitors were having more success. The pairing of Jordan Spieth and Patrick Reed, with a combined age of 45, had been another last-minute decision. Assistant captain Steve Stricker provided statistics to persuade Watson to change some of his original thoughts. The plan was for Spieth to play with Matt Kuchar, and Reed to go with Jim Furyk. Stricker, though, noticed the PGA Tour numbers that showed both youngsters ranked well in the 'total birdies' category making them an ideal fit for better-ball golf. Watson told them on the Wednesday about his new plan to put them together.

Vindication for the move came instantly. The Texan pair were thrashing Ian Poulter and Stephen Gallacher. Europe's captain had wanted Poulter to play the senior role in introducing his Scottish partner to the rarefied atmosphere of the Ryder Cup. The thinking was that Poulter becomes an inspirational force in these matches, regardless of his overall form. It was a gamble, though, and one that did not pay off from the moment Poulter missed a three-footer at the first.

The young Americans, meanwhile, played inspired golf. Spieth's par at the first was enough to put the Americans one up. Losing a hole to par in the better-ball format is regarded as a crime and the European pair showed little sign of recovering their poise. When Reed birdied the 11th the American rookies had collected three birdies apiece and were six up. Gallacher won the 12th with a par but the youngsters closed out a 5 and 4 victory two holes later.

That tied the opening session at one point apiece. The remaining matches on the course were much closer to call.

Martin Kaymer and Thomas Bjørn made a blistering start against Rickie Fowler and Jimmy Walker. Three birdies in the first four holes, two of them from Kaymer, put the Europeans in control. But Fowler birdied the fifth and Walker the ninth to trim the arrears to a single hole at the turn. Bjørn's birdie at the 13th put the home duo two up with five to play — an advantage preserved until the 16th. The debutant Walker then shone like one of those stars he loves to photograph. The Centenary Course finishes with a two par-fives sandwiching the par-three 17th. Walker birdied both to snatch an unlikely half. 'Any time you are two up with three to play and don't deliver your point you are disappointed,' Kaymer said.

The balance of power now lay in the hands of McIlroy and his chosen partner García, up against the crack American combination of Phil Mickelson and Keegan Bradley. McIlroy was using his new driver — Nike's Vapor model that had just been approved for competitive use. Although the Ulsterman said he had been testing it all summer, it seemed a curious move to put it straight into the bag at such a high-profile event, particularly as he had become undisputedly the best driver in the world with the previous model. He even contemplated introducing a new set of irons at Gleneagles, but decided against it for fear of a media backlash. He waited until the following week and with them finished in a share of second place at the Alfred Dunhill Links Championship.

The decision regarding his new driver at Gleneagles was initially made to look even more questionable during a relatively shaky opening display, although García's birdie at the sixth gave Europe the early advantage. At that time the blue of Europe was appearing all over the scoreboard. They were ahead in the first, second and now fourth match. But as Kaymer and Bjørn were pegged back and Spieth and Reed continued to dominate against Poulter and Gallacher, the morning momentum swung back in America's favour.

On cue, the visiting pair in the bottom match pounced. Three birdies in four holes from the seventh – two of them to Bradley – put the US two up with seven holes to go. In the tough, cool breeze the Europeans could not buy a birdie but pars were enough to win the 11th, 13th and 15th holes, enabling them to nudge ahead again. Bradley then struck with a stunning eagle at the 16th and Mickelson's birdie at the last was enough to claim a sensational 1-up victory that gave the session to the Americans. Not only that, they had taken points from McIlroy and Poulter, the two key players they were targeting in the European team. The theory was to take points from them and, additionally, gain a crucial psychological boost.

Although the session had gone against them, Europe were not overly concerned. 'I thought my job was not to be a cheerleader out there for the players and I told them that from the very first meeting. My job was to plot our next move as a team,' McGinley later revealed. 'Wave after wave of attack. I was plotting that next wave and, once that wave was underway, I was plotting the wave after that.'

This is where the choice of using five vice captains came into play. That first morning, Harrington, José María Olazábal, Miguel Ángel Jiménez and Torrance were out on the course, relaying information back to the skipper on walkie-talkies. The fifth man was Des Smyth, who had been detailed to look after the four players who had been left out. McDowell, Victor Dubuisson, Lee Westwood and Jamie Donaldson were told to sleep in and prepare themselves for the afternoon. McGinley did not want them on the tee, first thing in the morning, burning up energy. Those players had breakfast with Smyth, as a collective unit. The message was clear; they should ready themselves as they saw fit while Smyth provided the conduit to the captain.

'The fifth vice captain was a huge part of that,' McGinley said. 'We talked about a fresh wave coming out. If we don't hit them with the first wave, we hit them with the second. And if you see red on the board, you are not to panic or worry, there's another wave coming behind.'

Westwood had been picked for his experience. This was his ninth Ryder Cup and his sardonic sense of humour was a perfect foil for Donaldson on his debut. The articulate, intelligent McDowell had been detailed to look after the enigmatic Dubuisson and make him feel at ease in his first Ryder Cup. They duly practised together throughout the week.

During one of those sessions, the Frenchman was fretting. 'Dubuisson came up to me when he was playing with Graeme,' Pete Cowen, who also coaches McDowell, revealed. 'He said: "It's difficult for me, I've grown up admiring these nine players that I'm playing with. I've watched them on TV, I even watched Graeme win the US Open. I was shouting at the TV, you know: 'Come on GMac, come on GMac!' Now I'm playing with him and it seems a bit surreal and it's difficult to get my head round it."

'I told him not to worry about it,' Cowen went on. 'And then I said to Graeme that he needed to go and talk to him. Victor was playing great in the practice rounds and I pointed out to Graeme that he wouldn't be a bad partner for him. Graeme sat down and chatted to him and he was great. Then, on the Friday morning, they played a few practice holes. It was difficult because it was so windy. It was then that they made the decision to use Victor's ball. He told Graeme he was finding it very difficult to spin and control the make of ball that GMac used. Graeme just said: "No problem, we'll use your ball – perfect." And Dubuisson thought this was great, it made him feel like he was the most important thing.'

McDowell and Dubuisson had to wait until the final match of the day before they could start their Ryder Cup. They were up against Mickelson and Bradley, buoyed by their morning success against the world's first- and third-ranked players. The American line-up was curious, though. Watson left out his two best performers of the morning. Spieth and Reed were benched with little explanation. 'They were very upset with me for not playing them this afternoon,' Watson admitted. 'I said: "I know you're going to be mad at me, but you'll be playing tomorrow for sure."'

Watson sent out Jim Furyk and Matt Kuchar to face the Westwood/Donaldson combination. In the second match, Zach Johnson partnered Hunter Mahan against Stenson and Rose and, in the third contest, Fowler and Walker were up against McIlroy and García.

McGinley's plan to hit back hard in those foursomes worked brilliantly. The four players who sat out the morning had been made to feel an integral part of the team rather than also-rans. In fact, they had been given a specific and vital task. They had been handed the strategically important slots at the top and bottom of the afternoon draw and were imbued by the confidence their captain had invested in them.

Donaldson and Westwood fell behind early but hit back with a birdie at the sixth while a par at the next was enough to take them ahead. The lead was stretched at the 11th and the chemistry between the two was palpable. Kuchar and Furyk managed only their second birdie at the 16th to give the US some hope but it was extinguished at the last, where the European pair bravely birdied to claim a 2-up victory.

Rose and Stenson, meanwhile, picked up from where they had left off. They birdied the first and sixth holes to go two up on Johnson and Mahan, a gritty combination that the Europeans were in no danger of underestimating. The Americans showed why when they birdied the next two holes, and it was clear this was a match that was likely to go the distance. Europe went ahead again on the 11th, only to be pegged back on the 14th. One hole later, the Americans buckled as they carded their first bogey and two holes later they contrived to three-putt from the back of the penultimate green to lose 2 and 1.

'That's a fantastic point for us,' Rose told me in the

immediate aftermath. 'They were a really strong combination and we knew they wouldn't go away.' Rose's only discomfort was his swollen right thumb, but it had not prevented him from playing brilliant golf during an outstanding first day for the Englishman. It was two points out of two for this new partnership. Indeed, it was the first time in three Ryder Cups that Stenson had played with the same partner twice.

The McDowell/Dubuisson combination was equally impressive. The Frenchman, in particular, stood out. All the work that had gone into making the 'mystery man' fit into a team environment – the dinners with the captain in Malaysia during the EurAsia Cup, the meeting with motor-racing hero Eddie Jordan, the surreptitious tee-times shared with McDowell on the European Tour – paid dividends. The pair won three of the first five holes and controlled their contest against Mickelson and Bradley. Ultimately they won 3 and 2. Not only did they collect a valuable point, they dealt a mortal wound to what was expected to be one of the America's strongest partnerships. It never returned to the fray.

McIlroy and García were struggling, though. Beaten in the morning, they were up against it again after lunch. Walker was making an impressive debut and Fowler was showing the temperament that had brought him three runner-up finishes in the last three majors. The American pair went two up when they won the 12th and the much-vaunted Europeans were staring down the barrel of a second defeat. They did win the 13th with a par, but a bogey at the 15th left them two down with three to play. A guaranteed half point came the way of the US when they shared the par-five 16th in birdies and a full point seemed assured one hole later.

The American pair were on the green of the par-three 17th and seemingly certain of a par, while García's tee shot finished 40 feet away. It was time for McIlroy to make a statement, just as he had been doing throughout the summer. He sized up his birdie putt and generated the biggest roar of the day when it rammed into the back of the hole. It felt as though the entire 50,000 crowd had congregated to follow the final match on the course and it was now a cavalry charge to the 18th to see whether the Europeans could snatch an unlikely half.

It did not look promising when McIlroy's drive flew right into the trees, but the ball rebounded into the rough and García had a lie and a view that enabled him to get the ball up to the green with a five wood that carved round the trees for arguably the shot of the day. It enabled the Europeans to birdie and snatch that half. The home side won the afternoon sequence by a record 3½ points to a lone ½ and, after trailing at lunch, the holders were 5–3 ahead going into the second day.

McGinley's strategy had been justified while Watson was facing uncomfortable questions. As the week progressed, his news conferences became increasingly awkward. For someone who had spent the previous decades as a revered figure, this was unfamiliar territory. His audience no longer wanted rose-tinted reminiscences of past glories, they wanted explanations for what looked increasingly like flawed policies.

His wildcard selection of Simpson was a prime example but so, too, was the resting of Spieth and Reed. 'I know the question is going to be asked about Jordan Spieth and Patrick Reed, whether I should have played them in the afternoon,' Watson admitted. 'I thought at the time it was the best decision not to play them. There were a variety of reasons, but I won't go into those. It was a decision that my vice captains and I made. That was a decision that we felt very strongly for.

'I can tell you one comical thing, though. When I told Patrick that he wasn't going to play in the afternoon, it was comical at the time, not so comical now. I said: "How does that make you feel?" He said: "Well, I'm alright with it." Then he said: "Well, really, Captain, I'm not alright with it." I said: "That's the way I want you to be."'

It was a muddled explanation and, under cross-examination, Watson went further: 'I had some doubt in making that decision, but my gut feeling said that was the right decision.'

The contrast between the captains could not have been greater. Watson was working off the instincts that made him such a champion, while McGinley was far more strategic and the Irishman appeared in full control. 'For our guys to react the way they did, for all four matches to be up, I think, after six holes, there was blue on the board for every single match, that was a terrific response,' he stated. 'It shows a huge amount of character that we have on the team, a huge amount of talent. That we can come out with such strong pairings in the afternoon shows a great response and resilience.'

The pairs for the following morning's fourballs were announced and, again, the American line-up raised eyebrows. Watson omitted Mickelson and Bradley – his supposed on-course leader and the wildcard he had selected for his inspirational qualities. 'It's really just common sense,' Watson insisted. 'They played 36 holes. They are tired. Give them a break in the morning, get their legs back and there's a good chance they'll go in the afternoon in some way, shape or form. They may not go together but they will go in the afternoon.' It was not a convincing argument and, as it transpired, we did not see them together again.

Here's how they lined up for the second morning of fourballs:

Justin Rose & Henrik Stenson	v	Bubba Watson & Matt Kuchar
Jamie Donaldson & Lee Westwood	v	Jim Furyk & Hunter Mahan
Thomas Bjørn & Martin Kaymer	v	Patrick Reed & Jordan Spieth
Rory McIlroy & Sergio García	v	Jimmy Walker & Rickie Fowler

The only surprise from the European point of view was the absence of the outstanding McDowell and Dubuisson. Both were disappointed to learn that they would sit out another session, but McGinley explained: 'It was very tempting, but I'm looking at the big picture, something I can't reveal at the moment but you'll see on Sunday night. I'm working to a plan. I'll reveal a little bit more on Sunday night. Victor and Graeme played particularly strong today. It was very tempting, but I was in a very privileged position that I had a lot of options.'

There was little doubt which captain slept easier, that Friday night.

CHAPTER 16

Gleneagles Day Two

27 September 2014

'If we go on to win this Ryder Cup, that,
to me, was a pivotal moment.'
Paul McGinley on Justin Rose's
final putt of Day Two

If the atmosphere had been comparatively subdued on the first tee ahead of the opening day's action, it was anything but on Saturday. Once again, it was a dry and fresh day and Paul McGinley instructed one of his assistants, Miguel Ángel Jiménez, to make an early visit to the cauldron where the opening drives would be dispatched. Jiménez is one of the most popular figures in European golf. He knows how to play to a crowd and those were just the qualities the captain wanted. The ponytailed Spaniard with the ready smile worked the fans into a frenzy, ensuring a noisy and intense atmosphere before the players finally arrived for their 7.35 tee-off.

Once again, it was Justin Rose and Henrik Stenson who led off for the home side, while Matt Kuchar replaced Webb Simpson as Bubba Watson's partner. This quartet served up one of the greatest matches the Ryder Cup has ever seen. The wind had dropped compared with the difficult first day, the pins were more generous and there were birdie opportunities aplenty. The players fed off them voraciously. The Americans were a highly creditable seven under par and yet still lost 3 and 2. Rose holed almost every putt he looked at as the Europeans overturned an early deficit to register a convincing point. Rose and Stenson had now won three out of three points, even though Stenson's back was starting to ache. 'Justin played phenomenal golf, I just backed him up,' said the Swede.

The visitors were in better shape in the match behind, where Jim Furyk and Hunter Mahan dominated Lee Westwood and Jamie Donaldson. The Americans were convincing winners, four ahead with only three holes to go. McGinley was concerned. He had big plans for Westwood and Donaldson in the afternoon and needed to know whether they would be up to the job.

Sam Torrance was following the match and McGinley approached him to ask what had happened. 'I had been plotting and not seen the scores,' McGinley recalled. 'I came up and said: "Sam, where are we? Have they lost the dynamic? What's the body language? How are they playing?" All of the things you would ask. And Sam just looked at me and said: "Americans are playing great." That's why it was so important to have vice captains I could trust, who could read the game and read the players. And because of that endorsement from Sam they kept their places for the afternoon.'

But it was a precious point for the Americans, and a second was never in doubt in the next game. Jordan Spieth and Patrick Reed played with a controlled fury after being left out the previous afternoon. Thomas Bjørn and Martin Kaymer never stood a chance, despite going two up after the first three holes. Spieth won the fifth, sixth, ninth and 10th before Reed took over with birdies at the 13th and 14th holes. The younger of the pair then added a further birdie at the next to complete a crushing victory. They had dovetailed beautifully, demonstrating a synergy that had been sadly lacking from the previous afternoon's foursomes. It was a welcome result for Tom Watson, but ironically also provided more ammunition for his growing army of critics.

The bottom match did not hit the heights of the Stenson/ Rose victory in the top game, but it was still a compelling encounter that went the distance. Despite birdies at the first two holes, Ian Poulter remained badly out of sorts. Rory McIlroy was left playing a solitary role in trying to hold Rickie Fowler and Jimmy Walker at bay. Birdies at the eighth and ninth put the Europeans two up at the turn. Fowler responded by holing from a green-side bunker to win the next and, at the 11th, Walker birdied to level the contest. Two holes later Walker did it again to put the US ahead for the first time.

Poulter could not hit his hat at this stage and, on the 15th, drove into the rough. He hacked it short of the greenside trap guarding the front right of the putting surface. Fowler, meanwhile, played a brilliant approach and a birdie was almost certain. McIlroy was on the green in two but much further away. Poulter surveyed a tricky downhill chip. His crisp wedge sent the ball over the hazard and the ball ran out towards the flag, back left of the green. It took a right-to-left borrow and the crowd began to roar. The ball turned towards the hole and, dead weight, dropped in. From nowhere, the man detailed with the talismanic role had made a dramatic impact. He had denied the Americans the chance of going two up with three to play.

It was bedlam as he celebrated in typical Poulter fashion; McIlroy grinned in appreciation. At last he had had some help. The Englishman then birdied the par-five 16th to level the contest. It remained all square going up the last and McIlroy and Walker traded birdies to ensure an enthralling encounter finished honours even.

America had hit back, though. As on Friday, they edged the session by a point and now only trailed 6½–5½. Surely it was time for Watson to reintroduce his rested and inspirational pairing of Phil Mickelson and Keegan Bradley for the afternoon foursomes? The US skipper had a different view. His most decorated player had argued for the chance to play that Saturday afternoon, and had warmed up on the range only to find out by text that he had been dropped. It was the first time in a Ryder Cup career stretching back to 1995 that he had been left out for an entire day.

On the other hand, Fowler and Walker were named for the fourth match running. All three of their previous contests had gone to the 18th. The Centenary Course was an exhausting layout, with big undulating holes and long walks from greens to tees. Watson paid little heed to this as his decisions became ever more haphazard. Seven of his side were asked to play two rounds on that Saturday. His team required a big afternoon. They needed to build on an encouraging morning, but Watson was trying to do it with only nine players. Simpson also sat out the duration of that Saturday, along with Bradley. It meant two wildcards and the team's most experienced player were not used while Europe fielded all but Stephen Gallacher in their search for a commanding lead.

Donaldson and Westwood were given another opportunity and they faced Zach Johnson and Kuchar. McIlroy and García were re-united and played Furyk and Mahan. Kaymer replaced Stenson as Rose's partner to face Spieth and Reed, while McDowell and Victor Dubuisson again played the anchor role against Walker and Fowler.

In the top match the Americans drew first blood and Westwood and Donaldson twice had to come from a hole down before a par at the short sixth took them one up. Johnson and Kuchar combined to bring it back to all square after eight but then the European pair hit the accelerator to win the next two holes. Thereafter they never surrendered their advantage and a birdie at the 16th and a par on the penultimate green saw them home.

The victory took Westwood to a career 23 points, past Seve Ballesteros and into second place in the European all-time list. Later that evening, he sat with a handful of teammates in the interview room. As the likes of Rose and Graeme McDowell chatted animatedly about the day, the Englishman stared distractedly into the distance. James Corrigan, of the *Daily Telegraph*, wondered what was wrong. 'I sent him a direct message on Twitter to see if he was okay,' Corrigan told me. 'He replied that he was simply overcome with emotion that he'd overtaken Seve in the points table, adding that he was a bit of a softie, really.'

McIlroy and García finally hit form in the second of the foursomes. They lost only one hole to Furyk and Mahan in a match that began with victories on the first two holes and ended with two birdies in the last three for Europe's leading pair. They won 3 and 2, by which time McDowell and Dubuisson had thrashed the exhausted Walker and Fowler 5 and 4. This left one match out on the course.

Rose struggled to harness the putting touch of the morning and, along with Kaymer, barely held on against the youthful Spieth and Reed. McGinley's plan had been to put Rose together with Poulter for this match but, with the latter misfiring for much of the morning, he had a late change of heart. The captain was worried that he had not been able to tell this Ryder Cup colossus first hand. He had been forced to leave that task to one of his assistants. Those fears were quickly alleviated when Poulter put his arm round the skipper on one of the fairways early in the afternoon to say that he fully understood.

Spieth and Reed led two up after eight holes and were still ahead by a single hole coming up the last. On their way up that par five, Kaymer told Rose: 'Come on, we deserve a half here.' It was just the message the Englishman, who had been Europe's standout performer, needed to hear. The German left his partner with a five-foot birdie putt on the home green to force a tie and Rose did not waste the chance.

The importance of that putt should not be underestimated. It denied America the slightest momentum heading into the final-day singles. It guaranteed Europe went unbeaten in all eight foursomes matches as they repeated their record haul from the previous day of 3½–½. Consequently, the home side led the US 10–6.

America were in disarray. 'We got shellacked this afternoon,' Watson admitted. The captain also confessed to potential errors of judgement. 'It may have been a mistake that I put Jimmy and Rickie out for four matches. I thought they could handle it. Jimmy got a little bit tired,' he said. 'That was my calculated decision because I thought they were playing very well.'

Looking every bit of his 65 years, he searched for positives: 'As I recall, there's been a bit of history of 10–6 comebacks, most recently the Europeans last time and, of course, in 1999 at Brookline. The players are already talking about that.'

But Watson was clearly disappointed and spoke in critical terms about his team's performance. 'They just didn't live up to the standards that the Europeans did this afternoon,' he said.

Inevitably, he was quizzed on his benching of Mickelson. 'I played him two rounds yesterday and he was tired last night,' the skipper explained. 'I sat at the table with him. He was exhausted and maybe that was the wrong choice, me playing him two rounds. But he wanted to play in the alternate-shot, and I had to give him his due. He says: "I've got a good record in the alternate-shot."

'Today I came back up to the clubhouse and talked to him and Keegan and Webb, and said they would be sitting out the afternoon as well. I tell you, I expected exactly what Phil said to me. He said: "We can get it done, Captain. We want the chance." He lobbied again. He texted me, he said: "Give us a chance." I had to tell him no. I felt we had the best four teams possible in the afternoon for alternate shot.'

Those four teams brought home just half a point between them.

On Mickelson, Watson added: 'He didn't play very well yesterday. I told him that. Whether that was from being tired or the course not being set up for his type of game, I had to make that decision.'

The captain spoke of organising a get-together of all the players, their caddies and wives in the team room that evening, to try to inspire the sort of comeback Europe had managed at Medinah.

But the evening was not entirely positive. After trying to rally his team, Watson asked vice captains Ray Floyd, Andy North and Steve Stricker to provide their thoughts before Mickelson addressed his teammates. The man who had seethed at being left out of Saturday's action pointedly sat with his back to his captain and spoke individually to all of the players, offering personal messages of inspiration. Sources suggest this had the desired effect in motivating the team, but it also undermined Watson, the golfing legend who was supposed to be leading them.

Further details from that meeting were soon in the public domain. ESPN.com's respected writer Bob Harig located four people who were involved and they corroborated extraordinary revelations. Harig reported: 'Watson started by saying, according to all of the sources: "You stink at foursomes." After praising the rookie team of Reed and Spieth, Watson went through the Sunday singles pairings and ridiculed several members of the European side as he went through the match-ups.

'Soon after, Watson was presented a gift by Furyk, a replica of the Ryder Cup trophy that was signed by every member of the team. Instead of thanking them, the sources said Watson said the gift meant nothing to him if the players did not get the real Ryder Cup on Sunday and that he wanted to be holding it aloft on the green in victory. One of the sources said: "That's almost verbatim. He said it basically means nothing to me." Another added: "It was fairly shocking that he treated this thoughtful gift with such disdain."'

Other sources suggest that Watson expressed gratitude for

the gift but then turned to his team to say that he would prefer them to deliver the real Ryder Cup the following day. In their opinion, it was not the slight portrayed elsewhere.

Nevertheless, these revelations exposed Watson's captaincy and tarnished a man who had enjoyed a glowing reputation throughout a distinguished career. The captaincy was a job too far. The fact that he had not been to a Ryder Cup since his team's victory at the Belfry in 1993 contributed to the feeling that he was out of his depth. His ego made him belittle his players, and he entirely misjudged his treatment of Mickelson.

It was far more harmonious in the blue and gold environs of the European team room. Their success in the afternoon foursomes left them ecstatic, and within four points of defending the trophy. Rose's closing putt was highly significant. It showed Europe could dig out vital contributions when they needed them most. 'That half point was absolutely huge,' McGinley acknowledged. 'If we go on to win this Ryder Cup, that, to me, was a pivotal moment. But, as I say, let's not talk too far forward yet.'

This was the tenor of the evening meeting. It was time to revisit the words of Sir Alex Ferguson, about how successful teams banish complacency. They had to anticipate an American storm and Europe needed to be the team that stood firm as a rock. Westwood was invited to address his teammates. He had been in the 1999 side that surrendered a 10–6 advantage at Brookline. McGinley then warned: 'We have won seven of the last nine Ryder Cups, it's easy to be complacent.' He went on to remind them of the sort of messages that would stop them thinking the job was already done: 'We have a huge, big graphic in our team room: "Passion has determined our past and attitude will determine our future." I don't think anybody who has ever played for Alex Ferguson can ever accuse him or his teams of ever being complacent.'

For the final-day singles, the captains draw up the order they want to send out their 12 players and they are then matched together. McGinley's caution against complacency was reflected in his decision to send out his top performers early. He was going for an early kill. Equally, Watson had to respond in kind and this set up an intriguing running order for the last day at Gleneagles.

11.36	Graeme McDowell	v	Jordan Spieth
11.48	Henrik Stenson	v	Patrick Reed
12.00	Rory McIlroy	v	Rickie Fowler
12.12	Justin Rose	v	Hunter Mahan
12.24	Stephen Gallacher	v	Phil Mickelson
12.36	Martin Kaymer	v	Bubba Watson
12.48	Thomas Bjørn	v	Matt Kuchar
13.00	Sergio García	v	Jim Furyk
13.12	Ian Poulter	v	Webb Simpson
13.24	Jamie Donaldson	v	Keegan Bradley
13.36	Lee Westwood	v	Jimmy Walker
13.48	Victor Dubuisson	v	Zach Johnson

The big question was whether Watson's youngest players – Spieth and Reed – could continue their impressive debuts and give hope and inspiration to their teammates. Or would the likes of McDowell, Stenson, McIlroy and Rose snuff out any notion of an American fightback?

CHAPTER 17

Gleneagles Day Three

28 September 2014

'We had a real plan and we had a structure, with three or four big ideas that we kept going back to and we kept feeding into – ultimately, they proved to be right.'
Paul McGinley

The final-day line-up revealed a key element of Paul McGinley's master plan for this showdown in the heart of Scotland. He had held back Graeme McDowell and Victor Dubuisson to perform pivotal roles. They had won both of their foursomes matches and now it was time for them to occupy the crucial positions at the top and bottom of the singles. Any notion of dissent at being left out of the fourballs had been extinguished at source by thorough communication. The players were made aware at the start of the week that they would have a specific role and that they were key to the overall strategy of the European effort.

'He was worried at first about going out at the top of the order,' McDowell's coach Pete Cowen revealed. 'He said that he'd never been out first and that he always thought his role would be to go out last and anchor the order. To be fair, it was his caddie, Ken Comboy, who said to him: "Look, it's like a World Matchplay. You've got to knock the other guy out to get to the next round. And that's how we've got to think of it. It's no problem being first out, it's just another match and we've got to think of it as World Matchplay. We're going to knock

him out and we don't worry about what the others are doing."
And Graeme was happy to take that on board.'

The only problem with this plan was that McDowell had
only played alternate-shot golf that week. 'I just hadn't seen
enough putts fall,' the Northern Irishman later said. His coach
concurred. 'He was like a racehorse under-raced, really. He hadn't
hit certain tee shots, like drives at the second and the fourth and
so on. It almost took him five or six holes to get into the game.'

McDowell, though, showed few signs of apprehension as he
made his way to a boisterous first tee. Once again, Miguel Ángel
Jiménez entertained the crowd, recreating the famous dance of
his compatriot José María Olazábal which had been the signature moment following Europe's first away win back in 1987.
McDowell and his opponent, Jordan Spieth, strode to the first
tee through that evocative tunnel to find the entire par-four
hole again surrounded by thousands upon thousands of people.

It was a carnival atmosphere and McDowell bounced on his
toes and played to the crowd with his own little dance before
the players were announced. The final day of the 40th Ryder
Cup was underway when Spieth unleashed a fine three wood
down the fairway. It comfortably outstripped McDowell's accurate driver, but the home player nailed a fine approach while
the American found sand.

Spieth hit an excellent bunker shot, but the mood
demanded an early birdie for the buoyant Europeans. And
McDowell was certain he had delivered as his putt from 11 feet
headed towards the hole. Only at the last second did it deviate,
lipping out as the player was shaping to collect it from the cup.
Nervelessly, Spieth holed a tester to halve the hole in par.

Back on the tee, Patrick Reed and Henrik Stenson were
starting their match, while Rory McIlroy and Rickie Fowler,
who had shared major leaderboards all summer long, made the
final preparations for their contest.

One after another, the matches began. Spieth delivered the

start demanded by his captain. He birdied the second to take the lead and pars were enough to give the 21-year-old victories on the third and fifth. McDowell looked rusty and his putter was cold. Behind, Stenson held the early advantage over Reed while McIlroy made a blistering start against Fowler, winning five of the first six holes. For the Americans, Hunter Mahan took charge by going four up on the previously impregnable Justin Rose. Phil Mickelson nudged ahead of Stephen Gallacher and Thomas Bjørn was struggling against Matt Kuchar.

There was enough early American success to suggest the possibility of reversing the 'Miracle of Medinah'. 'Glory in the Glen' might just be on the agenda, but the electronic score-boards on the course were slow to reflect this. One American caddie complained that they should be more up to date, to inspire the rest of his team.

The pressure on McDowell, in particular, was immense. He had to find a foothold in a match that was rapidly slipping from his grasp.

At the seventh Spieth, who had not put a foot wrong and almost chipped in for birdie on the previous hole, dispatched another magnificent approach to the elevated green. He had a seven-foot birdie chance to go four up. Even for a man of McDowell's renowned fighting qualities, that would have been hard to overturn. But the young American's putt lacked the authority of his previous efforts and Europe's lead-out man was offered a significant reprieve. 'Something clicked at that very moment,' McDowell would reveal. He birdied the eighth and ninth holes but Spieth replied in kind. This, though, was the last joy for Spieth. His game started to unravel, in the way that it had during his final rounds at the Masters and Players' Championship earlier in the year.

Spieth three-putted the 10th to lose a hole for the first time in the match. It was the first of four holes in a row for McDowell, who visibly grew in confidence as his opponent fell apart. It was during this sequence that the tide of the whole contest turned decisively Europe's way. McIlroy, who claimed four birdies and an eagle in his first six holes, romped to a 5 and 4 victory over Fowler in a performance befitting his status as the world's best player. After an uncertain start to the week, McIlroy contributed massively to the European cause. Given the nature of a year in which he confirmed himself as golf's next superstar, it was entirely appropriate that he put the first point on the board for the home team on the final day. Emblematic of his career, the 25-year-old did it ahead of schedule, having started in the third match out.

McDowell waited until the par-three 17th to complete his win. A six-foot par putt after escaping from a greenside bunker was enough to close out a remarkable win. The Ulster golfer had come from three down at the turn and contributed five birdies to justify his captain's faith. It was a crucial point and, as he acknowledged in the Foreword to this book, one of which he may be most proud – quite a statement from someone who claimed the decisive win over Mahan four years earlier at Celtic Manor. This one put Europe 12–6 ahead and within two points of retaining the trophy.

The United States needed a rapid reversal in fortunes. Reed provided hope by inflicting the only defeat suffered by Stenson all week. It was a tight tussle. The young American went two up with birdies at the 11th and 12th but a bogey at the next, compounded by a Swedish birdie at the 15th, levelled the contest. They came up the last and, with Reed making a brave birdie, it came down to Stenson's short-range attempt to force a half. It was probably Stenson's worst putt of the week. He yanked it left and the pugnacious Reed, who had been booed after he provocatively held his finger to his lips to celebrate an earlier birdie, was now able to celebrate a brilliant Ryder Cup debut. It was 12–7 and there was a faint glimmer of American hope.

Europe, though, were realising their captain's aspiration of hitting the opposition in wave after wave. In the 10th match, Jamie Donaldson won the fifth with a par and then birdied the seventh to go two up on Keegan Bradley. These holes were won before only a handful of spectators in the way that captain McGinley had experienced in 2002 against Jim Furyk. The hoards would be surrounding Donaldson soon enough, though, and these early successes for the Welshman put more blue on the board, despite the American wildcard soon halving the arrears.

Up ahead, Martin Kaymer completed a 4 and 2 demolition of Bubba Watson, who failed to contribute from any of his three appearances. Kaymer finished it on the 16th with a glorious bump-and-run from the right of the par-five green. The ball shaped to miss on the right edge, but the hole seemed to suck it in for a match-winning eagle. The resulting roar told everyone on the course that Europe had edged ever closer to victory. At 13–7, they were one point away.

Kuchar eased past Bjørn 4 and 3, the highlight coming when the popular American holed his second shot at the 410-yard par-four eighth to go three up. This US win made the score 13–8 and Mickelson then delivered his point with a 3 and 1 victory over Gallacher. The left-hander put to bed his captain's notion that the Gleneagles course was a bad fit for the five-times major champion. He collected seven birdies in a match of the highest quality.

Next to finish were Rose and Mahan. The Englishman clawed his way back from four down after six holes. He played a spectacular approach from under a bush on the left side of the 13th for a tap-in birdie to level the contest. It was an inspirational shot and little wonder Rose turned to a TV camera and said: 'A bit of Seve for you.' The match finished all square and the Englishman remained unbeaten over the three days.

Ever closer — 13½–9½. Now all the attention switched to Donaldson's match with Bradley.

The Welshman had birdied the ninth, 11th and 12th holes to go four up. If he won the 14th, the contest would be over. But the hole was shared. It meant a guaranteed half, though, and Europe knew they had retained the trophy, even if it wasn't yet official. Players who had finished their rounds, both captains and the vast majority of the 50,000 fans, gravitated towards the 15th green. They watched Donaldson fire off a perfect drive, leaving a 146-yard wedge to the pin. 'It was a perfect yardage,' the 39-year-old would reflect. All he needed was to halve the hole and Europe would win the 2014 Ryder Cup. The pin was cut on the right edge of the green. Donaldson's only problem all week had been short irons flying left so he took dead aim on the flag. He reasoned that if the fault crept in he would still hit the middle of the green.

McGinley and Watson walked down that 15th fairway in deep conversation. Watson knew the game was up. Redemption had eluded his team, and McGinley was about to beat his golfing hero.

Donaldson confirmed that fact with a magnificent approach that didn't deviate from its target and finished within tap-in range. He raised his right arm, pointing his index finger in celebration as he triumphantly marched down the fairway. The crowds erupted. His captain ran from the sidelines to congratulate the Welshman and slap him on the back. Donaldson was still in the moment, glancing over at his opponent. Bradley, in turn, was looking to his captain because he did not want to bow to the inevitable concession without Watson's say-so. His skipper nodded and Bradley took off his cap, the signal that it was, indeed, all over. Europe's players wanted to mob the golfer who had sealed a famous victory, but Donaldson classily had eyes only for the man he had beaten 4 and 3. He made the handshake to spark unbridled celebrations as players, caddies and assistants engulfed the putting surface. 14½–9½. Job done. Masterplan executed. The showdown was over.

Donaldson described it as the 'wedge shot of my life'. He added: 'I can't really put words to it. It's unbelievable. Obviously I knew it was all getting tight there at the end . . . I was just trying to not spend too much time looking at the scoreboard and just concentrate on my match, and that's what I did, and was able to do it well enough to close it out.'

It was entirely appropriate that it was this European Tour stalwart who finished the job. It had taken him all but one week of the qualifying period to earn his place in the team. He had done it in style, too, with his victory in the Czech Republic. Donaldson had made himself one of the top dozen golfers on the continent, having overcome a serious back problem that once threatened his career. Having made it to the Ryder Cup, he was the beneficiary of McGinley's guile and detailed planning. The captain had made sure he knew this rookie inside out and recognised that he would prosper in the company of Lee Westwood. Now Donaldson had delivered three points from a possible four. Justifiably, he celebrated long into the night despite an early flight the following morning. As he came out of the Gleneagles hotel he was met by a television reporter. 'Jamie, are you able to take it all in yet, having claimed the winning point in the Ryder Cup?' Donaldson looked at the lens, paused, and said: 'Erm, no. Because I'm still drunk.'

The previous afternoon, back on the course, the Welshman had effusive praise for the skipper before embracing and kissing him. Donaldson said: 'He's been sensational. Paul captained one of the Seve Trophies I played in and I told everybody that he was going to be unbelievable here, and he's certainly done a lot more than that. He's been incredible. It's been a hell of a week.'

There was also a kiss for Donaldson's mum, Jackie, who joined the celebrations on the green. She chose the moment to jokingly tell him he didn't need to get 'a proper job' anymore. Europe's newest golfing hero informed the *Sunday Telegraph*: 'There's a funny, but very important story for me behind that. When I was an amateur and it wasn't really happening for me after two years of dedicating myself full-time to the game, my mum came up and said: "Right, I've had a chat with your dad and we think it's time you found yourself a proper job."

'That's her – straight to the point, no messing. It was the kick up the backside I needed and from that moment I never looked back. I always remembered that, whenever I went through dips and there were many, what with the back injury and losing my Tour card and everything.'

Reacting to the fact that the Cup had, at last, been won McGinley responded by looking at Donaldson: 'The highlight? The pleasure when you look at a face like that!' he said. 'We had a real plan and we had a structure, with three or four big ideas that we kept going back to and we kept feeding into – ultimately, they proved to be right.'

The remaining action was academic. Sergio García edged home to inflict yet another defeat on Jim Furyk on the home green and Ian Poulter won the last hole to preserve his unbeaten singles record with a half against Webb Simpson. Westwood fell to the impressive Jimmy Walker 3 and 2 and the final match was halved between Victor Dubuisson and Zach Johnson.

Given Europe's commanding position, that contest was never likely to become significant. But it might have done, so McGinley had his insurance policy in place. He accompanied the Frenchman through the early holes, remembering the sense of isolation he had felt on his own debut in 2002 at the Belfry. 'I said: "Remember, this is what we spoke about last night, Victor. The crowds will come back. Hang in. Don't worry about it, we are all there for you." And he was off and running.'

Once McDowell finished the top match he was sent back to offer his partner moral support. 'Graeme came running up the fairway, underneath the crowd, through the crowd, to get to Victor's shoulder. There was that sense of bonding,' McGinley said.

By the end, McDowell was standing next to McIlroy to the side of the final green. Two men, who had been partners in the past but were going through the strain of a bitter legal dispute, had re-united under the umbrella of Europe. They stood giggling like schoolboy best buddies as Zach Johnson contemplated the final putt of an extraordinary three days. McIlroy was clutching a large bottle of champagne and, prematurely, the cork popped. Laughing, he wheeled away, trying to contain the spray to avoid distracting the American.

It was an extremely rare moment in the summer of his life where McIlroy's timing was a touch out. As the final match finished honours even, leaving Dubuisson unbeaten and a final score in the home side's favour of 16½–11½, the spray was suddenly unleashed. It was a vivid metaphor for the unconfined and hard-earned joy European golf was once again able to experience.

Epilogue

*'If this precipitates some changes, then
that's probably a good thing.'*
PGA President Ted Bishop

In a break with tradition, the Ryder Cup was presented on the 18th fairway rather than at the site of the opening ceremony. In a further change from the norm, the closing American news conference exposed the beaten team's dissatisfaction with their leadership. These occasions, when the entire team and their captain sit before the press, have previously been expressions of unity. In 2008, a beaten Europe rallied around Nick Faldo when his stewardship had come under scrutiny, two years later Corey Pavin was praised by the losing Americans, and they did the same for Davis Love at Medinah.

But not this time.

In the media melee on the 18th green, Phil Mickelson told the cameras of the American network NBC that the US had failed to incorporate the lessons learned during Paul Azinger's leadership of the victorious 2008 team. Now he was ready to repeat those criticisms in front of their current leader as well as the world's press.

It was an extraordinary moment. Mickelson sat at the far left of the desk as we looked on. Watson was in the centre. Asked to explain America's eighth defeat in the last 10 Ryder Cups, Watson blamed his players. He said: 'The obvious answer is that our team has to play better. That's the obvious answer, and they do. I think they recognise that fact; that somehow, collectively, 12 players have to play better.'

Moments later came this question: 'Anyone that was on the team at Valhalla, can you put your finger on what worked in 2008 and what hasn't worked since?'

Mickelson pounced. 'There were two things that allowed us to play our best that I think Paul Azinger did,' he said. 'And one was he got everybody invested in the process. He got everybody invested in who they were going to play with, who the picks were going to be, who was going to be in their pod, when would they play and they had a great leader for each pod. In my case we had Ray Floyd, and we hung out together and we were all invested in each other's play. We were invested in picking Hunter that week; Anthony Kim and myself and Justin were in a pod. So we were invested in the process. And the other thing that Paul did really well was he had a great game plan for us.'

The man who had been so desperate to play the day before and who had been told he was benched by text message went on: 'Those two things helped us bring out our best golf. We all do the best we can and we are all trying our hardest, and I'm just looking back at what gave us our best success. We use the same process in the Presidents Cup and we always do really well. Unfortunately, we have strayed from a winning formula in 2008 for the last three Ryder Cups and we need to consider, maybe, getting back to that formula that helped us play our best.'

Mickelson, who the night before had addressed the team with his back to his captain, denied he had just issued a brutal assault on the US's Gleneagles regime. However, as the Associated Press's Doug Ferguson pointed out: 'It was like going on a date and raving all night about how great your previous girlfriend was.'

In truth, Mickelson had made a devastating critique of what was wrong with the current set-up. 'Nobody here was in on any decision,' added the player who was expected to have been the on-course leader for the US team.

Asked if he thought Mickelson was being disloyal with his comments, Watson stared ahead and said: 'Not at all. He has a difference of opinion. That's okay. My management philosophy is different than his.'

American players shifted uneasily in their seats. No one spoke up for the captain. The closest anyone came was when Jim Furyk, sitting at the opposite end of the podium to Mickelson, was asked for his thoughts. 'Gee, thanks. Just sitting over here, minding my own business,' Furyk dead-panned. Then, more seriously, he said: 'I have a lot of respect for both gentlemen. I've known Phil my entire life. Since I was 16, I've competed against him. He's one of my dearest friends on the PGA Tour. And I have a lot of respect for our captain. I know he put his heart and soul in it for two years. He worked his ass off to try to provide what he thought would be the best opportunity for us. I don't think it's wise for either one of us to be pitted in the middle of that.'

Mickelson had chosen his words carefully and the underlying message was clear. It exposed what he perceived to be serious flaws in the leadership of the American team and the way it is run by the PGA of America. Almost immediately, it was branded a 'one-man mutiny' on the US Golf Channel network by respected commentator and former PGA Tour player Brandel Chamblee. Probably the most popular golfer in the US, Mickelson was being roundly criticised for a serious breach of collective responsibility.

The writer Doug Ferguson, who covers more American golf than any other journalist, held a more considered view. The correspondent, whose reports are circulated worldwide, told me: 'I think a lot of people would say it was the right message at the wrong time. I think it was the right message at the right time.

'I admire Phil, I think he showed a lot of courage. It made Tom look bad and it made Phil look bad and Phil knew that.

He's not an idiot. He knew to say it the way he did, that was very well thought out. He knew what the ramifications were going to be. He's got a huge following and a lot of people were going to turn on him. If he did it in private, nobody would remember. But nobody will forget that press conference. If you are the PGA of America, you can't run from that press conference. It was staggering.'

PGA President Ted Bishop, the man who had appointed Watson, later said that he would have preferred Mickelson to have addressed his views to the captain behind closed doors. 'He did what he did with a purpose, whether you agree with it or not, he's passionate about the Ryder Cup,' Bishop stated. 'It was definitely an uncomfortable setting and just watching the body language of the players on the podium, I think everybody was uncomfortable. It really wasn't the way we wanted to end this Ryder Cup. It poured a little bit of salt in the wounds for us.'

But Bishop also acknowledged that the way the team's most decorated player had aired his views would probably help prompt much-needed change. 'It would have been great if that conversation had been confidential between Phil and Tom. I think he was speaking as much to the PGA of America as to Tom Watson, but as some changes unfold down the road I think he will probably feel that what he did was a good thing. And, at the end of the day, maybe it was.

'If this precipitates some changes, then that's probably a good thing,' Bishop added. 'We're looking to assemble a task force comprising some former Ryder Cup captains and some current players, along with a handful of PGA of America officials, to create a review of everything to do with the Ryder Cup.'

Mickelson spoke with Watson after they returned to the US and a week after the defeat Watson posted an open letter on the PGA website. In it he said: 'I take complete and full responsibility for my communication, and I regret that my words may have made the players feel that I didn't appreciate their commitment and dedication to winning the Ryder Cup. My intentions throughout my term as captain were both to inspire and to be honest.

'Secondly, the guys gave everything. They played their hearts out. I was proud to get to know each and every one of them. I know they are all going to win tournaments, be on future Ryder Cup teams and have wonderful careers.

'Our team certainly showed guts when it took it to the other team early in Sunday's singles matches. We were indeed tied with them as the scoreboard turned wonderfully red. Our players started fast, as I had asked them to in my comments the night before. I asked them to really concentrate on holes 2–5, as the Europeans had won too many early battles on these particular holes. But, in the end, the facts are that the other team played better. My hat's off and congratulations to them.

'As for Phil's comments, I completely understand his reaction in the moment. Earlier this week I had an open and candid conversation with him and it ended with a better understanding of each other's perspectives. Phil's heart and intentions for our team's success have always been in the right place. Phil is a great player, has great passion and I admire what he's done for golf.

'The bottom line is this. I was their captain. In hindsight, whatever mistakes that were made were mine. And I take complete and full responsibility for them. I want to say again to the players, their families, the PGA and our country how proud and honoured I was to captain this talented group of golfers, and how privileged I was to spend the past two years working this labour of my love for the Ryder Cup.'

Mickelson, meanwhile, talked to Bishop about the way America should approach the biennial matches in future. 'We need to blow the model up and start over,' the out-going President accepted. 'We need the input of the players. Not that we are trying to copy Team Europe, but they have certainly developed a formula for success. We can certainly steal a page from their book.'

McGinley had put together a blueprint based on playing in three winning Ryder Cups, on two victorious vice captaincies and on his leadership roles in successful Seve Trophy matches. He built on those experiences and allowed the captaincy role to evolve, adding extra dimensions, many of them taken from his experience of team sports while growing up in Ireland. He took the job of the captain to a new level, as each and every one of his players acknowledged as they sat in champagne-soaked blazers after the match.

Martin Kaymer, for whom 2014 had been such a landmark year, with his US Open and Players' Championship victories, summed up the team's view. He told me: 'Even though all the players have different characters he made them feel like a unit. We were all very, very close that week and very strong. It was always a team and such a good spirit, especially after the Saturday when we led 10–6. The way Paul talked to us with a very strong speech to say that it was not over yet, I just thought he had a very strong connection with all the players. He knew all the different characters and that was something I haven't seen before in a captain. I think it was very, very impressive, the job that he did.

'It was definitely the best and most enjoyable Ryder Cup that I have played. Obviously at Medinah there was less support not playing on your home soil, so I could really, really enjoy every single moment, every single game I played this time. We played very controlled because we were always in charge of our plan. Paul had a brilliant game plan and we never backed off. I think we can be very proud of the achievement of just keeping going and we never gave them a chance of a comeback on the Sunday,' added Kaymer who contributed two from a possible four points.

The European team partied hard, that victorious Sunday

night, mingling with the opposition as the two team rooms came together. Perhaps the only advice the Europeans did not heed from their captain was to not drink too much so as to help preserve great memories. Fortunately, they had the pictures on their mobile phones to remind them. One picture in particular, of Rory McIlroy wearing only a short kilt and a long wig alongside rookie Stephen Gallacher, summed up the celebratory mood.

McGinley, ever the deep thinker, felt that image held a deeper resonance. 'To see that photograph in the papers on the Monday morning with Stevie and Rory, Rory wearing the kilt; that to me, just summarised everything that we wanted to achieve as a team. That sense of bonding. You could see they were so comfortable in each other's company, Stevie had a drink in his hand and Rory had a kilt on. That sense of bonding will last them for ever and ever.

'I look back at my dad, he's from a Gaelic football background in Donegal, and he would go to Donegal and I would go to the games with him sometimes. And to see him meet a guy that he might not have seen for 20 or 30 years, maybe 40 years; someone he'd not seen since they played together and immediately that bonding is straight there. They are sitting down, reminiscing about old times. I would love to see Stevie and Rory doing that in 50 years' time, having a conversation.'

The morning after the night before, the blue and gold fish were still swimming in their tank in the team room. Henrik Stenson's caddie Gareth Lord sipped his coffee, and his mate Jamie sneaked a crafty Heineken. Scott Crockett, the European Tour's Director of Media, helped orchestrate his captain's next round of interviews. Stenson popped down to say farewell to his skipper, as did Sergio García and his girlfriend Katharina Boehm. McGinley instructed his son to alert his mum, Ali – the girl he had met during his student days in San Diego – that she would soon be needed to wave off the departing Americans.

Already the out-going skipper was plotting his next move. To organise a Dublin exhibition of those motivational posters. More immediately, he was about to return to the ranks as a European Tour player, but first it was time to return to his Sunningdale home to ready the family for a return to school the following morning.

His son was watching the Ryder Cup highlights and beckoned his dad to come and look. 'Watching that for half an hour, not having seen any of it on television before, straight away I got the sense of bonding. I could see the players' body language with each other. I could see the way they were hanging out and hugging each other. I could see the caddie involvement, the vice captains being part of it. I could see the crowd interaction. That half an hour was probably the most emotional I've been all week, because that, to me, was . . .'

He paused, only briefly. Emotion was welling again.

'That, for me, was confirmation of so many things I wanted. That was just it. We nailed it.'

Not only that, America's Ryder Cup set-up had been left in pieces. When they are put back together, they will need to be assembled in a far more enlightened fashion.

Europe – tight knit. Job done.

Afterword

*By Colin Montgomerie,
European Captain 2010*

Paul McGinley simply did not put a foot wrong in his victorious captaincy of the 2014 European Ryder Cup team. He deserves every ounce of the credit he has received in the aftermath of such a convincing and clinical victory.

From the outset, I knew his meticulous attention to detail would stand him in good stead. Likewise, I knew that through all his years of experience as a player and vice captain he would have been taking careful note at each Ryder Cup, and learning from each and every captain and player, as to what worked and what did not. He certainly brought all that knowledge to great effect at Gleneagles last month.

Paul was a very popular choice amongst the players, having done a great job as both my vice captain in 2010 and José María Olazábal's in 2012 and he had their backing and confidence from the moment he was touted as a possible candidate. That is such an important foundation for any successful captaincy. During the build-up, the match itself and during the analysis since, the players have loudly chorused their appreciation and respect for Paul.

Up against his childhood hero, Paul was not in the least bit intimidated and indeed proved more than a match for Tom Watson in every Ryder Cup duty, ranging from his public pronouncements to his captain's picks and his team selection.

He led the team with perfectly scripted and delivered speeches and created an ideal atmosphere that brought out the best in his players out on the course.

I believe his decision to select five vice captains was another inspired move. Where some said it would be too many, Paul knew what an important role his supporting quintet would play in helping him deliver his carefully thought-out strategy. And he was proven right.

I know that the US side will be anxious to restore the balance of power, with Europe having been so dominant of late. If they are looking for a blueprint for success, they should look no further than Paul McGinley. His faultless performance, a culmination of all his Ryder Cup learnings and passion, would be a great model for them to copy as they look to turn the tide.

All in all, it was a flawless performance from Paul and one he can proudly relive for the rest of his life.

Ryder Cup Results

Europe		USA
Friday Morning Fourballs		
Justin Rose & Henrik Stenson	5 & 4 beat	Bubba Watson & Webb Simpson
Thomas Bjørn & Martin Kaymer	HALVED with	Rickie Fowler & Jimmy Walker
Stephen Gallacher & Ian Poulter	lost 5 & 4	Jordan Spieth & Patrick Reed
Sergio García & Rory McIlroy	lost by 1 hole	Phil Mickelson & Keegan Bradley
	Europe 1½ USA 2½	
Friday Afternoon Foursomes		
Jamie Donaldson & Lee Westwood	won by 2 holes	Jim Furyk & Matt Kuchar
Justin Rose & Henrik Stenson	2 & 1 beat	Hunter Mahan & Zach Johnson
Rory McIlroy & Sergio García	HALVED with	Jimmy Walker & Rickie Fowler
Victor Dubuisson & Graeme McDowell	3 & 2 beat	Phil Mickelson & Keegan Bradley
	Europe 3½ USA ½	
	End of Day One Europe 5 USA 3	

Europe		USA
Saturday Morning Fourballs		
Justin Rose & Henrik Stenson	3 & 2 beat	Bubba Watson & Matt Kuchar
Jamie Donaldson & Lee Westwood	4 & 3 lost to	Jim Furyk & Hunter Mahan
Thomas Bjørn & Martin Kaymer	5 & 3 lost to	Patrick Reed & Jordan Spieth
Rory McIlroy & Ian Poulter	HALVED with	Jimmy Walker & Rickie Fowler
Europe 1½ USA 2½		
Saturday Afternoon Foursomes		
Jamie Donaldson & Lee Westwood	2 & 1 beat	Zach Johnson & Matt Kuchar
Sergio García & Rory McIlroy	3 & 2 beat	Jim Furyk & Hunter Mahan
Martin Kaymer & Justin Rose	HALVED with	Jordan Spieth & Patrick Reed
Victory Dubuisson & Graeme McDowell	5 & 4 beat	Jimmy Walker & Rickie Fowler
Europe 3½ USA ½		
End of Day Two Europe 10 USA 6		

Europe		USA
Sunday Singles		
Graeme McDowell	2 & 1 beat	Jordan Spieth
Henrik Stenson	lost by 1 hole	Patrick Reed
Rory McIlroy	5 & 4 beat	Rickie Fowler
Justin Rose	HALVED with	Hunter Mahan
Stephen Gallacher	3 & 1 lost to	Phil Mickelson
Martin Kaymer	4 & 2 beat	Bubba Watson
Thomas Bjørn	4 & 3 lost to	Matt Kuchar
Sergio García	1 up beat	Jim Furyk
Ian Poulter	HALVED with	Webb Simpson
Jamie Donaldson	4 & 3 beat	Keegan Bradley
Lee Westwood	3 & 2 lost to	Jimmy Walker
Victor Dubuisson	HALVED with	Zach Johnson
Europe 6½ USA 5½		
OVERALL Europe 16½ USA 11½		

2014 Individual Ryder Cup Records – After Singles

	Played	Won	Lost	Halved	Points
Europe					
Justin Rose	5	3	0	2	4
Graeme McDowell	3	3	0	0	3
Henrik Stenson	4	3	1	0	3
Jamie Donaldson	4	3	1	0	3
Rory McIlroy	5	2	1	2	3
Victor Dubuisson	3	2	0	1	2½
Sergio García	4	2	1	1	2½
Lee Westwood	4	2	2	0	2
Martin Kaymer	4	1	1	2	2
Ian Poulter	3	0	1	2	1
Thomas Bjørn	3	0	2	1	½
Stephen Gallacher	2	0	2	0	0
United States					
Patrick Reed	4	3	0	1	3½
Jordan Spieth	4	2	1	1	2½
Jimmy Walker	5	1	1	3	2½
Phil Mickelson	3	2	1	0	2
Hunter Mahan	4	1	2	1	1½
Rickie Fowler	5	0	2	3	1½
Keegan Bradley	3	1	2	0	1
Jim Furyk	4	1	3	0	1
Matt Kuchar	4	1	3	0	1
Webb Simpson	2	0	1	1	½
Zach Johnson	3	0	2	1	½
Bubba Watson	3	0	3	0	0

Acknowledgements

There are many people to thank for their help in writing this book and this is by no means a comprehensive list. The biggest debt of gratitude goes to Sarah and Ollie, who not only put up with me being away at golf tournaments for too long, but then had to live with me spending my time at home hunched over a laptop. Sarah, though, was a constant source of encouragement, not to mention the scariest of proofreaders.

To Lorne Forsyth and Jennie Condell at Elliott and Thompson, thank you for the lunch where the *Showdown* idea was conceived and commissioned. Within ten months it was on the shelves! Lorne and Jennie were great enthusiasts and wonderful sounding boards. So was editor Pippa Crane, who helped ensure the book was swiftly on the shelves – probably before Team Europe had dry-cleaned the champagne from their blazers. Thanks also to copy editor Tony Lawrence and publicist Alison Menzies. To my neighbour Ken Jackson, thanks, again, for the mugshot.

To my fellow golf correspondents, James Corrigan (*Daily Telegraph*), Derek Lawrenson (*Daily Mail*), David Facey (*Sun*) and Ewan Murray (*Guardian*) thank you for your friendship and insights over dinner that inevitably informed this book. Kim Crawford (a wine label rather than a person) probably deserves some credit too. Special mention to James for sharing the week that followed the Ryder Cup and for helping ensure I stayed on top of all that happened at Gleneagles.

To my BBC Head of Radio Sport, Richard Burgess, thank you for supporting this project and likewise golf editor

Michael Carr and producer Graham McMillan. Having spent most of the last decade travelling with me to the majors and Ryder Cups, this particular GMac has been a great help on and off air.

The other GMac to thank is the man who led out Europe on the final day of the Ryder Cup. It's a real thrill to have Graeme McDowell's foreword at the start of this book and I'm very grateful. Thanks also to Colin Montgomerie for his afterword on the man who beat him to the Gleneagles captaincy. Paul McGinley was an extraordinary skipper and I'm very grateful for the vast number of interviews he granted BBC Radio during his captaincy. Thanks also to Paul's parents, Michael and Julia, for their time spent providing so much information on the upbringing of Europe's leader in the fortieth Ryder Cup. To my good friend Greg Allen at RTÉ, thanks also for your insights.

European Tour media director Scott Crockett leads the best communications team in sport and they have all played a huge part helping with this project. Special thanks to Michael Gibbons for his help in nailing awkward-to-verify facts and figures.

This was not a solely European project, although the final result ultimately tipped it in that direction. Ted Bishop at the PGA of America was very helpful with his time and thoughts and thanks also go to Communications Director Julius Mason. To Alex Miceli, Doug Ferguson and Bob Harig, thank you for your time, friendship and insights.

Former European captain Bernard Gallacher was another great help as was my on-air sidekick Jay Townsend. Somewhere in amongst our arguments we arrive upon a greater understanding of this great game.

A huge thank you to all of the players involved in an extraordinary golfing year. So many of these golfers have been generous with their thoughts and insights. There are too many to name individually, but special mention to Rory McIlroy for being such a grounded and willing interviewee despite his amazing success that made so much of the narrative in this book and made covering golf such an exciting pursuit in 2014.

Finally thanks to my dad for introducing me to the game. Without that I would never have gravitated towards a job I regard as the best I could ever do.

Index